EARLY AMERICAN
BOOKS & PRINTING

EARLIEST KNOWN REPRESENTATION (ABOUT 1795) OF
AN AMERICAN BOOKSTORE

The spelling 'stationary' was standard for many years. From a trade
card, believed to be unique, in the Robert Fridenberg collection

EARLY AMERICAN
BOOKS & PRINTING

By

JOHN T. WINTERICH

DOVER PUBLICATIONS, INC.

NEW YORK

Published in Canada by General Publishing Company,
Ltd., 30 Lesmill Road, Don Mills, Toronto, Ontario.
Published in the United Kingdom by Constable and Com-
pany, Ltd., 10 Orange Street, London WC2H 7EG.

This Dover edition, first published in 1981, is an unabridged
and unaltered republication of the work originally published
by the Houghton Mifflin Company, Boston, in 1935.

International Standard Book Number: 0-486-24171-8
Library of Congress Catalog Card Number: 81-66245

Manufactured in the United States of America
Dover Publications, Inc.
180 Varick Street
New York, N.Y. 10014

TO
B. E. W.

PREFACE

THE Walrus said it was time to talk of many things, but his agenda specified only seven, and he never mentioned any of them again.

Any book, particularly any book about books, that attempts a compact survey of a broad field must be an exercise in superficialities. Let the commentator confine his province as closely as he may, it will bulge out in some spots and collapse in others — he projects an area as quadrangular as Wyoming, and by the time he has it plotted, it is as amorphous as Switzerland.

Consider momentarily the casual group photograph. Nothing is quite so uninteresting unless it be a second casual group photograph. But in the most casual of such representations of self-consciously posed humanity, one notes a face or two, or half a dozen, over which one lingers as Keats lingered over the lover and the lady of the Attic shape. The notes which follow flit similarly from face to face, from title-page to title-page, from imprint to imprint, in the crowded group photograph of early American books.

At the outset it was essential to decide whether to essay the utilitarian detail and inclusiveness of the telephone directory or to loiter, agreeably to one's self, over more or less arbitrary choices and to attempt at the same time to lend the presentation a semblance of narrative — whether to make the product a reference manual or something that might conceivably be read for its own continuity. For in the subject itself there is continuity and there is a story, whether or no its spirit has been caught in the pages that follow.

The result, whatever it may be, is distinctly not a source book. It is, one may hope, a partial guide to sources; and in view of the heavy dependence placed on these, and the fact that the sources are listed as they occur in the text, they are not summarized at the conclusion of these notes. The compiler is particularly indebted to Lawrence C. Wroth's *The Colonial Printer* (New York: The Grolier Club, 1931), of which Chapter VII is little more than a summary — made, it should be added, with Mr. Wroth's express consent for the pilfering.

The difficulty inherent in the effort to keep the modifier *early* from getting completely out of hand will become obvious to the reader as he progresses toward lateness and finds *early* striving valiantly to keep up with him. Time is merely a projection of something or other into space (or is it the other way about?), a truth which was brought well home to one previously three-dimensional mind in the preparation of these data.

The compiler wishes to express his gratitude to the editors of the *Publishers' Weekly* and of the *Saturday Review of Literature* for permission to use material which has appeared in their pages.

J. T. W.

CONTENTS

I. Westward Ho!   1

II. Cambridge Points the Road   25

III. Mr. Bradford Understands a Want   50

IV. Benjamin Franklin, Printer and Publisher   70

V. Gentlemen of the Press   91

VI. The Rise of the Magazine   113

VII. Tools of the Trade   126

VIII. Muses Ten to Twelve   136

IX. Over the Hills and Far Away   161

X. Enter the Professional Author   175

XI. Once More Westward Ho!   204

XII. Means — and an End   217

Index   239

ILLUSTRATIONS

EARLIEST KNOWN REPRESENTATION (ABOUT 1795) OF
AN AMERICAN BOOKSTORE *Frontispiece*

COLUMBUS TELLS THE WORLD 10

THE BAY PSALM BOOK 28

THE EARLIEST EXTANT 'NEW ENGLAND PRIMER' 46

THE FIRST NATIVE NEWSPAPER 92

PAUL REVERE, CARTOONIST 118

FRONTISPIECE OF 'THE POWER OF SYMPATHY' (1789) 150

FIRST SEPARATE AMERICAN EDITION (1846) OF
KEATS'S POEMS 218

EARLY AMERICAN
BOOKS & PRINTING

.·.

CHAPTER I

Westward Ho!

IF THE shade of Martin Waldseemüller had been
able to return to St. Dié in July, 1918, some four
centuries after he had departed this life, he would
have remarked with undoubted interest the presence
of many men clad in olive-drab uniforms and speaking an English which was unlike any he may have
heard on earth. Could he have inquired of his latter-
day fellow-townsmen who these newcomers were, he
would probably have been startled at the response —
startled and most immensely pleased.

Americans! Then his little effort in propaganda
far back in 1507 had succeeded. It did pay to ad-
vertise. For in this little town on the Lorraine
frontier two continents and their peoples had been
christened — christened by neither prince nor pre-
late, courtier nor knight-at-arms, but by this obscure
professor in the local gymnasium — most decidedly
a fresh-water college, many days' journey from the
sea and from the populous capitals of Renaissance
Europe.

Little enough is known of Martin Waldseemüller,
or Hylacomylus, according to the rendering of his
name in Greek, after the reigning fashion among

scholars. He was a native of Freiburg, was a student
there in 1490, established a library at St. Dié sometime before 1507, published his epochal *Cosmographiæ Introductio* the same year, and died at some
unguessable date before 1552, for a scholastic treatise
of that year alludes to him as 'piously defunct.'

The *Cosmographiæ Introductio* was simply a little
manual of geography — a description of the world,
followed by narratives of the four voyages of Amerigo
Vespucci. Many harsh words have been leveled at
Vespucci's possibly innocent memory; at the worst he
may have been a charlatan who attempted to steal the
prestige that belonged to others; at the best he may
have been the first adventurer of his adventurous day
to set foot on the mainland of North America. At all
events, there is no evidence to show that he made the
slightest effort to foist his name on the New World,
although the name New World itself was an invention
of his own and one for which he is entitled to due
credit.

Vespucci's *Mundus Novus* (almost certainly not
written by himself) first appeared before 1504 —
possibly as early as 1502 — as a leaflet of four un-
numbered leaves. The place of printing is as uncer-
tain as the date. This letter (in Latin, translated
from a lost Italian original) described his third voyage (1501–02). It went through many editions from
many presses, as did accounts of the three other voyages ascribed to Vespucci. Copies of these widely disseminated little chronicles inevitably found their way
to the hands of Martin Waldseemüller, to whom
they seemed the most exciting reading he had come
upon in a long time. He assembled them, therefore,
in his geographical handbook, and in the first part of
his manual made this plea:

2

But now that those parts [i.e., Europe, Asia, and Africa] have been more extensively examined and a fourth part has been discovered by Americus (as will be seen in the sequel), I do not see why we should rightly refuse to name it Amerigen or America, namely, the land of Americus, after its discoverer Americus, a man of shrewd intelligence, since both Europe and Asia took their names from women.

The *Cosmographiæ Introductio* became that agreeable phenomenon of the publishing world, a bestseller. Its plea was carried far and wide, and its suggestion was almost unconsciously and automatically adopted. Vespucci himself died in 1512, and can have borne no great share in the campaign to assure his immortality, though he could hardly have avoided hearing about it.

Almost exactly a year before the appearance of the original edition of the *Cosmographiæ Introductio* at St. Dié, Christopher Columbus himself had died at Valladolid. What Columbus would have thought of Waldseemüller's project for the naming of a hemisphere, had he lived to learn of it, is matter for interesting conjecture. The Waldseemüller episode has been put first in the present summary (even ahead of the incalculably important Columbus letter) only because it is perhaps the most striking instance that can be adduced to demonstrate the power of the printed word in the era of discovery — an era in which the printed word itself was such a novelty in Europe that men were not yet fully awakened to a realization of its tremendous potentialities in the scheme of civilization, or, if they were somewhat gropingly aware of them, were a little afraid of them.

The publication of the Latin Bible printed at Mainz about 1455 by Johann Gutenberg is generally accepted as signalizing the birth of the book as we know it today. Gutenberg probably and pardonably wanted the wonderful discovery to remain a secret, but the second half of the fifteenth century was too alert an age in which to keep so good a secret for very long. Gutenberg could not conduct the enterprise single-handed, and he could not employ and train journeymen without acquainting them with the whole of the mystery. In 1462 the burghers of Mainz had the ill luck to choose the losing side in a struggle between rival archbishops, and some of Gutenberg's apprentices and skilled workers were quite probably among those who were sent into exile as a result. The incident thus became a definite impulse to the diffusion of printing. Two Mainz printers, Conrad Sweynheim and Arnold Pannartz, familiar to every reader of Charles Reade's *The Cloister and the Hearth*, went as far afield as Italy, and at Subiaco, near Rome, issued in 1465 the earliest books known to have been printed in Italy. The art continued to spread, and was flourishing in at least eight other European countries by the end of the next ten years. It reached England in 1476, when William Caxton set up his press at Westminster, but Caxton himself, the preceding year, had issued at Bruges the first book ever printed in English.

By the end of the fifteenth century, printing had been introduced to well over two hundred European communities. In some instances the introduction had been casual and transitory. Itinerant journeymen might stop in a town, do a job or two, and then pass on. In other centers, such as Venice, Paris, Strassburg, and Nuremberg, the new art was soon inaugurating an enduring contribution to the local economic, industrial, and cultural life. Knowledge

4

and practice of the craft spread amazingly, and it is probable that the monumental *Gesamtcatalog der Wiegendrucke*, now being assembled under the direction of the German government, will, when completed, list well over thirty thousand different editions of books issued in Europe before 1501. As to the number of titles which will not be listed because no copies survive, one guess is as good as another. The total would include, unfortunately, many of the very books which one would most like to know about — the popular reading of the day. The survival of nearly fifty copies of the Gutenberg Bible is, after all, no great feat of preservation — most of the edition became the property of monasteries, cathedrals, and universities, and copies were rarely touched by clumsy lay hands.

More than half the fifteenth-century books which have come down to us are ecclesiastical or theological in character — sermons, commentaries, polemics, lives of the saints, church histories, breviaries, psalters, Bibles. There are treatises on the sciences and pseudo-sciences, for it was a day when astrology rubbed shoulders with astronomy and alchemy with chemistry, and any collector of medical books must set aside ample shelf-room for the earliest expositions in print of the art and practice of healing. The Greek and Latin classics were inevitably among the first writings to win the immortality of type, and there was an abundance of grammatical and philological textbooks which were made necessary by the spread of the printed word itself. But far scarcer and in general far more desirable, not alone by reason of their scarcity, but because they were made for, and absorbed by, the man in the street and in the cottage, the man who had to buy the bread, pay the taxes, and fight the wars, are the romances and fables in prose or verse, the treatises on household economics, farming, cookery, home remedies (the how-to books of their day), nearly all of them in the language of the country of their origin — French, German, Italian, English.

Books which were printed before the end of the year 1500 are called *incunabula* — cradle books. They are the only books which are valuable on account of their age (some of them can be had for a few dollars, but not many, and certainly none that have anything to do with America). They may be valuable on other counts as well, but age alone is sufficient to hallow them. Of no other group of books can this be said without qualification. Once a qualification is admitted, once age is regarded in a relative rather than in an absolute sense, it becomes another matter. Thus, if a book should come to light which was printed in Cambridge, Massachusetts, in 1635, it would be worth more than a Gutenberg Bible, and a book printed in English in California in 1845, unless it were unusually bulky, would be worth many times its weight in gold. But crumbly calf-bound readers issued in Boston or Philadelphia or New York 'more than a hundred years ago' are not old books in the sense in which the bibliographer, the collector, and the librarian reckon antiquity.

By the time Columbus sailed out of Palos in the *Santa Maria*, the printed book was as familiar, though not so obtrusive, a phenomenon as was the automobile when Theodore Roosevelt left the White House. The most critical hours of Columbus's momentous argosy did not come until the expedition was within a few leagues of home. Off the coastal islands a severe storm arose, and the leader was ap-

palled, not at the imminence of physical disaster, but
at the prospect that word of the glorious success of
the voyage might never reach his patrons and the
world. Accordingly, on February 14, 1493, during
the height of the hurricane, he wrote a careful account of the expedition on a piece of parchment.
Then, according to the kindly and accurate Bartolomé de Las Casas (who accompanied Columbus on
his three other voyages, and whose father was present
on the first), 'he wrapped this parchment in a large
piece of waxed cloth, hermetically sealed the package,
fastened it securely in a large wooden cask, conceal-
ing it in such a way that no one could know what it
was.' The cask was duly committed to the waves,
and the waves, up to this writing, have refused to
give it up.

The marvel is, considering the number of Lost
Dauphins, John Wilkes Booths, and Charley Rosses
who are matter of record, that so few reputed discoveries of this romantic cache have won their way
to print. Perhaps the most unusual account dates
back to 1852, when the American brig *Chieftain*, of
Boston, found itself due for a blow off the coast of
Morocco. The captain, according to the story, let
down a drag in order to increase ballast. The menace
of the storm passed, and when the drag was hauled in,
it brought up 'a coffer of cedar wood' inside which
was disclosed 'a cocoa-nut, hollow, and containing a
document written in Gothic letters upon parchment.'
The parchment was exhibited to 'an American bookseller' at Gibraltar (Heaven knows who he was, and
what he was doing at Gibraltar!) and the bookseller
immediately offered the captain one hundred dollars
for it. The cagey Yankee declined to sell, and 'thereupon the bookseller read to the astonished captain

7

the document, which was no other than the holograph relation of the discovery committed to the sea three hundred and fifty-nine years before.' John Boyd Thacher (whose collection is now in the Library of Congress) chronicles the incident in a footnote, in his *Christopher Columbus*, without, of course, lending it the slightest credence, though he cites one authority who was inclined to set some store by it. 'This document and its safe-deposit, the cocoanut, have disappeared,' says Thacher, 'though they are likely to appear again at some future time.' Perhaps the most suspicious element in the story is the ready ease with which the 'American bookseller' was able to read the fantastic scrawl that passed for handwriting in the fifteenth century.

But the tempest relented, the caravel did not founder, and on the following day (February 15), under less stressful circumstances, Columbus wrote another letter. It was addressed to Luis de Santangel, who had had faith in his idea when others doubted or scoffed, and whose proximity to Ferdinand and Isabella (history should set them down as Isabella and Ferdinand) had endowed that faith with substance. The following day, safe in port, Columbus wrote still another letter, addressed to Gabriel Sanchez, Chancellor of the Royal Household, which was merely a courteously roundabout way of getting the news to the sovereigns themselves.

Señor [began the letter to Santangel], por que se aureis plazer — Sir, as I know that you will have pleasure of the great victory which our Lord hath given me in my voyage, I write you this, by which you shall know that ... I passed over to the Indies with the fleet... where I found very many islands peopled with inhabitants beyond number. And of them all I have taken possession

for their Highnesses, with proclamation and the royal
standard displayed; and I was not gainsaid.

The letters were duly delivered, and that to Santangel was immediately put in print in Barcelona,
possibly with the type of Pedro Posa. It was an unpretentious piece of work — more than that, a
slovenly — and it is to be hoped that Señor Posa
spoke sharply to whoever botched it, and then
thought evil of himself for letting it go out of his shop.
It was, perhaps, all in the day's work; Señor Posa
doubtless did not appreciate the epochal importance
of this wretched sample of his handiwork. The
printed letter occupied three and a half pages of a
single folded sheet, each page measuring some seven
by ten inches. It was not intended to be anything
so ambitious as a book — it was a mere handbill, a
speedy means of making known to Spain, and to so
much of the world as cared to read, the success of the
expedition.

No one knows how many copies of the Santangel
letter were printed, but the marvel is, no matter how
large the edition, that a single example should survive. But a single copy has (though its existence
was unknown until forty years ago), and is now in the
possession of the New York Public Library — unquestionably the most valuable piece of printing
known to exist today.

The letter to Santangel may have been copied far
and wide — printing was being carried on in twenty
Spanish cities in 1493 — but no other example of an
early issue in Spanish is known with the exception of
a copy (also unique) of an edition printed at Valladolid
about 1497 which is now in the Biblioteca Ambrosiana
at Milan. The Sanchez letter, however, was quickly
translated into Latin and issued from presses in Rome,

Paris, Basel, and Antwerp. Of the three Rome editions of 1493, between forty and fifty examples altogether are known today — a remarkable total in view of the ephemerality of the productions. Of the Antwerp edition of the same year, only a single copy is known. It is preserved in the Bibliothèque Royale at Brussels. A German edition published at Strassburg in 1497 by Bartholomew Kustler has this naïvely charming title: '*Eyn schön hübsch lesen von etlichen inszlen die do in kurtzen zyten funden synd durch den Künig von Hispania, und sagt von grossen wunderlichen dingen die in den selbe inszlen synd*' — 'A very pretty story of sundry islands which were discovered a short time since through the King of Spain, and tells of great and marvelous things which are in these same islands.' Versions in rhyme were issued in Rome, one of them accompanied by a woodcut representation of the discovery.

There was no reason, obviously, why most of Europe, high and low, should not have heard of the exploit of Columbus before the end of 1493. The very multiplicity of editions of the Columbus letters is testimony, not alone to the swift dissemination of the news, but also to the importance with which it was regarded and the eagerness with which its romantic details were absorbed.

Books [says Thacher] may be printed in the first instance as voluntary contributions to the public store, without a desire for their birth and without support for their existence. But books are not reprinted except in response to public desire and public interest. We know of no other work which in the short space of ten or twelve months at the close of the fifteenth century passed through thirteen editions and from the presses of five of the great States of Europe.

COLUMBUS TELLS THE WORLD

First page of the four-page Spanish letter (Barcelona, 1493) announcing the discovery of America. From the unique original (11⅚₁₆ × 8⅝ inches) in the New York Public Library

The mariners who braved the rigors of the Atlantic in that pre-steam and pre-wireless day were, of course, men of action rather than chroniclers. It was their destiny to make history and to leave the perpetuation of it to others. The Columbus letters, therefore, are a notable and very happy exception. Much of our information on the era of discovery comes to us at second, third, or even a later hand, but much of it is none the less thoroughly credible and authoritative, and even where it is not, it cannot be thrown utterly out of court on that account. Better bad testimony from which the expert can winnow a grain or two of truth or even probability than utter silence. A minor chronicler, moreover, might chance to include a scrap of information that the others had missed. Thus, everyone knows that Columbus brought back several Indians as samples of the strange new humanity he had discovered in the Indies, but Columbus himself does not say how many. An Italian courtier who happened to be at Barcelona when Columbus returned sent home a letter (soon put in type) summarizing the results of the expedition and declaring that Columbus had six natives with him. To the casual inclusion of this scrap of information do we owe the only actual census of transplanted aborigines given in any contemporary source.

Several chronicles of transcendent importance were not compiled and published until a comparatively late date. Richard Hakluyt died a few months after Shakespeare — long after the end of the great epoch of discovery and well within the dawn of the era of colonization. He stands, therefore, midway between the Renaissance and the new age of historical research, not too remote from the one to breathe its quickening atmosphere, and close enough to the other to have brought to his investigations something of the spirit of modern scholarship. His *magnum opus* was his *Principall Navigations, Voiages, Traffiques and Discoueries of the English Nation*, the complete edition of which (three volumes in two, London, 1599–1600) should contain the account of the voyage to Cadiz which Elizabeth ordered suppressed after the Earl of Essex had fallen from royal favor. The *Principall Navigations* contains narratives of more than two hundred voyages, ably documented and competently edited by a zealous authority whose efforts lent immeasurable impetus to the rearing of British North America. Hakluyt died before his task was completed, and it was taken up by Samuel Purchas, who toiled with plodding diligence, but lacked the magnificent enthusiasm that had characterized his great forerunner.

It was a day of spaciousness and splendor, and the world of publishers caught its spirit and translated it into lavish and synoptic title-pages. For example: *A Description of New England: or the Observations, and Discoueries, of Captain Iohn Smith (Admirall of that Country) in the North of America, in the year of our Lord 1614: with the Successe of sixe Ships, that went the next yeare 1615; and the accidents befell him among the French men of warre: With the proofe of the present benefit this Countrey affoords: whither this present yeare, 1616, eight voluntary Ships are gone to make further tryall. At London: Printed by Humfrey Lownes, for Robert Clerke; and are to be sould at his house called the Lodge, in Chancery Lane ouer against Lincolnes Inne, 1616.* Thus was New England named, though the designation included much more territory than it does now.

Captain John Smith was a romantic figure even for

his blustery and belligerent day. Two years before his death appeared his *True Travels*, the title-page of which exploited his prowess to a degree that makes the most fulsome numbers in Beadle's Dime Library read like pallid understatements by comparison: *The True Travels, Adventures, and Observations of Captaine Iohn Smith, in Europe, Asia, Affrica, and America from Anno Domini 1593, to 1629. His Accidents and Sea-fights in the Straights; his Service and Strategems of Warre in Hungaria, Transilvania, Wallachia and Moldavia, against the Turks, and Tartars; his Three Single Combats betwixt the Christian Armie and the Turkes. After how he was taken prisoner by the Turks, sold for a Slave, sent into Tartaria; his Description of the Tartars, their strange manners and customes of Religions, Diets, Buildings, Warres, Feasts, Ceremonies, and Living; how hee slew the Bashaw of Nalbrits in Cambia, and escaped from the Turkes and Tartars. Together with a continuation of his generall History of Virginia, Summer-Iles, New-England, and their proceedings, since 1624, to this present 1629; as also of the new Plantations of the great River of the Amazons, the Iles of St. Christopher, Mevis, and Barbados in the West Indies. All written by actuall Authours, whose names you shall finde along the History. London, Printed by J. H. for Thomas Slater, and are to bee sold at the Blew Bible in Greene Arbour, 1630.*

It is a noble company, this multitudinous assembly of early and middle Americana, a company that includes such disparate (but rare and costly) units as the Nuremberg *Chronicle* of 1493, scarcer in Latin than in German, one of the most elaborate of early picture books, with its attempt to assign credit for the discovery of America to Martin Behaim (a remarkable instance of local pride); Sebastian Brandt's popular *Narrenschiff* (1494), done into English fifteen years later and printed at London by Richard Pynson with this ample explanatory title: *This present Boke named the Shyp of folys of the worlde was translated in the College of saynt mary Otery in the counte of Deuonshyre, out of Laten, Frenche, and Doche into Englysshe tonge by Alexander Barclay Preste: and at that tyme Chaplen in the sayde College, translated the yere of our Lorde god M.CCCCC.VIII. Imprentyd in the Cyte of London in Fletestre at the signe of Saynt George by Rycharde Pynson to hys Coste and charge: Ended the yere of our Sauiour M.d.ix. The xiiii day of Decembre;* Fracanzano de Montalboddo's *Paesi Nouamente Retrovati* of 1507; Peter Martyr's *Decades* of various dates from 1511 on (translated into English in 1555, and exercising a vast influence); Giovanni Battista Ramusio's *Summario* of 1534, with a map of superlative rarity; Thomas Hariot's *Briefe and True Report of the New Found Land of Virginia* (1588), the earliest book in English of English origin relating to what is now a part of the United States; the various editions of Samuel de Champlain's voyages from 1604 to 1632; *Histoire de la Nouvelle France* (1609), by Marc Lescarbot, 'eye-witness to some of the events here related'; the *Grands Voyages* and the *Petits Voyages* of Theodor de Bry, initiated in 1590, continued after De Bry's death mainly by his widow and sons, and completed in 1634, a description of which in the Brayton Ives sale catalogue of 1891 occupies seven pages.

Consider, too, the account by George Beste, who was master of a ship in the third expedition, of Martin Frobisher's three voyages 'for the finding of a passage to Cathaya' (London, 1578), containing two maps which seem to have survived in fewer than ten copies;

equally rare, *The Navigators Supply* (London, 1597) of William Barlow, inventor of the compass-box (the Americana section of the library of the Marquess of Lothian, dispersed at auction at the American Art Association Anderson Galleries in 1932, was particularly rich in manuals of navigation); Baptist Goodall's *The tryall of Travell* (London, 1630), with one of the few references to Columbus in English verse within a century and a half of his voyages; *Plain Dealing: or, Newes from New England* (London, 1642), wherein Thomas Lechford, lawyer, set forth his experiences in Boston and vicinity from 1638 to 1641; William Castell's *Short Discoverie of the Coasts and Continent of America* (London, 1644), with what has been pronounced the most accurate description of New York in English before 1650; *A Perfect Description of Virginia: being a full and true Relation of the present State of the Plantation, their Health, Peace, and Plenty: the number of people, with their abundance of Cattell, Fowl, Fish, &c.... Being sent from Virginia, at the request of a Gentleman of worthy note, who desired to know the true State of Virginia as it now stands. Also, a Narration of the Countrey, within a few dayes journey of Virginia, West and by South, where people come to trade... With the manner how the Emperor Nichotawance came to Sir William Berckley, attended with five petty Kings, to do Homage* (London, 1649); and Edward Johnson's *History of New-England. From the English planting in the Yeere 1628, until the Yeere 1652. Declaring the form of their Government, Civill, Military, and Ecclesiastique. Their Wars with the Indians, their Troubles with the Gortonists, and other Heretiques. Their manner of gathering of Churches, the commodities of the Country, and description of the principall Towns and Havens, with the great encouragements to increase Trade betwixt them and*

Old England. With the names of all their Governours, Magistrates, and eminent Ministers (London, 1654), called by W. F. Poole 'the most important record of New England's life which the first hundred years brought forth.'

No one of the books that have thus far been enumerated — no one of hundreds of comparable others that might be enumerated if this were a catalogue of a hypothetical library instead of a descriptive essay — is ever likely to grace the shelves of him who runs, reads, and would retain. Most of us can count ourselves fortunate if we are within a few hundred miles of a repository of such treasures, twice fortunate if we can visit that repository and view the treasures. They are not, obviously, of that company of print which might appeal to him who 'always has been interested in old books.' It is not wholly a question of dollars and cents, though dollars and cents, especially dollars, are helpful in many a book-collecting crisis. The wealthiest man alive, whoever he may be and however many there may be of him, could not today hope to assemble a tithe of the items that the great collectors of a century or a half-century since (or of yesterday) contrived, after years of intensive, painstaking, specialized effort, to put upon their roomy and well-tended shelves. It is simply too late.

Nor is there the slightest likelihood that valuables of such magnitude will turn up at the casual seeker's whispered 'Open sesame!' in some stuffy New England attic, or along New York's Fourth Avenue, or in Ye Olde Antique Shoppe on the Boston Post Road, or at a Westchester County auction, or in an Indianapolis second-hand furniture establishment. The chances are better, by fifty or more to one, anywhere in Europe — and this area has been explored and exploited for generations. Booksellers and book-collectors, be it remembered, have been looking for first editions of *Ben-Hur* and *Ten Nights in a Bar Room* only since 1920 or later, but they have been looking for Columbus letters for two or three centuries.

And if these statements produce vanity and vexation of spirit, let it be said at once that, for one field forever closed to the collector of moderate means, a hundred are still open or, better yet, await his hand upon the gate. Attention will be paid to these in season.

It is dangerous to lay down general rules in the rare-book field, particularly in that intricate acre of it devoted to such bedrock Americana as has been discussed in this chapter. Almost every generality that one dare venture must be hedged about with exceptions, restrictions, and qualifications as soon as it is uttered. But it is safe to make the statement that any book published anywhere before the middle of the seventeenth century which makes any definite (or, in some instances, indefinite) allusion to America is on that account of more than trivial value. That value may be comparatively trifling, or may be reckonable at a purely fantastic figure that puts it, if not beyond the dreams of avarice, at least far beyond the likelihood of attainability. Avarice may be endowed with the wealth of those Indies which Columbus died thinking he had entered by the front door, and still sigh for many great examples of Americana in vain. So many of them are known by single examples, or twos, or threes, or half-dozens, and others which may exist to the full dozen are all the property of institutional collections which are not likely to be broken up until the crack of doom, when each of us will have a Columbus letter in Spanish. Rarity must be computed not so much by the number of copies in existence as by the number of copies available, or likely to be available, to a desiring or intending purchaser. It is a grand old economic principle that operates with beans and blubber as with books. It is called the law of supply and demand.

Books published anywhere in Europe, particularly in England, from 1640 or 1650 to the end of the seventeenth century which mention America are *likely* to be of value on that account, though the generalization is somewhat more risky than the earlier one. This period, of course, includes many significant and costly items, some of them of far more importance and worth than several published a century and more earlier. After 1700 an item of Americana published abroad must be of special importance to be a grand desideratum, but a sufficient quantity of books fall within this category to make a long and impressive list, since the period includes such strongpoints of historical and collector interest as the French and Indian Wars and the American Revolution.

Inevitably, many problems raised in the study of early and middle Americana are still in dispute. Some of them are likely never to be solved — a consideration that does not prevent the attempt to solve them from exercising an enduring fascination. Bibliography, far from being a dry-as-dust pursuit, is as absorbing an enterprise as criminology and involves many of the identical principles — a knack of deduction, the application of common sense, and no insignificant appreciation of the fundamentals of psychology.

The earliest bibliographer of Americana was White Kennett, Bishop of Peterborough (1660–1728). Bishop Kennett, as a means of aiding the efforts of the Society for the Propagation of the Gospel in Foreign Parts (an organization of considerable importance in the history of the book in America), formed a collection of maps, documents, pamphlets, and books of American interest which was designed to assist him in the preparation of *A History of the Propagation of Christianity in the English-American Colonies*. Unfortunately this project was abandoned (had it been carried through it would have added much to the sum of our historical and bibliographical knowledge), but fortunately the Bishop found time to assemble a catalogue of his collection before he presented it to the Society. His *Bibliothecæ Americanæ Primordia* (London, 1713) is itself an occasional visitor to the auction room and commands a considerable premium.

Not quite half a century after Bishop Kennett's death, the first great native bibliographer of Americana was born in Truro, Massachusetts. Obadiah Rich served for several years as a consular officer in Spain, and, thus fortunately set close to one of the fountain-heads of American source material, assembled a remarkable library and collection of documents and manuscripts. He published at London, in 1832, *A Catalogue of Books Relating Principally to America, Arranged Under the Years in Which They Were Printed, 1500–1700*, which was followed in 1835 and 1846 by compilations covering the later periods. The manuscript of still another important catalogue was left in a hackney-coach and never recovered — it has happened in our day (though not with bibliographical copy) to Edgar Lee Masters and (substituting his own car for a hackney-coach) to Booth Tarkington.

Rich was of great assistance to Irving while the latter was busy with the investigations that pro-

19

duced *A History of the Life and Voyages of Christopher Columbus* (1828) and *Voyages and Discoveries of the Companions of Columbus* (1831). In the preface to the former work Irving paid fitting tribute to Rich's aid by calling him 'one of the most indefatigable bibliographers in Europe, who, for several years, had made particular researches after every document relative to the early history of America. In his extensive and curious library I found one of the best collections extant of Spanish colonial history.' Irving himself would have made a competent assistant to his acquisitive friend.

In the course of my rummaging [he wrote Alexander H. Everett (older brother of the great Edward) from Seville on July 11, 1828], I have come by chance upon a work on Cosmography, &c., by the Cardinal Pedro Alideo, which is cited by Las Casas as having been several times in his hands, and full of marginal notes by Columbus and his brother, the Adelantado. I found the precise work, with all the marginal notes, mostly in Latin, remarkably neatly written. It is curious in the extreme, as containing relations, &c., of Columbus, of various things bearing upon his theory, and written prior to the discovery. None of the people of the library knew of its being the handwriting of Columbus; or, indeed, seemed to attach any particular value to the book until I made them sensible of it. What a prize this would have been for friend Rich.

American bibliography owes an immeasurable debt to Henry Stevens the younger (1819–86), who followed in the footsteps of a wise father. Stevens went to London in 1845 to look for Americana, arriving at a moment when the British Museum had decided to let bygones be bygones and to increase its then somewhat unimpressive store of American books. Stevens was engaged for the task, and continued at it until his death forty years later. He had a very important share in the formation of the John Carter Brown and James Lenox collections, especially the latter. Despite his long residence in England, he never forgot that he was a native Vermonter, often signing himself 'Henry Stevens of Vermont' or adding 'G. M. B.' — that is, Green Mountain Boy — after his name. He was assisted in his researches by his younger brother, Benjamin Franklin Stevens, who later assumed charge of the famous Chiswick Press.

The first important bookseller to specialize in Americana was Thomas Rodd (1796–1849), from whose shop in Great Newport Street, London, went forth catalogues which the present-day collector scans with most acute distress. Rodd, like Stevens, was a member of a bibliophilic family. His father, Thomas before him, was bookseller, editor, historian, and poet, and his brother Horatio (who later lived in Philadelphia) was a book and print dealer and an authority on Shakespeare.

Of the later scientific bibliographers, the pioneer in the field of early Americana was Henry Harrisse. Harrisse, born in Paris in 1830, became a citizen of the United States and practiced law in New York. His *Bibliotheca Americana Vetustissima*, published in New York in 1866 (followed by *Additions*, Paris, 1872), was the principal work of reference in its field for more than forty years — until the appearance of the great Church catalogue, to be discussed presently. Harrisse worked in collaboration with Samuel Latham Mitchell Barlow, whose collection of Americana, impressive though it was, ranked below those of George Brinley, John Carter Brown, and James Lenox. Virtually every important book in these four libraries is now in an institutional collection — the Brown collection went directly to Brown University and the Lenox collection to the Lenox Library, which has since been absorbed into the New York Public Library.

Foremost among bibliographies of the earliest Americana is the monumental *Catalogue of Books Relating to the Discovery and Early History of North and South America Forming a Part of the Library of E. D. Church* (New York, 1907), compiled and annotated by George Watson Cole, now librarian emeritus of the Huntington Library at San Marino, California. No private library can ever again hope to approximate the Church collection even remotely for completeness, and the Church catalogue atones for such shortcomings and omissions as it could not avoid by including references to other known copies of rarities represented in it and by listing other rarities (such as the first Columbus letter) which Mr. Church's diligence was unable to secure. E. Dwight Church was a manufacturing chemist of Brooklyn, New York. Quietly, modestly, methodically, intelligently, he assembled over many years the fine collection which was sold on his death in 1912 to the late Henry E. Huntington, in whose library, now forever the property of the people of California, the collection remains virtually *en bloc*.

The Church catalogue itself is a rare and valuable manual. Originally published in an edition of one hundred and fifty copies, most of which were presented to institutional libraries, it appears much less frequently in auction catalogues than many of the books it describes. It is arranged in chronological order, like the Harrisse — the only logical arrangement in a work of this character — and its usefulness is augmented by the inclusion of some fourteen hundred facsimiles of colophons, title-pages, and woodcuts.

To the technical expert the Church catalogue offers an amazing conspectus of books most of which, in any copies, are not likely ever again to be represented in the auction room or the dealer's catalogue. To the collector a glance through its pages is both a disappointment and an inspiration. If he is more susceptible to the former emotion, he will say, 'Behold this marvel! It could be done once, but it can never be done again!' But if he have also the capacity for inspiration, he will add, 'But perhaps something of impressive note in a more closely specialized, more strictly limited field can be done that will still be an impressive and important contribution to scholarship, that will give me as much joy in the doing, and that will cost me infinitely less.'

The student of American books will not have gone far before he encounters the name of Joseph Sabin. A native of Northamptonshire, Sabin came to America in 1848, at the age of twenty-seven, after considerable experience in England as bookseller and publisher, despite his slender schooling. He was in the book business for many years in Philadelphia, and in the early 1860's he moved to New York, where he became one of the earliest specialists in rare books. In 1867 he began publication of *A Dictionary of Books Relating to America, from its Discovery to the Present Time*. The prospectus to this all-embracing compendium stated:

Had the magnitude and extreme difficulty of the undertaking been presented to my mind in full proportions at the outset, I should never have attempted it; and, indeed, I may remark, that I have more than once almost determined upon its abandonment; but a deep sense of its importance, however imperfectly it may be executed, and a strong partiality for bibliographical pursuits, have stimulated me to continue my labor, until the work has attained such a degree of completeness as to justify its publication, and render its completion a task of comparative ease.

Despite the 'comparative ease,' completion was denied Joseph Sabin. On his death in 1881 thirteen volumes were ready; the work is not even yet complete, having attained a twentieth volume, and the rest, from 'S' on (the dictionary is perforce in alphabetical order), is now being prepared by the Bibliographical Society of America.

The very magnitude of Sabin's *Dictionary* makes it necessary for it to confine itself to the briefest description of the books it lists — to identification, in fact, rather than to description. The twenty volumes list well in excess of eighty thousand titles, but there are inevitable omissions, particularly in the earlier volumes, so that the familiar phrase 'not in Sabin' is not necessarily an indication of excessive rarity, desirability, or value. It is, however, an indication that further research regarding the item under consideration is well worth making.

The bulk of Sabin's *Dictionary* makes it a manual which the average student and collector is not likely to have on his shelves. It is, indeed, no more readily available than the Church catalogue, but copies are to be consulted in the larger university libraries, particularly those which have impressive specialized Americana collections, and in the larger public libraries.

CHAPTER II

Cambridge Points the Road

BOOKS did not make up any considerable share of the dunnage which the Pilgrims crammed into the *Mayflower* and the less famous craft which followed in her wake to populate the Massachusetts Bay Colony. The colonists needed only a few familiar specimens of imported printing to do battle with each other and the devil, and none at all to fight Indians. But there were those among them who looked forward to a contemplative life even in the midst of inevitable privation — who foresaw, indeed, a greater need for the solace of letters on that very account. Chief among these was John Harvard, who bequeathed his library of some three hundred volumes and half his estate to the college at Newtowne, and who died in September, 1638, ignorant of the immortality which his simple act of generosity would win for him. For the General Court not alone ordered the college to take his name, but changed that of Newtowne to Cambridge in his honor.

Harvard's death must almost have coincided with the arrival of the ship *John* from London bearing, among other curiosities, a printing press. Its owner, the Reverend Jose Glover, had died on the voyage, broken down, perhaps, by his efforts to raise funds for the new college (of which he had had hopes of being president) and to prepare the way for his publishing venture. Just how greatly his passing altered the plan for the establishment of the first press in British North America there is no means of knowing;

25

the important thing is that it did not prevent the actual establishment, however greatly it may have affected the details. The equipment became the property of Glover's widow, and curious bystanders who watched it being unloaded must have been at least mildly amused at the knowledge that this queer contraption belonged to a woman.

Accompanying Glover and his wife on the *John* was Stephen Daye or Day, with his wife, their two children, Stephen, Jr., and Matthew (aged probably nineteen and seventeen respectively), William Boardman, who was Mrs. Daye's son by a former marriage, and three men servants. It is possible that Stephen Daye the elder, who was a locksmith by trade (that is, a skilled mechanic), was not intended to have anything to do with the operation of the press beyond its setting up and assembly, but the death of Glover on the high seas must have altered this arrangement and given him a prominence in the history of American printing which, if this view is correct, was not intended to be his. At all events, the press was duly established in Cambridge toward the end of 1638, with Stephen Daye in charge.

Of the first two productions of the Cambridge press which there is good evidence to show were actually produced, no examples survive. The earliest was a broadside, *The Freeman's Oath*, a putting into type of the document to which every male resident of the colony more than twenty years old, and a householder for at least six months, had to subscribe in order to become a citizen of the Massachusetts Bay Colony: 'I do solemnly bind myself in the sight of God, when I shall be called to give my voice touching any such matter of this State, in which freemen are to deal, I will give my vote and suffrage as I shall judge in mine own conscience may best conduce and tend to the public weal of that body, without respect of persons, or favor of any man.' It was a noble pronouncement — the original draft, in the hand of John Winthrop, is now in the Boston Public Library — and an example of it in its first printed form would bring a noble price in the auction room.

The second production of the Daye press, and the first in book form, was William Peirce's *Almanack* for 1639 — issued, presumably, toward the end of 1638. Peirce was a noted mariner — the doyen, in fact, of New England sailmasters. It is regrettable that not all of his activities were so commendable as the compilation of almanacs — in the very year in which he was preparing the vanished issue of 1639 he found time to transport a company of captive Pequots to the West Indies and to bring back a shipload of Negro slaves, the first to reach New England. He died a violent sailor's death in the Bahamas in 1641, little recking that if a copy of his 1639 almanac should come to light nearly three centuries later, it would be worth rather more than any cargo he ever carried.

The reasons for the disappearance of *The Freeman's Oath* and the Peirce *Almanack* are not far to seek. Both were fragile productions which were put to sturdy use. The *Almanack* was probably thumbed to bits before the last sun of 1639 had set. The chance that a copy of either production exists somewhere is excessively remote, but not beyond the bounds of possibility. The only known copy of the first issue of the Columbus letter, be it remembered, was not discovered until nearly four centuries after its publication.

Meanwhile, the Daye press was busy on a much

27

more elaborate and durable production. The Bay colonists, except those at Plymouth, had been using the Sternhold and Hopkins version of the Psalms, to their growing dissatisfaction. The need was felt for a version which would adhere more closely to the words and sense of the original, and a company of divines, some in England and some in America, assumed the task of preparing it. Chief of these were the Reverend Richard Mather, of Dorchester, and his fellow clerics Thomas Welde and John Eliot, of Roxbury. The new translation was apparently made in 1637 and 1638, and was therefore nearly ready for Stephen Daye when he established the Glover press at Cambridge. The book was issued sometime in 1640 as *The Whole Booke of Psalmes Faithfully Translated into English Metre*, and has become a pearl of exceeding price as the first surviving example of printing made in British North America. The specific geographical identification is important, for the Bay Psalm Book (that is, the Psalm Book of the Massachusetts Bay Colony), as it is popularly and properly called to distinguish it from all preceding and succeeding *Whole Bookes of Psalmes*, was far from being the first book to be printed in the New World. That honor belongs to Mexico, which beat Massachusetts by a full century.

There is evidence to show that some seventeen hundred copies of the Bay Psalm Book were printed. The survival of so specific a figure is noteworthy; there are books published as late as 1900 (or 1934, for that matter) regarding which the bibliographer could not hope to assemble such definite data. But all seventeen hundred copies were made for use, and they were used. Eleven copies only are known to exist today, and several of these give abundant indi-

24 Concerning thee shall be my prayse
   in the great assembly:
   before them that him reverence
   performe my vowes will I.
25 The meek shall eat & be suffic'd:
   Iehovah prayse shall they
   that doe him seek: your heart shall live
   unto perpetuall aye.
27 All ends of th'earth remember shall
   and turne unto the Lord:
   and thee all heathen-families
   to worship shall accord.
28 Because unto Iehovah doth
   the kingdome appertaine:
   and he among the nations
   is ruler Soveraigne.
29 Earths-fat-ones, eat & worship shall
   all who to dust descend,
   (though none can make alive his soule)
   before his face shall bend.
30 With service a posterity
   him shall attend upon,
   to God it shall accounted bee
   a generation:
31 Come shall they, & his righteousnes
   by them declar'd shall bee,
   unto a people yet unborne,
   that done this thing hath hee.
      23 A Psalme of David.
THe Lord to mee a shepheard is,
   want therefore shall not I.

                                    2 Hee

2 Hee in the folds of tender-grasse,
   doth cause mee downe to lie:
   To waters calme me gently leads
3 Restore my soule doth hee:
   he doth in paths of righteousnes:
   for his names sake leade mee.
4 Yea though in valley of deaths shade
   I walk, none ill I'le feare:
   because thou art with mee, thy rod,
   and staffe my comfort are.
5 For mee a table thou hast spread,
   in presence of my foes:
   thou dost annoynt my head with oyle,
   my cup it over-flowes.
6 Goodnes & mercy surely shall
   all my dayes follow mee:
   and in the Lords house I shall dwell
   so long as dayes shall bee.
         Psalme 24
      A psalme of david.
THe earth Iehovahs is,
   and the fulnesse of it:
   the habitable world, & they
   that there upon doe sit.
2 Because upon the seas,
   hee hath it firmly layd:
   and it upon the water-floods
   most sollidly hath stayd.
3 The mountaine of the Lord,
   who shall thereto ascend?
   and in his place of holynes,

   E 3   who

THE BAY PSALM BOOK

The John Carter Brown copy, once Richard Mather's, opened at the
Twenty-Third Psalm

cation of long and arduous service. A census of the first ten (the eleventh is a more recent discovery) is given in the facsimile edition of the Bay Psalm Book published in 1903, containing an introduction by Wilberforce Eames. Dr. Eames's summary showed that at that time seven of the ten copies were in public institutions (all except one of these being in this country) and three in the hands of private collectors in America. Of these three, two have since changed hands, one to enter an institutional collection and the other to become the crown jewel of a private library. At present, therefore, only two of the ten copies are in private hands, as is the since-discovered eleventh. All these, inevitably, will one day gravitate to public collections.

The last perfect copy to appear at public sale was that owned by George Brinley, of Hartford, Connecticut, whose library formed the most comprehensive collection of books relating to America ever assembled, and one probably forever impossible of duplication. The Brinley collection was catalogued by Dr. James Hammond Trumbull, who accomplished the task with such competence that the Brinley catalogue, despite the fact that the sale was initiated in 1879, remains today a reference manual of highly practical worth. Dr. Trumbull was too good a scholar to permit himself to become ecstatic in print, and it may therefore have been the auctioneer rather than himself who appended this note to the description of the Bay Psalm Book:

> To offer any remarks on the RARITY or the IM-PORTANCE of this precious volume would be sheer impertinence. The acquisition of a copy of the original edition of the Bay Psalm Book must always be the crowning triumph to which every American collector

aspires — while the chances of acquisition are constantly diminishing. It is by no means probable that another copy will be offered for competition within the next quarter of a century at least.

The prophet, whoever he was, erred by ten years, because the Livermore copy came up for sale in 1894. But with that single exception (which was not a particularly striking exception) he was more than accurate, for no copy has been offered at auction since the Livermore. The Livermore copy lacked thirty-six pages of text and, far more important, the title-leaf.

Only one other copy has met the test of the auction block in America, but that one happens to be the most desirable copy known. As long ago as 1703, when the Bay Psalm Book was no further removed from contemporaneity than *Little Women* is today, Thomas Prince, of Boston, then a youth in his teens, conceived the idea of forming a collection of New England books and documents. By the date of his death (1758) the collection had grown to notable proportions — so notable, indeed, that had it by some happy chance been maintained intact until today, its appearance in the market would create a sensation without parallel in the history of book and autograph collecting in America. In addition to his books and manuscripts, Prince left a worthy monument to himself in his own career. He was graduated from Harvard in 1707, traveled widely for his inconvenient day, become co-pastor (with his classmate Dr. Joseph Sewall, 'the weeping prophet') of Old South Church, Boston, and compiled historical and bibliographical data of enduring importance.

Prince willed his collection to Old South, and it remained in the steeple for a century, accumulating dust, prestige, and value. Some of it vanished when the British held Boston, though there appears to be no direct evidence that the invaders themselves took any of it — it is simply easier to blame them than anyone else. One may at least be grateful that they did not set fire to the town. For high overhead reposed no fewer than five copies of the Bay Psalm Book — five of the eleven known to survive today. One of these had once been the property of Richard Mather, the principal translator, and bore his autograph.

The Mather copy has had an exciting history that did not lapse into dullness with the departure of General Gage's redcoats. In 1860 it came into the possession of Dr. Nathaniel Shurtleff, physician, scientist, historian, genealogist, and three times mayor of Boston. Dr. Shurtleff seems to have rated a Bay Psalm Book if any individual ever did, for he could trace his lineage to no fewer than eleven of the *Mayflower's* passengers. He died in 1874, and a little more than a year later, his library was put up for sale and duly sold — save for the Bay Psalm Book. Officials of Old South, complacent enough while the Prince books were in storage in the steeple, were granted an injunction staying the sale. The Shurtleff estate at length won the right to dispose of the book, and on October 12, 1876, it was knocked down to Sidney S. Rider, of Providence, for $1025. For the next five years it was in the library of a private collector, and following his death in 1881 it became the property of the John Carter Brown Library, Brown University. Since it is forever removed from the market, speculation regarding its present-day value is to little purpose.

No fewer than four of the eleven extant copies of the Bay Psalm Book lack the title-page — clamorous testimony to the fact that the rugged Christians of the colony responded as lustily with their hands as with their voices. A book without a title-page is in general as valueless as a building without a roof. But there are many buildings without roofs which are carefully preserved as survivals of significant civilizations, just as there are statues without arms and heads on which are bestowed the tender ministrations of great governments. But it is only the Parthenons and the Venuses of Milo and the Winged Victories of Samothrace, only the Gutenberg Bibles and the First Folio Shakespeares and the Bay Psalm Books, which continue to merit preservation after suffering the casual amputations wrought by carelessness and ignorance and the flight of time. Booth Tarkington's *The Gentleman from Indiana*, Edwin Arlington Robinson's *The Torrent and the Night Before*, H. L. Mencken's *Ventures into Verse* — these, in first edition, may be valuable books in their own right, but strip them of their title-pages and they deflate audibly to zero. Only the company of the great elect of printing can hope to retain some shred of monetary value in truncated or fragmentary form.

Between 1638 and 1692 more than two hundred books, pamphlets, and broadsides appeared from the Cambridge press. Of forty or so of these titles, no copies are known to survive. Many of the others exist only in unique or imperfect exemplars. No one of the two-hundred-odd is abundant, to put the case at the extreme of optimism. Any early Cambridge imprint, obviously, is not only excessively rare but of considerable value. A significant measure of the unattainability of this aristocratic group is the fact that the earliest Cambridge imprint in the Library of Congress is Richard Mather's *The Summe of Certaine Sermons Upon Genes: 25. 6*, issued in 1652.

The fact that theology was writ with a big, big **T** in primeval New England would be sufficiently apparent from a glance at the Cambridge titles were other evidence lacking. For the rest, there were almanacs, Harvard theses (a sort of program of Commencement exercises), spellers, a *Capital Lawes* of 1643 of which no copy is known to exist, and a *Book of Lawes and Liberties* of 1648. There was little frivolity in the Massachusetts Bay Colony in the seventeenth century.

Cambridge imprints fall into two classes so far as their collecting prestige is concerned. The first group includes any book printed before 1675, the date of the earliest Boston imprint. The second includes books appearing between 1675 and the end of the century, during which period Boston was establishing that primacy in the publishing world which was to attain its magnificent height not quite two centuries later. Early Boston imprints are of value as imprints up to about 1725, after which year they must possess some special distinction beyond mere place and date to make them items of moment — an exception broad enough to let in numerous important books of much later appearance. The selection of the year 1725 is frankly and conservatively arbitrary; there are few bookmen who would sniff at a 1726 Boston imprint, and some who would look at least twice at one of, say, 1737, falling within the first century of printing in New England. Both booksellers and collectors are a somewhat impious crew, and it must regretfully be explained that an early New England item whose contents are concerned with the things of this world is likely to be many times more valuable, sentimentally and practically, than one having to do solely with the Kingdom of God.

33

Yet the most romantically interesting product of the Cambridge press itself was quite definitely concerned with the affairs of the spirit. In the autumn of 1631, well before the arrival of the Reverend Jose Glover's printing press, John Eliot reached Boston in the ship *Lyon*. Eliot had been born before Milton and was to survive until after the birth of Pope, thus providing, quite unconsciously, a long and sturdy link between two disparate Englands. Receiving his degree from Jesus College, Cambridge, in 1622, Eliot taught school, became a preacher, and then underwent a travail of soul that sent him into the camp of the dissenters. Arrived in the Bay Colony, he soon became 'teacher' in the church at Roxbury, inaugurating thereby an affiliation that lasted almost sixty years.

Eliot's interest in the Indians probably dated from his first sight of them. What a wealth of material to win to the Lord! Before many years had passed, he was studying their language, and eventually mastered it in accordance with a recipe whose terms, as pronounced by himself, have become famous: 'We must not sit still, and look for miracles: Up, and be doing, and the Lord will be with thee. Prayer and Pains, through Faith in Jesus Christ, will do any thing.' It was probably in 1654 that Eliot published his *Primer of the Massachusetts Indian Language* — one of the vanished Cambridge imprints. He had already, as has been noted, borne a share in the preparation of the Bay Psalm Book.

But he had a larger project in view than the mere compilation of Indian vocabularies. It was nothing less ambitious than a Bible in the native dialect. Consider for a moment the difficulties that the task imposed. It involved, first, the rendering of an utterly alien speech into English sounds and characters, to be followed by the transposition of hundreds of thousands of words of unintelligible copy into type at the hands of compositors who had no knowledge of what they were setting (apart from the recurrence of the familiar proper names of Scripture), and who worked with primitive equipment in a land in which the printing press itself was still a somewhat mysterious novelty. The keystone of this fragile arch was certainly James the Printer, later officially christened James Printer, a bright Indian lad whom Eliot trained for the task with the assistance of the experts, and who thus became the first native-born craftsman — or at least the first craftsman of native ancestry — to learn and practice the art of typography in the British colonies.

The financing of the publication was not the least of the problems connected with it, but this was accomplished by the establishment, by act of Parliament, of 'a Corporation for the Promoting and Propagating the Gospel of Jesus Christ in New England,' which came to be generally known as the New England Company. A quantity of paper and a new press were sent over from England, and an assistant printer, Marmaduke Johnson, was dispatched in the summer of 1660 to help Samuel Green, who was carrying on where Stephen Daye had left off.

The New Testament was ready in 1661, appearing in an edition of fifteen hundred copies, of which a thousand were reserved for binding with the Old Testament on its completion two years later. The New Testament separately, therefore, is much scarcer than the two Testaments together. Forty copies of the New Testament were sent to England,

and these (with perhaps a few more) had an English title-page in addition to the Indian, and a leaf dedicating the work to King Charles II, not long since returned in triumph to his royal perquisites. In the whole range of Christendom probably nobody was less impressed by the performance than the dedicatee.

John Eliot's Bible enjoys the distinction of being the first edition of the Scriptures to be printed in the New World. In 1743, Christoph Sauer, of Germantown, Pennsylvania, published a Bible in German, but forty-nine more years were to elapse before the appearance of an American-made Bible in English from the press of Robert Aitken, of Philadelphia.

The economic supremacy of such rarities as the Bay Psalm Book and the Eliot Indian Bible in the history of the book in America can never be questioned, but there is one other title whose transcending sentimental importance must ever outweigh that of these and other great predecessors, and whose monetary worth as well in its early issues can scarcely be called negligible. The beginnings of the *New England Primer* are shrouded in a mystery that may never be dissipated, although in bibliography it is folly to assume that the solution of any problem is hopeless. The idea of the *Primer* seems to have originated with a humble London printer named John Gaine, who in the fall of 1683 deposited with the Stationers' Company a book called *The New England Primer or Milk for babes*. A year and a half later no copies seem to have been available, for a Boston bookseller inquired for them and was told none were to be had. Nor, in the quarter-millennium that has since elapsed, has a single copy come to light.

In 1686, another London printer, Benjamin Harris, emigrated to Boston, and, sometime between that year and the end of 1690, issued the earliest native *New England Primer*. Toward the close of the latter year a second edition was in process, for at the end of Henry Newman's *News from the Stars*, an almanac for 1691 (printed, doubtless at the end of 1690, 'by R. Peirce for Benjamin Harris'), appeared this advertisement:

> There is now in the Press, and will suddenly be extant, a Second Impression of *The New-England Primer enlarged*, to which is added, more *Directions for Spelling:* the *Prayer of K Edward* the *6th*. and *Verses made by Mr. Rogers the Martyr, left as a legacy to his Children:* (Sold by Benjamin Harris).

Such unequivocal evidence admits of no gainsaying. And considering the subsequent popularity of the *New England Primer*, it is almost equally certain that impression succeeded impression, to the great profit of Mr. Harris, and, after his return to England, to the profit of such publishers as continued to carry on the good work. Yet the earliest issue of the *Primer* to survive is that printed at Boston by S. Kneeland & T. Green in 1727, and of this edition but one example, now in the New York Public Library, is known. It is incredible that young America then stopped reading for eight years; on the contrary, young America read to such enthusiastic purpose that the next surviving issue (likewise represented today by only a single copy, which is in the Huntington Library) is that of 1735. Copies dated 1737, 1738, 1744, 1746, and 1749 also are known, some of these later years also being represented by unique examples. All of the earliest issues were printed in Boston; the earliest surviving copy with a New York imprint

(James Parker) is dated 1750, and the earliest
Philadelphia example (James Chattin), 1757. Yet
the Philadelphia firm of Franklin and Hall is known
to have issued edition after edition from 1749 on,
though the earliest survivor bearing this imprint is
dated 1764.

Charles F. Heartman, in *The New-England Primer
Issued Prior to 1830* (1934), estimates that in the pre-
sumptive century and a half between the earliest issues
of the *Primer* and the dawn of the railroad era, between
six and eight million copies of this immensely popular
guide to little minds and souls were printed. 'Of this
number,' he adds, 'probably less than fifteen hundred
are still extant.' There have been numerous editions
since 1830, but after that date the *Primer* came to
be issued more and more as a curiosity for the benefit of an America that was beginning to be conscious
of its romantic past. Accepting Mr. Heartman's estimate, how many million tiny native sons and daughters first learned through the pages of the *Primer*
that

In Adam's Fall
We Sinned all,

or read breathlessly of the tree-climbing prowess of
Zacchæus? There must have been three or four
readers to a copy oftener than there was a single
reader, for it was a day of ample families and frugal
book budgets.

Chronologically, the story of printing in British
North America shifts from Massachusetts to the
Middle Colonies, but for geographical convenience
the rest of New England will here be considered
before the Harlem and the Hudson are crossed.

The hegemony of Boston in the field of printing

and publishing remained secure throughout the last quarter of the seventeenth century, and has, of course, never been threatened since that day by any other center in New England. In 1709, Thomas Short, who had probably learned his trade from Bartholomew Green, went to New London, Connecticut, and set up a press there. Connecticut's official printing had previously been done in Cambridge or Boston, and Short left the latter city with the assurance that the colony's business would be given to him. His first imprints, and thus the first to be issued in Connecticut, were a proclamation for a fast and *An Act for Making and Emitting Bills of Publick Credit*, both broadsides, which were followed by the first book to be printed in Connecticut, *A Confession of Faith, Owned and Consented to by the Elders and Messengers of the Churches in the Colony of Connecticut in New-England*, the printing of which, although the title-page was dated 1710, was probably not completed until the following year. The book is better known as the Saybrook Platform. Short was succeeded by Timothy Green, of the Massachusetts Greens, who came to New London in 1714 by invitation of the Connecticut Assembly and until his retirement some years before his death in 1757 remained the colony's official printer. A press was established at New Haven in 1754 by James Parker, and its first production was a compilation, in Latin, of the laws of Yale College, dated 1755. So exhilarated was Parker by the thought that he was issuing the first book ever printed in New Haven that he called special attention to the fact on the title-page: 'Liber Primus Novo-Portu impressus.' Not until 1764 did the first Hartford imprint appear under the sponsorship of Thomas Green, a great-great-grandson of the

39

Samuel Green who had himself succeeded Stephen
Daye at Cambridge. Yet Hartford swiftly made up
for lost time, and during the early years of the nineteenth century became one of the most important
publishing centers in the United States, as well as the
site of a literary colony of impressive numbers and
importance. It reasserted its publishing prominence
soon after the Civil War with the rise of the American
Publishing Company and the almost coincident
appearance, Lochinvar-like out of the West, of
Samuel Langhorne Clemens. *The Innocents Abroad*,
*Roughing It, Mark Twain's Sketches, The Adventures
of Tom Sawyer, A Tramp Abroad, The Tragedy of
Pudd'nhead Wilson*, and *Following the Equator* first
appeared with Hartford imprints, the earliest of them
little more than a century after Thomas Green had
set up shop.

Printing was not introduced into Rhode Island
until 1727, when James Franklin, brother of Benjamin, and his elder by nine years, sought in Newport
that felicity of peace which was so difficult of acquisition in the politico-theological storm-center that
was Boston. His *New-England Courant* had aroused
the ire of Cotton and Increase Mather, the former of
whom charged it with being 'full freighted with
nonsense, unmannerliness, raillery, profaneness, im-
morality, arrogance, calumnies, lies, contradictions,
and what not, all tending to quarrels and divisions.'
Sometime previously Cotton Mather had canceled
his subscription to the *Courant*, in the manner of
outraged subscribers before and since, and James
Franklin had charged him in print with sending his
grandson to buy it surreptitiously thereafter. It was
a splendid advertisement for the *Courant*, but Mather
was not the man to yield as long as there was anyone

to fight with, and James Franklin ultimately spent a month in jail for his nose-thumbing. Not until 1726, however, did he decide he had had enough and go to Newport. Here he issued, the following year, a pamphlet, *John Hammett's Vindication and Relation*, followed soon after by an *Almanack* for 1728, of which a single copy survives. On his death in 1735, the business was conducted by his widow, Anne, assisted by her two daughters and, as soon as he was old enough, by a son James. The daughters, declared Isaiah Thomas, in his *History of Printing in America* (Worcester, 1810), 'were correct and quick compositors at case' and likewise 'sensible and amiable women.' In Providence, then and for many years later the second city of the colony, printing was not introduced until 1762, when William Goddard (who, like James Parker, of New Haven, was a product of New York training) established a business into which, a few years later, his mother entered as an active partner. The important share borne by women in the spread of printing in colonial America, beginning with the widow of the Reverend Jose Glover, is noteworthy, though Old England could offer an occasional precedent, such as that Mary Fenner who carried on for four years as Cambridge University printer after the death of her husband William in 1734.

James Franklin had had a taste of prison for his temerity with the types; Daniel Fowle was to suffer for the temerity of another, and as a consequence printing was soon established in New Hampshire. Fowle had been a printing proprietor in Boston since 1740, when he was twenty-five years old. In 1754 he was charged with having issued an allegorical pamphlet, *The Monster of Monsters*, attacking the recently passed Excise Act. He spent three days in jail, relieved his feelings during the next few months by writing and publishing two pamphlets about the injustice, and in 1756 was invited to come to Portsmouth. In November of that year he issued the inevitable *Almanack*. His main concern, however, was his newspaper, the *New Hampshire Gazette*, the first number of which antedated the *Almanack* by several weeks. Not alone was the *Gazette* the first newspaper in New Hampshire, but it enjoys a unique distinction for all America in the fact that it survives to this day as the oldest continuously published newspaper in the United States.

The first Vermont press was established in 1778 in the village of Dresden, on the east bank of the Connecticut — now Hanover, New Hampshire, where the backs go tearing by. Here Alden Spooner issued in that year, among other ephemera, a Thanksgiving proclamation — a fitting example of original printing in view of the subsequent and deserved repute of the Vermont turkey. Two years later his brother, Judah Padock Spooner, began to print in the village of Westminster, on soil that was then and is yet unequivocal Vermont.

Printing was introduced into Maine (then still a part of Massachusetts) in 1785 with the establishment at Falmouth of *The Falmouth Gazette and Weekly Advertiser* by Benjamin Titcomb and Thomas B. Wait, who moved to Portland that same year. In 1786 appeared at Portland, with the Wait imprint, an edition of David Fenning's *Universal Spelling-Book*, a popular English importation, and Eleazar Moody's (or Moodey's) *The School of Good Manners. Composed for the Help of Parents — Teaching Children How to Behave During Their Minority*.

Numerous useful state and local bibliographies are

available to student and collector (if not often for purchase, then at least for consultation in university and public libraries), and the most recent index of these manuals is to be found in Margaret Bingham Stillwell's *Incunabula and Americana, 1450–1800: A Key to Bibliographical Study* (New York: Columbia University Press, 1931). Several of these bibliographies, however, originally compiled with fidelity and accuracy, have now become, through no fault of their compilers, sadly out of date, and the seeker after book knowledge should perpetually bear in mind Miss Stillwell's admonition to consult the latest authorities as well as the earlier, regardless of the merited prestige won by earlier scholars.

The monumental and inclusive bibliographical reference work on early American books and printing is Charles Evans's *American Bibliography*, the purpose of which is clearly defined in its secondary title: *A Chronological Dictionary of all Books, Pamphlets and Periodical Publications Printed in the United States of America from the Genesis in 1639 down to and Including the Year 1820*. The first volume of this vast undertaking appeared in 1903, published by the compiler himself, and was preceded (since he was his own vice-president in charge of sales) by a prospectus explaining the purpose of the work, defining its spheres of usefulness, and appealing *seriatim* to the various groups who would be technically interested in it. Thus specifically did he address the booksellers, and this apostrophe is here given both for its own sake and also by way of proof that a bibliographer is not necessarily a pedantic, two-footed crustacean without heart or humor:

To my dear friend, and enemy, the Dealer in old books, I would also address a few words of pious regard;

43

for, on my soul, I love thee, thou half-starved picker-up of unconsidered trifles! With all contrition I confess that, as I have pored over the blurred and ill-digested pages of your Catalogues, thee have I damned. Yea! even with a damn which reached from Dan to Beer-sheba. But I love thy tribe. There is a bond of sympathy between us. And I would be thy Moses. I love thy musty, dim, ill-lighted shops; but more do I love thy stalls in the warm sunlight; for there thy crass ignorance of thy wares is shown me to my profit. For have not mine eyes seen, on the populous street of a great city, exposed to the rude gaze of every passer-by, Samuel Willard's *Compleat Body of Divinity* (Boston, 1726) — the first folio volume, other than laws, printed in the United States — standing upon an open stall, its nearly thousand pages sagging in its covers; its full calf binding stained by the falling rain — teardrops of Heaven! And, tied around it with string, as if to conceal its nakedness, was a leaf, on which was rudely written with red ink: This book, over one hundred and fifty years old, only one dollar! So, too, did Hester Prynne stand in the market place with the Scarlet letter on her breast for the sin of another! Go to, thou dullard! if thou art fortunate to possess a copy, hie thee to the dusty shelf on which this treasure lies neglected; add fifty dollars to thy selling price, or, better still, encase it in a plush-lined case, for the time is at hand when its value will increase an hundred-fold, even as has the first folio of the divine William. And is it also left to me, thou purblind and bald-headed thief of Time! to teach thee, after all these years, how thou shalt print thy Catalogues to thy profit? Then arrange thy wares in an orderly and chronological manner. Compel not thy customer to wade through pages filled with modern abominations of printed books in search of the rare editions of the past, to his sore disappointment and loss of time. Then will he see at a glance whether thou possessest that which he desires. Verily, verily! will the ducats flow into the coffers of him who followeth this my admonition. Hark thee! it is by words of wisdom like unto these, scattered through my pages, that I expect to win and hold thy love. By these, and many more like unto them, shalt thou profit if thou subscribest, and that quickly, for my book of books. But, if thou do it not, then will thy flesh be mortified by seeing thy detested rival across the way, Smirk, him, whom thou in thy heart hast so often anathematized as an old junk dealer, who doesn't know a book from a brick; yet, who is wiser than thou if thou do it not, him wilt thou see flourish like the green bay tree, even as the chariots of the wealthy stand without his door and wait. If thou subscribest quickly, in place of the lean and grimy paw in which I drop the pennies for my purchase now, then will I see thy plump, well-favored hand stroking the sides of my book of books, and fondly calling it the Old Bookseller's Bible.

Evans's *American Bibliography* has indeed become the bookseller's Bible, even though its Revelation is yet to be written. When the first volume appeared in 1903, its compiler had already devoted some sixteen years to the task; when he died in February, 1935, he was hard at work on the twelfth volume. The eleventh volume, completing the year 1797, appeared in 1931, so that Mr. Evans was then able to add twenty-eight years to the sixteen he had given to the work before the first volume appeared. The drudgery implicit in the effort may be measured in part by the inevitable growth in the number of titles year after year. Thus, the years 1639 and 1640 together occupy only three pages (including a full-page description of the Bay Psalm Book), whereas the year 1797 requires two hundred and seventy-five pages. The arrangement is necessarily chronological, but alphabetical within the separate years, and cross-indexes in each volume supply convenient references to authors, subjects, and places.

The announcement 'not in Evans' occasionally appears proudly in auction and booksellers' catalogues, but such a designation is a tribute to a reference manual whose serviceability has been vastly enhanced with the passage of the years and the tremendous growth in the interest in American books. The tag 'not in Sabin' is also familiar, and this duplication of negatives has occasionally given rise to the supposition that the manuals cover identical fields. But, as Mr. Evans points out, Sabin's *Dictionary* is concerned with books *relating to* America, wherever printed, whereas Evans's *American Bibliography* has to do solely with books *produced in* America.

What and when is rarity among colonial imprints? Albert Carlos Bates discussed this question and offered an abundance of examples in a paper, 'Some Notes on Early Connecticut Printing,' which he contributed to *The Papers of the Bibliographical Society of America* (Volume XXVII, Part I, 1933). The fact that Mr. Bates was concerned with the imprints of a single colony is incidental; he properly chose a field to the study of which he had devoted 'a considerable number of years — more, perhaps, than I would care to admit'; a similar survey of the other colonies would exhibit a parallel condition. The period embraced in Mr. Bates's study was from 1709 to the end of the eighteenth century — roughly the first century of printing in Connecticut. Of the proclamation for a fast printed by Thomas Short at New London in 1709, already referred to, one copy survives. Twelve other similar pronouncements were presumably issued under Short's direction; none is

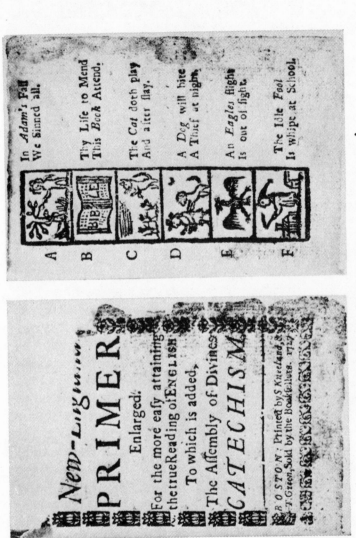

THE EARLIEST EXTANT 'NEW-ENGLAND PRIMER'
Title and first page of alphabet of the unique copy of the 1727 Boston edition
in the New York Public Library

known. One of the earliest imprints by Timothy Green, Short's successor, was also a proclamation for a fast, of which one copy is known. A bridge under construction at Norwich collapsed in 1728 and the catastrophe was duly celebrated in a pamphlet printed by Green; the fact that the pamphlet had once existed was known, but no copy came to light until the twentieth century, and that copy remains so far unique. Connecticut's last official printer of this era was another Timothy Green, whose tenure of office (1763-94) included the busy period of the Revolution. Broadsides were emitted from his press almost with the zeal and rapidity of balls from flint-locks — and with about as much likelihood of surviving as the powder flashes that sped the theoretically deadlier missiles. The fugitive character of these imprints is set forth statistically by Mr. Bates:

The last week in April, 1775, a proclamation for an embargo on the exportation of provision was issued. No one of the 80 copies printed is now known. Then came a proclamation of 400 copies stating the wages of soldiers — no copy known. Next a vote of the assembly to encourage the making of firelocks — no copy known. This was followed by 400 'beating orders,' so-called, authorizing enlistments, of which one, possibly two, have survived. The same number of copies were printed of a vote of the assembly 'recommending sobriety' to the people, only one or two copies of which are known. In May another embargo was laid — 80 copies printed, none to be found. Again in August came still another embargo — 140 copies printed, none to be found. An act for raising and equipping a body of minutemen was passed in December, 1775; only one of the 350 copies printed can now be found.

Nor is this shortage confined exclusively to such tenuous productions as broadsides. *The American*

47

Singing Book, by Daniel Reed, was published in New Haven as late as 1785; one copy is extant. Twelve years later there appeared at New Haven a summary of *The Advantages and Disadvantages of the Marriage State*. Mr. Bates comments that 'it certainly is to be regretted that but one copy of this tract is now to be found.' Post-Revolutionary New Haven devoured the literature of crime with equal avidity; *A Faithful Narrative of Elizabeth Wilson*, executed (both the narrative and Elizabeth) in Pennsylvania in 1786, which was reprinted in Connecticut the same year, was conned with such zeal that the edition is represented today by a single copy. Lightning killed three Suffield youths in 1767 and the Reverend Ebenezer Gay pounced on the event and gave the world a *Sermon*; one copy is known, but, oddly enough, a broadside chronicle of the tragedy in verse is known by two copies.

There is, Mr. Bates concedes, danger in stressing the singleness of single copies, the uniquity of the 'only one known.' 'There may be other copies,' he explains, 'on the shelves of collectors who prefer to have their treasures remain unknown to others, or libraries which have not been examined may be found to contain copies of publications which had previously been thought to be unique. And at any time, one or a number of copies of a publication not previously known may come to light.' And he mentions, without identifying, a Connecticut pamphlet 'a copy of which will appear perhaps once in five years in an auction or a dealer's catalogue, where it will be noted as "very rare." Probably there are only two or three readers of the catalogue who are aware that there is a remainder being held back by one party, evidently in the hope of a further advance in the price.' This contingency, it should be added, is not likely to arise with sufficient frequency to give the collector of colonial imprints grave concern.

CHAPTER III

Mr. Bradford Understands a Want

NOT quite sixty-two years to the day after the *Mayflower* had pushed a tentative prow westward, the ship *Welcome* set out from Deal with one hundred souls on board, inaugurating thereby an argosy which eventually was to prove as fruitful as that of its highly publicized predecessor — and which immediately proved far more horrible. For smallpox came to ravage the packed little vessel, and when, at the end of November, 1682, it anchored in the Delaware River off the settlement of Newcastle, thirty of the hundred, including the master of the ship, had gone a darker and more arduous journey.

Of the seventy who were spared, certainly the most important was the head of the expedition, who had come to America as proprietor of a considerable domain which had been granted him by Charles II in lieu of moneys due the proprietor's father. The new continent (though by his day it was hardly so new as it had once been) was manna from heaven to the most spendthrift of the Stuarts. The proprietor wanted to call his allotment New Wales, and then, when this suggestion was amiably frowned on, Sylvania. Charles, out of the fullness of his heart and the emptiness of his pocket, suggested prefixing the name of Penn to this woody derivative as a gesture of honor, not to young William Penn, but to his father, Admiral Sir William Penn, who will endure forever as one of the vivid personalities of his time through the accident of having been a next-door neighbor of Samuel Pepys. Young Penn objected vigorously, and even went so far as to offer money to the King's secretary in an effort to hire a friend at court. But Charles was obdurate. Pennsylvania it must be.

Accompanying Penn on the *Welcome's* grisly voyage may have been a youth of nineteen named William Bradford. Born in Leicestershire in 1663, Bradford had served an apprenticeship to Andrew Sowle, Quaker printer, accomplishing thereby a threefold destiny. He learned printing, he became a Quaker (though he did not die one), and he fell in love with Sowle's daughter Elizabeth.

It makes a better story, naturally, if Bradford accompanied Penn, but the scales of historical evidence incline against the probability. If Bradford did reach America in 1682, there was little for him to do save look about him, watch the rapid growth of the city of Philadelphia (which within a year boasted a hundred houses), and contemplate the opportunity that would soon await a skilled printer. At all events, Bradford was in London at the end of April, 1685, to claim his Elizabeth, and a few weeks later bride and groom embarked for America, the latter fortified with a letter of recommendation and introduction bearing no less impressive a signature than that of George Fox, the founder of the Society of Friends.

Arrived in Philadelphia (it was Elizabeth's first visit, anyway), Bradford, now twenty-two years old, seems to have set up shop almost immediately, and by the end of the year he had issued the first example of printing to appear in the Middle Colonies. Its title-page, of an amplitude common to the times, merits reproduction in full: *Kalendarium Pennsilvaniense, or, America's Messinger. Being an Almanack for the Year of Grace, 1686. Wherein is contained both the English & Forreign Account, the Motions of the Planets Through the Signs, with the Luminaries, Conjunctions, Aspects, Eclipses; the rising, southing and setting of the Moon, with the time when she passeth by, or is with the most eminent fixed Stars: Sun rising and setting, and the time of High-Water at the City of Philadelphia, &c. With Chronologies, and many other Notes, Rules and Tables, very fitting for every man to know & have; all which is accomodated to the Longitude of the Province of Pennsilvania, and Latitude of 40 Degr. north, with a Table of Houses for the same, which may indifferently serve New-England, New York, East & West Jersey, Maryland, and most parts of Virginia. By Samuel Atkins. Student in the Mathamaticks and Astrology. And the Stars in their Courses fought against Sesera, Judg. 5. 29. Printed and Sold by William Bradford at Philadelphia in Pennsilvania, 1685.*

Little is known of Samuel Atkins beyond the fact that he compiled and edited this earliest Pennsylvania imprint. He makes one other sortie into recorded history, as will presently be noted, and then is seen no more, according to Charles P. Hildeburn in *A Century of Printing: The Issues of the Press in Pennsylvania, 1685–1784* (Philadelphia, two volumes, 1885–86). Hildeburn quotes Atkins's foreword to the *Kalendarium,* an ingenuous and entertaining combination of apologia and sales talk.

I had thoughts [Atkins adds after his preliminary detailed explanation of the plan of the compilation] to have incerted a Figure of the Moons Eclips, a small Draught of the form of this City, and a Table to find the hour of the day by the Shadow of a Staff; but we having not Tools to carve them in that form that I would have them, nor time to calculate the other, I pass it for this year, and not only promise it in the next, but likewise several other more particular Notes and Observations, which shall not only be useful to this Province, but likewise to the neighboring Provinces on both sides. In the meantime, except this my Mite, being my first Fruits, and you will encourage me, according to my Ability, to serve you in what I may, or can, whilst I am SAMUELL ATKINS.

How long he remained 'Samuell Atkins' there is no way of knowing. Clearly he was an itinerant starmonger, a troubadour of the sciences, who made his living as best he might at that thin trade up and down the Middle Colonies. One would like to know more about him, for he personified a romantic tradition that did not long survive him.

An almanac seems a harmless enough initiatory product for a pioneer of printing, but, for all that, his *Kalendarium Pennsilvaniense* got Bradford, and Atkins along with him, into difficulty. The almanac contained the customary schedule of important events in history, and opposite one date was the entry: 'The beginning of the Government here by the Lord Penn.' Samuel Atkins was called before the provincial council and commanded to blot out the courtesy title, and William Bradford was ordered thereafter 'not to print anything but what shall have lycence from the council.'

Bradford himself was a contributor to the *Kalendarium*, and his address, 'The Printer to the Readers,' offers an admirable first-hand picture of the state of printing in Pennsylvania at the end of 1685:

Hereby understand that after great Charge and Trouble, I have brought that great Art and Mystery of *Printing* to this part of *America* believing it may be of great service to you in several respects, hoping to find

Encouragement, not only in this Almanack, but what else I shall enter upon for the use and service of the Inhabitants of these Parts. Some Irregularities, there be in this Diary, which I desire you to pass by this year; for being lately come hither, my Matereals were Mis placed, and out of order, whereupon I was forced to use Figures & Letters of various sizes, but understanding the want of something of this nature, and being importuned thereto, I ventured to make publick this, desiring you to accept thereof, and by the next, (as I find encouragement) shall endeavour to have things compleat. And for the ease of Clarks, Scrivniers, &c. I propose to print blank Bills, Bonds, Letters of Attourney, Indentures, Warrants, &c. and what else presents itself, wherein I shall be ready to serve you; and remain your Friend W. BRADFORD.

Bradford's announcement was dated at Philadelphia, 'the 28th 10th Month [i.e., December], 1685'; Atkins's, twenty-five days earlier.

That 'great Art and Mystery of Printing,' however, continued, from the point of view of vested authority, to be regarded as a black art and an unhallowed mystery. Four years later difficulties arose between the governor and the populace, and Bradford put the charter of the colony in print, to the high anger of the governor. The printer was summoned before the council, and an account of the hearing survives in his own hand. One passage in his testimony has all the dignity and nobility of Milton's *Areopagitica*:

Governour, it is my imploy, my trade and calling, and that by which I get my living, to print; and if I may not print such things as come to my hand, which are innocent, I cannot live.... If I print one thing to-day, and the contrary party bring me another to-morrow, to contradict it, I cannot say that I shall not print it. Printing is a manufacture of the nation, and therefore ought rather to be encouraged than suppressed.

Despite this courageous manifesto, worse was to come. In 1692 the Society of Friends in Pennsylvania became a house divided. Bradford printed a tract for the weaker of the warring groups, and was forthwith put under arrest and his plant seized, including the chase which held the types from which the fatal pamphlet had been printed. The case came to trial, and it was for the prosecution to prove that Bradford had actually printed the offending declaration. No witness could be produced who had seen him print it, but the prosecution had the locked chase as a telling Exhibit A with which to confound the defense. The chase was passed around among the jury, until one clumsy juror, none too type-wise, let the form drop, and the case for the prosecution dissolved in pi.

Toward the end of April, 1693, Bradford's equipment was restored to him. About a month previously, however, the New York Council had offered him the position of public printer, and Bradford accepted, influenced doubtless by a variety of reasons. Perhaps not least among these was a willingness to be quit of the controversial atmosphere of the City of Brotherly Love and a complementary and human-natural eagerness to goad the flanks of his oppressors from a safe remove. At all events the presumed first issue of Bradford's press in Manhattan, and thus the first example of printing in New York City and State, was *New-England's Spirit of Persecution Transmitted to Pennsilvania, And the Pretended Quaker found Persecuting the True Christian-Quaker, in the Tryal of Peter Boss, George Keith, Thomas Budd, and William Bradford, At the Sessions held at Philadelphia the Nineth,*

Tenth and Twelfth Day of December, 1692. Giving an Account of the most Arbitrary Procedure of that Court. Printed in the Year 1693.

This quarto pamphlet of thirty-eight text pages (with page 33 misnumbered 31 in Bradford's excitement) is reproduced entire in facsimile in Douglas C. McMurtrie's *New York Printing MDCXCIII* (Chicago: The John Calhoun Club, 1928), and here the student of wordy battles of long ago may read it if he will. He should also devote at least a passing glance to the reproduction in full of the second (or possibly the first) product of Bradford's New York press, a companion piece to the first (or possibly the second): *A Paraphrastical Exposition on a Letter from a Gentleman in Philadelphia to his Friend in Boston Concerning a certain Person who compared himself to Mordecai.* The author of this labored and dull, rhymed polemic, of which a single copy survives, now in the collection of Dr. A. S. W. Rosenbach, was John Philly or Phillips. The object of his attack was Samuel Jennings, who had presided at the Bradford trial, and whose name is given in acrostic in the proemium. There is a possibility that both these pamphlets were actually printed in Philadelphia, but in view of Bradford's most recent and sharpest skirmish with the authorities it would have been folly for him to have defied them on their home grounds when his transfer to a city of refuge was so near at hand. And if Bradford actually issued the pamphlets, out of bravado, under the very noses of his oppressors, would he not in all likelihood have stressed this fact by using a Philadelphia imprint instead of none at all?

During his first year as 'Printer to King William and Queen Mary' in New York, Bradford issued between thirty and forty specimens of his art, mainly acts, proclamations, and circular letters. Of more romantic interest was *A Narrative of an Attempt Made by the French of Canada upon the Mohaques Country*, known today by one copy, which is in the Public Record Office in London. Early in 1694 appeared his *magnum opus* up to that time, *The Laws & Acts of the General Assembly for Their Majesties Province of New-York*, followed by other similar compilations bearing his imprint in 1710, 1713, 1716, and 1726. From 1693 to 1724, according to Victor Hugo Paltsits's sketch of Bradford in the *Dictionary of American Biography*, he printed 'more than 250 pieces, and from 1725 to 1743 about 150 more.' Among other accomplishments, as Dr. Paltsits summarizes them, Bradford 'printed the first New York paper currency (May 31, 1709), the first American Book of Common Prayer (1710), the first drama written in English America (1714), the first history of New York (1727), and the first copperplate plan of New York (Lyne's survey, undated, but 1730).' Of Bradford's highly important place in the history of the newspaper in America there will be more to say.

Confusion may always exist as to the priority of the early issues of Bradford's New York press. Such evidence as has become available in the intervening two and a half centuries is summarized and evaluated in Wilberforce Eames's *The First Year of Printing in New York* (New York, 1928), which lists and describes the thirty-eight known or inferred Bradford issues from May, 1693, to April, 1694. 'A dozen titles,' says Dr. Eames, 'are represented by a single surviving copy, and half a dozen more known only from the records.' What is 'probably the earliest piece with a full New York imprint' is Eames No. 6, *An Act for raising six Thousand Pound for the payment of three Hundred Volunteers, and their Officers, to be imployed in the Re-inforcement of the Frontiers of this Province at Albany...* of which the colophon reads, 'Printed and Sold by William Bradford, Printer to King William and Queen Mary, at the City of New-York, 1693.'

Two interesting and significant incidents of Bradford's Pennsylvania activities must be summarized in the briefest discussion of his busy career. In 1690 he was an important member of the company which established the first paper mill in America, and in all likelihood was the prime mover in the enterprise. John William Wallace, who delivered the address at the two hundredth anniversary of Bradford's birth in New York in 1863, with Gettysburg not two months away (the address was published at Albany the same year), quoted a rhymed account of the establishment from John Holme's *The Flourishing State of Pennsylvania*:

> Here dwelt a Printer, and, I find,
> That he can both print books and bind;
> He wants not paper, ink, nor skill;
> He's owner of a paper-mill:
> The paper-mill is here, hard by,
> And makes good paper frequently.

Rather less than a century ago a Philadelphia bookseller and member of the Society of Friends, Nathan Kite, was inspecting an old quarto volume in the Society's library when he chanced to note that one of the lining-papers was obviously a printed sheet of which the printed side had been pasted down. He moistened the leaf, removed it, and found it to be 'Proposals for the Printing of a large Bible, by William Bradford,' dated 1688. The proposals, nine in number, are given in full in the Wallace monograph. The fourth on the list announces 'that the pay shall be half Silver Money, and half Country Produce at Money price. One half down now, and the other half on the delivery of the Bibles.' Nothing came of the project. Almost a century was to elapse before another Philadelphian issued the first Bible in English to be printed in America.

William Bradford's pioneership was not to end with the establishment of his New York press in 1693. In 1723, when he was sixty years old, he issued from Perth Amboy, then the capital of the province of New Jersey, a compilation of the session laws of the province. The title-page declares unequivocally that the compilation was 'printed... *in* the City of Perth Amboy.' Doubt has been cast on the literal intent of this statement; it has been argued that as Perth Amboy was a good four hours' sail down the bay and into the Kill van Kull in the most favoring weather, it would have been highly unbusinesslike for Bradford to transport his heavy equipment to the Jersey shore, reassemble it, print his book, dismantle his apparatus, and return it to New York, fifteen miles away, when he could much more conveniently have printed the session laws in New York with any title-page he chose and shipped the copies to Perth Amboy.

For all that, the evidence tends to show that the book actually was printed *in* Perth Amboy, exactly as Bradford announced. The case is clearly set forth in the chapter on early printing in British North America which Lawrence C. Wroth, librarian of the John Carter Brown Library at Providence, contributed to *Printing: A Short History of the Art*, edited by R. A. Peddie (London, 1927). In 1723 the province of New Jersey authorized a paper-money issue, and as Bradford was already the province's official printer, operating from New York, the contract must have been awarded to him.

To prevent fraud on the part of the printer in the handling of these bills [writes Mr. Wroth], certain cautionary provisions of the Act made it almost imperative that he work, as Keimer was commissioned to do later, under the observation of commissioners appointed to represent the Government. For these reasons one may assume that Bradford printed the money in Perth-Amboy instead of in his New York office. The job was one of unusual profit for the printer, and the notes were made in this case, I believe, from woodcut blocks, which could be printed on an ordinary press. It is not difficult to think of Bradford for this reason moving a press and appurtenances from New York to Perth-Amboy and, after the money had been finished, of printing there an edition of the recent assembly statutes. At any rate we have the coincidence that in these two years, 1723 and 1728, when paper money issues were printed in New Jersey by outside printers, volumes of newly made statutes also appeared bearing the names of these printers and of the New Jersey towns in which the money had been put to press.

The precedence earned by paper money in the spread of printing in North America, it may here be noted, was not confined to the East or even to the early eighteenth century. When the followers of Brigham Young reached Great Salt Lake City, there was an instant need for currency, and a quantity of primitive dollar bills was issued in January, 1849 — the earliest exemplifications of typography in Utah. The printer was Brigham H. Young, nephew of the Mormon leader, 'with the perhaps unskilled aid of Thomas Bullock,' according to Douglas C. McMurtrie in *The Beginnings of Printing in Utah* (Chicago: The John Calhoun Club, 1931).

The Keimer mentioned by Mr. Wroth was Samuel of that ilk, Benjamin Franklin's first Philadelphia employer, who in 1728 issued, over a Burlington imprint, the session laws of 1727–28. In 1727 an issue of New Jersey paper money was printed by Keimer and Franklin on a press taken to Burlington for the purpose. This four-ply coincidence, Mr. Wroth believes, is too impressive to be ignored, and he concludes therefore that one should be 'willing to acknowledge as genuine the imprint in Bradford's case too, and to concede the year 1723 as marking the beginning of printing in New Jersey.'

Both the Perth Amboy and the Burlington enterprises, however, were temporary ventures. It was left for James Parker to establish the first permanent New Jersey press at Woodbridge, not far from Perth Amboy, where he issued in 1755 *An Ordinance for Regulating and Establishing the Fees of the Courts of Chancery of the Province of New Jersey* as his earliest surviving local imprint. Parker, a native of Woodbridge, was a graduate of Bradford's shop, and, as has been noted, established the first press in New Haven in 1754. Isaiah Thomas characterized him as 'well acquainted with printing, a neat workman, and active in business'—a satisfactory epitaph.

Virginia almost achieved the distinction of being the second colony, and the first outside of New England, to establish a press — an honor which it well merited owing to its transcendent importance in the provincial scheme. William Nuthead set up a press at Jamestown in 1682 and, from credible evidence, seems to have completed two or three minor productions, but orders came from London that the venture must halt, and halt it did. Thus was Virginia's typographical clock set back for almost fifty years, for not until 1730 did William Parks issue from his press at Williamsburg the first Virginia imprint which survives today — William Gooch's *Charge to the Grand Jury*.

Nuthead, after being estopped by royal decree from prosecuting his trade at Jamestown, thereupon anticipated William Bradford, James Franklin, and Daniel Fowle — if he could not print where he was, he would print elsewhere. Thus was printing introduced in Maryland, where, at St. Mary's City, Nuthead had established a press certainly by 1686. His first known imprint (and even of this no copy survives, the work being known only by a London reprint of 1689) was *The Declaration of Reasons and Motives for the Present Appearing in Arms of their Majesties Protestant Subjects in the Province of Maryland*. Nuthead's widow, Dinah, conducted his business after his death, subsequently transferring it to Annapolis. It is thus possible, from the above inconclusive data, that Maryland may have had a press before William Bradford set up shop in Philadelphia. At all events, it can claim the credit (leaving out of account Nuthead's abortive efforts at Jamestown in 1682) of being one of the four colonies in which the art was established before the close of the seventeenth century.

Destiny intervened to retard the development of printing in South Carolina when Eleazer Phillips, Jr., set up a press at Charleston in 1731. He died the following year and was succeeded by Thomas Whitmarsh, whom fate overtook after almost the same interval. Lewis Timothy, who succeeded Whitmarsh, was of somewhat hardier stuff, but unfortunately was not a good business man, according to the testimony of a former employer who was an excellent judge of such matters — Benjamin Franklin. After

Timothy's death his widow Elizabeth carried on the business for a few years, adding thus another name to the notable roster of women pioneers of American printing. Not until eighteen years after Phillips's brief tenure at Charleston did James Davis of Virginia establish the first North Carolina press at Newbern. A dozen years later still, presumably in 1761, James Adams introduced printing to Delaware. His earliest known production was a Wilmington *Almanac* for 1762.

With the inauguration of a press at Savannah by James Johnston in 1763 (or possibly in 1762), printing became a factor in the development of the last of the thirteen original colonies to take advantage of its benefits. It is worth while to pause a moment in the present narrative and to offer a summary of the status of the art at this moment measured in terms of its products — their number and their species. It had taken the printing press just short of a century and a quarter to accomplish the journey from Cambridge to Savannah. There were those among the weatherwise who detected the scent of storm clouds below the horizon, but hardly the shrewdest among them appreciated the imminence of a hurricane that would sunder the cluster of settlements along the Atlantic seaboard from the mother country.

The simplest way in which to make a survey of the printing field in America in 1763 is to turn to the third volume of Evans's bibliography and take a quick census. More than two hundred and thirty titles are listed for that year, but several of them are of newspapers newly established or recently transferred from weak to strong jurisdiction — or sometimes vice versa. Of the non-periodical issues that remain (not including almanacs as periodicals), nearly

63

one half fall within the category of religious and theological. It was a day, of course, in which the influence of the Church reached into every concern of existence. 'New England being a country whose interests are remarkably enwrapped in ecclesiastical circumstances,' said Cotton Mather, 'ministers ought to interest themselves in politics.' And ministers certainly did. The colonial printer would have been hard put to it to survive had it not been for the disputatiousness of the pulpit and its eagerness to take all human activity for its province — and by no means in New England alone.

Affairs of state occupied the press in only half as much abundance, though forming the next largest group of titles after theology. Then came that old standby, the almanac — more than thirty were issued in 1763, headed, both alphabetically and commercially, by Nathaniel Ames's *Astronomical Diary*, issued in Boston, New London, Newport, and New Haven.

These three groups account for well over three quarters of the American imprints of that year. The remaining titles fall under sundry miscellaneous headings, of which two are worth special consideration in that they touch the common man most intimately. These categories are the useful arts, of which there are half a dozen examples, and that division which can be most satisfactorily headed Entertainment—books of which the primary purpose may have been, in one or two instances, to instruct, but which, taken as a group, form the closest approach to books to be read for the pleasure of reading that that granite era could offer. In this connection two important considerations must perpetually be borne in mind. The first is that much of the printed matter of the day, including particularly the 'reading' books, was imported from England. The colonists, be it remembered, were still using English-made Bibles and continued to use them until the Revolution was almost over. The second is the fact that many of the entertainment books of the day were read to pieces, so that of dozens of these no examples survive for inclusion in Evans or for later discovery. The fate of the earliest issues of the *New England Primer* is ample corroboration.

In New York the enterprising Hugh Gaine published in 1763 James Boydell's *Merchant Freighters' and Captains of Ships' Assistant* and W. H. Dilworth's *Complete Letter Writer; or Polite English Secretary.* Stephen Sewall's *Hebrew Grammar* appeared the same year at Boston, 'printed by R. and S. Draper, for the Honorable and Reverend the President and Fellows of Harvard-College' — printed, too, just in time, for the Hebrew types were lost in a fire a few months later. From the press of B. Franklin and D. Hall, of Philadelphia, came *A New Set of Copies, in Large Modern Round Text, for the Use of Schools,* the work of William Thorne, 'Writing-Master and Accomptant' in that city, while William Goddard issued at Providence a highly useful *Table of the Value of the Lawful Money Bills of This Colony, in Old Tenor, at Twenty-three and One Third for One, Interest Included.* Certain of these titles may well be lacking in emotional stimulus to the jaded reader of a later generation, but he will at least grant them precedence of interest over Samuel How's *The Sufficiency of the Spirit's Teaching, Without Humane Learning: or a Treatise Tending to Prove Human Learning to Be No Help to the Spiritual Understanding of the Word of God* (Wilmington, John Adams), and Joseph Bellamy's

65

A Blow at the Root of the Refined Antinomianism of the Present Age, printed in Boston by Samuel Kneeland. It would be unjust, however, to permit the inference that the sermon and the almanac were not 'reading' books. The colonial sermon was more than a mere discourse pronounced in a church, and the colonial almanac was more than a solar time-table. 'The people demanded pious reading and their pastors saw that they got it,' declares Lawrence C. Wroth in *The Colonial Printer* (New York, 1931). 'The theological treatises, the sermons, the controversial matter generally, not to mention certain other remarkable productions, have a profounder significance in our cultural and political history than they are usually credited with.' And in extension of this thesis he quotes a vigorous paragraph from Vernon L. Parrington's *The Colonial Mind*:

> That our colonial literature seems to many readers meager and uninteresting, that it is commonly squeezed into the skimpiest of chapters in our handbooks of American literature, is due, I think, to an exaggerated regard for esthetic values. Our literary historians have labored under too heavy a handicap of the genteel tradition — to borrow Professor Santayana's happy phrase — to enter sympathetically into a world of masculine intellects and material struggles. They have sought daintier fare than polemics and in consequence mediocre verse has obscured political speculation, and poetasters have shouldered aside vigorous creative thinkers. The colonial period is meager and lean only to those whose 'disedged appetites' find no savor in old-fashioned beef and puddings.

Mr. Wroth does not hold it essential to 'settle down to a course of reading along the line suggested by these words to be willing to believe them true.'

He who has previously scorned the eighteenth-century almanac, moreover, can spend many enjoyable evenings over Samuel Briggs's *Essays, Humor, and Poems of Nathaniel Ames, Father and Son...from Their Almanacks, 1726–1775* (Cleveland, 1891), a bulky anthology into which, as into Pepys or Boswell, one may dip anywhere with a certainty of delight. Mr. Briggs's title-page quotes a passage from Moses Coit Tyler's *History of American Literature* in further testimony to the social essentiality of the almanac (the Ames annual, well before 1764, was selling at the rate of sixty thousand copies):

> No one who would penetrate to the core of early American literature, and would read in it the secret history of the people in whose minds it took root, and from whose minds it grew, may by any means turn away in lofty literary scorn from the Almanack — most despised, most prolific, most indispensable of books, which every man uses, and no man praises; the very quack, clown, pack-horse, and Pariah of modern literature; the supreme and only literary necessity even in households where the Bible and the newspaper are still undesired or unattainable luxuries.

Tyler wrote, of course, and Briggs quoted, at a time when no patent-medicine could aspire to any pretense of common acceptance unless it proclaimed its virtues annually on pages alternating with schedules of the sun, moon, and planets. On such ventures as these the Ameses would have cast an eye of unspoken derision — and impaled them with an epigram in their own next succeeding almanac.

Of examples of 'a tale which holdeth children from play and old men from the chimney corner' there was in 1763 a grievous lack. One might pass an enthralled half-hour with *Dying Speech of Bristol, a*

Negro Boy of 16 Years Old, Who Was Executed at Taunton, December 1, 1763, for the Murder of Mrs. Elizabeth M'Kinstry, rushed into type at Boston, but one would prefer to hear the matter after deft recasting by Mr. Edmund Pearson. There was doubtless an abundance of topical amusement in *New-Year Verses of the Carriers of the Pennsylvania Gazette* and *New-Year Verses of the Carriers of the Pennsylvania Journal*—a pleasant practice that survived at least into the time of the present commentator, and which in the early years of the nineteenth century (as will later be shown) was to have one or two illustrious names among its exemplars. For more certain delight one would have had to turn to two importations of sufficient appeal to merit reprinting in America, such as *Mother Midnight's Comical Pocket-Book: or, A Bone for the Criticks. Being a Sure and Certain Cure for the Hip. Containing the Nicest and Largest Dish of Novelties, That Ever Was Seen — Heard — Smelt — or Tasted; Carefully Cook'd-up by Mother Midnight's Merry Grandson; Containing Nothing but Originals, All Very Humorous, Prodigious Satyrical, and Quite Uncommon; Informing the Publick, That This Dish of Dishes Was Wrote in an Uncommon Place, at an Uncommon Time, by an Uncommon Hand, Humphrey Humdrum, Esq.* — to wit, Joseph Lewis — 'London: Printed. Boston, New-England; Re-printed and sold by Zechariah Fowle, in Marlborough-street, MDCCLXIII.' Better yet, the alert Christoph Sauer, of Germantown (a Germantown of which the accent was then heavily on the German), could forsake his native tongue for the moment and issue, for the joy of such as chose to buy, *The Dreadful Visitation in a Short Account of the Progress and Effects of the Plague, the Last Time It Spread in the City of London in the Year*

1665 Extracted from the Memoirs of a Person Who Resided There, During the Whole Time of That Infection — and thus was Daniel Defoe introduced to the New World. Eleven years were to elapse before a shriveled chapbook version of *Robinson Crusoe*, the first to appear in North America, was issued in New York.

There did exist an American literature of a sort, and it will be briefly surveyed in a succeeding chapter. One great American classic, however, was already in the living if not in the making — its author did not begin to put it into words until 1771, and it did not reach type until twenty years thereafter, when it inaugurated one of the strangest adventures in the history of publishing. Its author-to-be, meanwhile, was already a figure of such superlative importance in the chronicle of American printing (and was soon to assume such an important rôle in the critical affairs of his country) that he must be considered in rather more detail than any other individual who touches these notes.

CHAPTER IV

Benjamin Franklin, Printer and Publisher

JOSIAH FRANKLIN was reared a dyer in the village of Ecton in Northamptonshire, but soon after his arrival in America, about 1682, he foresaw a greater future in the trade of tallow-chandler and soap-boiler. It was a calling which seems humble enough in a day that has evolved such mouth-filling occupational designations as sales engineer, merchandising counsel, and mortician. Josiah Franklin, had the locution been available in his era, might have asserted with all accuracy that he was an important factor in public utilities — even our own catch-phrase epoch has not been quite equal to the coinage of the label 'public utilitarian.' For when the Boston town watch wanted fresh candles they bought them from Josiah Franklin — from other tallow-chandlers too, perhaps, but at least some, by documentary evidence, from Josiah Franklin.

The close relationship between progress in the science of artificial illumination and progress in the dissemination of the printed word could be charted with almost mathematical accuracy. In the preceding chapter stress was laid on the fact that an overwhelming proportion of early American imprints were concerned either with theology and ecclesiasticism or with politico-legal affairs. Had the electric lamp or the gaslight been available, the ratio might have been impressively otherwise. Most of the books of colonial days were designed for the use of those whose professions exacted some considerable amount of 're-quired reading' — ministers, physicians, lawyers, pub-

70

lic officials, schoolmen. The man who toiled with his hands (and hands are eminently useful in the building-up of a new country) labored while the light of heaven would let him and then returned to a home wherein the conveniences were hardly such as to make reading a pleasure. Lincoln studied by the glare of blazing pine-knots, but the middle-class Bostonian and New Yorker and Philadelphian of the generations immediately preceding Lincoln (to say nothing of their country cousins) had to depend on illuminants that offered no greater inducements to either the solace or the benefits of type.

Josiah Franklin's wife and their three children accompanied him to America. Before her death she bore him three more children. Josiah remarried, and of the second union ten children were born. Of this multitudinous offspring, thirteen grew to maturity — a remarkable proportion for the time and region. The eighth child and last son of the second marriage, christened Benjamin after a paternal uncle, was at first intended for the Church, but Josiah could not afford to give him the education which this most learned of the professions demanded, and at the age of ten, after receiving as thorough an intellectual rearing as could be expected in so short a space, Benjamin Franklin quit school to assist his father in the fabrication of candles and soap. An elder brother, John, had already become proficient in the twin arts of illumination and sanitation and had gone to the bustling colony of Rhode Island to practice them. Another brother (and another Josiah) had also investigated them, found them not to his liking, and run away to sea.

Benjamin, also, made it clear that the parental pursuits were not to his taste, and a wise father, fear-ing another abrupt departure, took Benjamin walking about Boston, that he might 'see joiners, bricklayers, turners, braziers, etc., at their work' and thereby, boywise, make known to his elder which way his inclinations lay. A patent leaning toward books at length persuaded the father to make him a printer, despite the fact that another brother, James, Benjamin's elder by nine years (and one day, as already related, to become the first printer in Rhode Island), had adopted the craft. Benjamin conceded a preference to the claims of printing over those of tallow-chandlery, but he still sniffed, with the true landsman's appetite, the tang of the salt breeze that blew in from the east. Josiah, however, was insistent, and the parental insistence of 1718 was no toy scepter to swing above the head of a sub-adolescent boy. Accordingly, Benjamin was duly indentured to James 'to serve as an apprentice till I was twenty-one years of age, only I was to be allowed journeyman's wages during the last year.'

Before long, Benjamin was writing odds and ends of verse, and James, with the inbred Franklin sagacity, encouraged him in his endeavors and let him put some of his compositions in type.

One [declared Benjamin] was called *The Lighthouse Tragedy*, and contained an account of the drowning of Captain Worthilake, with his two daughters: the other was a sailor's song, on the taking of *Teach* (or Blackbeard) the pirate. They were wretched stuff, in the Grub-street-ballad style; and when they were printed he sent me about the town to sell them. The first sold wonderfully, the event being recent, having made a great noise. This flattered my vanity; but my father discouraged me by ridiculing my performances, and telling me verse-makers were generally beggars.

The importance of these two pieces consists in the fact that they were 'the first with which Franklin's name can be identified as either author or printer,' according to Dr. William J. Campbell, who adds that 'no copy is known to exist, nor is the exact title of either of them known.' This was true in 1918, when Dr. Campbell's admirable catalogue of *The Collection of Franklin Imprints in the Museum of the Curtis Publishing Company* was issued, and it is unfortunately still true today. If they were at all like similar productions of both earlier and later date, they were broadsides — single sheets that were distributed like handbills, the main difference being that they commanded a price. They would command a fantastic price today, together or singly, and their eventual discovery is by no means beyond the bounds of possibility. A copy of one — or copies of both — may be tucked away in some forgotten contemporary theological compendium which has not been opened for a century.

The disappearance of these broadsides is regrettable on many counts, not least of which is the fact that even if Benjamin had never accomplished anything else, he could at least claim credit for sponsoring perhaps the most textually interesting productions of his brother's press. James Franklin was a skilled printer — London trained, and 'no slovenly self-taught colonial,' in Paul Leicester Ford's phrase — and James was not, of course, in any degree responsible for the dullness of the copy that was brought to his shop. A brief glance at a few of his imprints of this period is of interest mainly because of the certainty that Benjamin worked on many of them.

The product of James Franklin's press [says Ford in *The Many-Sided Franklin* (New York, 1899)] is a dreary

73

lot of 'gone-nothingness.' A few of the New England sermons of the day; Stoddard's *Treatise on Conversion*; Stone's *Short Catechism; A Prefatory Letter about Psalmody*, in defense of church singing, which many Puritans still held to be unholy; an allegory styled *The Isle of Man, or, Legal Proceedings in Manshire Against Sin*; Care's *English Liberties*; sundry pamphlets on the local politics of the moment, such as *A Letter from One in the Country to his Friend in Boston, News from the Moon, A Friendly Check from a Kind Relation to the Chief Cannonneer*, and *A Word of Comfort to a Melancholy Country*; two or three tractates on inoculation, and one aimed half at the Boston clergy and half at the fair sex, entitled *Hooped Petticoats Arraigned by the Light of Nature and the Law of God*, were the chief output of the new printer during the years his brother served him.

In the summer of 1721, James Franklin established a newspaper, *The New-England Courant*. Two years earlier he had been engaged to print the *Boston Gazette*, but with the transfer of its management a few months later the contract had gone elsewhere. The *Courant* was a new departure even for the novelty that was American journalism — so extensive and violent a departure, indeed, that in the following year the authorities sentenced the printer-proprietor to a month's imprisonment for his insolence. The punishment did not improve him; free again, he pressed the thorn of the *Courant* deeper into the flesh of his persecutors, with the consequence that he was soon forbidden 'to print or publish' either the *Courant* 'or any other pamphlet or paper of the like nature' unless it were first submitted to the secretary of the province.

There were two apparent ways out of the dilemma, and one was as eminently unsatisfactory as the other. The first was to quit printing and publishing. The second was to submit to the censorship. James hit upon a more ingenious solution. He turned the *Courant* over to sixteen-year-old Benjamin. Benjamin's indentures as apprentice to James had five years to run, and in order to forestall any objection on the part of the authorities that an apprentice was not competent to manage the paper, the indentures were ostentatiously canceled and a new document drawn up as a private and confidential (but none the less binding) memorandum which in theory was no one's affair save James's and Benjamin's. The half-sheet issue of the *Courant* for February 4–11, 1723, identified it as 'printed and sold by Benjamin Franklin in Queen street, where Advertisements are taken in.' Benjamin Franklin's name thus first appeared in an imprint. It remained on the tailboard of the *Courant* until the paper's discontinuance in 1726, long after Benjamin had left Boston.

The gratifying tableau of two stalwart brothers battling loyally side by side for the freedom of the press, however, was not the whole picture. James and Benjamin had differences, and Benjamin later admitted that he himself was 'perhaps... too saucy and provoking,' and that James, despite 'the blows his passion too often urged him to bestow upon me,' was 'otherwise not an ill-natur'd man.' Benjamin, at all events, decided to take advantage of the freedom accorded him by the cancellation of his indentures, which act he later conceded to have been 'not fair' and 'one of the first errata of my life.' James spread the tidings of this perfidy throughout Boston, and every local printing establishment thereupon became a closed shop to Benjamin Franklin.

If James assumed that Benjamin would thus be forced to return to his own shop, he reckoned without

75

his Benjamin. For not long thereafter, with the con-
nivance of a friend, John Collins, Benjamin was
smuggled aboard a New York-bound sloop, and three
days later, thanks to a fair wind, he was in a city
which was not yet a metropolis judged even by easy
colonial standards. He called on 'old Mr. William
Bradford' (aged sixty), who had nothing to offer, but
who suggested that his son Andrew, then flourishing
(after a fashion) in Philadelphia, might have a position for him, since Andrew's 'principal hand,' Aquila
Rose, had just died.

Franklin set out by water by way of Perth Amboy.
It is interesting to note, in view of the dispute regard-
ing the earliest New Jersey imprint which was sum-
marized in the preceding chapter, that the trip from
New York to the New Jersey port took thirty hours.
All in good time he reached Philadelphia.

Washington did not cut down a cherry tree and
then inform his father that he could not tell a lie;
Wellington did not say 'Up, Guards, and at 'em!' or
Pershing, 'Lafayette, we are here.' The dear old
legends explode all about us; it is gratifying to recall
that there is one at least the accuracy of which is unimpeachable. Walking up Market Street, Philadelphia, Benjamin Franklin did pass the home of his
wife-to-be with a roll under each arm and munching
a third, and his wife-to-be did see him and note that
he made 'a most awkward, ridiculous appearance.'

Andrew Bradford had nothing to offer — the vacancy left by the death of Aquila Rose had already
been filled. But Franklin was not yet done with the
ghostly trail of Aquila. At Andrew Bradford's suggestion he waited on Samuel Keimer, who had recently set up as a printer despite a meager endow-
ment of equipment, native ability, or acquired skill.

He found Keimer 'composing an Elegy on Aquila Rose' directly from the type.

> So there being no copy [recorded Franklin], but one pair of cases, and the Elegy likely to require all the letters, no one could help him. I endeavor'd to put his press (which he had not yet us'd, and of which he understood nothing) into order fit to be work'd with; and, promising to come and print off his Elegy as soon as he should have got it ready, I return'd to Bradford's, who gave me a little job to do for the present, and there I lodged and dieted. A few days after, Keimer sent for me to print off the Elegy. And now he had got another pair of cases, and a pamphlet to reprint, on which he set me to work.

This broadside poem, therefore, was the first piece of Philadelphia printing with which Franklin's name is clearly identified. The 'pamphlet to reprint' may have been *A Letter to a Friend in Ireland, The Doctrine of Absolute Reprobation Refuted, A Letter from One in the Country to His Friend in the City, A Parable,* or (and this would certainly have been Franklin's choice) *The Curiosities of Common Water,* all of which Keimer imprints of 1723 are listed in the short-title check list which follows the Curtis catalogue. No more specifically is it possible to identify the 'little job' which Andrew Bradford gave him.

It is not likely that Franklin would have long continued with Keimer (who was 'an odd fish; ignorant of common life, fond of rudely opposing receiv'd opinions, slovenly to extream dirtiness, enthusiastic in some points of religion, and a little knavish withal') even if a roundabout coincidence had not brought him to the attention of the governor of the province, Sir William Keith, whose quarrel with William Bradford had been one of the impulses that had estab-

lished the latter as New York's first printer. Keimer
'star'd like a pig poison'd' one day when no less a
worthy than Sir William entered the shop in search
of the new assistant from Boston. Governor and assistant adjourned to a tavern, where the former disclosed a grandiose idea for setting the newcomer up
in a shop of his own. He must first, of course, go to
London to buy equipment, and to this end the governor loaded him down with enthusiasm and letters
of credit. After a short visit to Boston (where all
'made me welcome, except my brother,' who 'receiv'd me not very frankly, look'd me all over, and
turn'd to his work again'), Franklin sailed for London, which he reached the day before Christmas,
1724 — to learn, to his intense mortification, that
Sir William's letters of credit were worthless, since
that gentleman's prowess as a promiser and his shortcomings as a performer were rather more familiar in
the old country than in the new.

Franklin, however, had little difficulty in extricat-
ing himself from the crisis into which he was precipi-
tated on his arrival in London by the non-negotiabil-
ity of Sir William Keith's commercial paper. 'I immediately got into work at Palmer's,' he says, 'then
a famous printing house in Bartholomew Close, and
here I continu'd near a year.' Samuel Palmer, declares John Clyde Oswald in *Benjamin Franklin
Printer* (New York, 1917), 'was more than an ordinary printer. He had visited America, was letter-
founder as well as printer, and was engaged in the
writing of "A History of Printing," only a third of
which he had completed when he died in 1732.'

Franklin identifies only one of the jobs on which
he worked at Palmer's. 'I was employed,' continues
the Autobiography, 'in composing for the second

78

edition of Wollaston's "Religion of Nature.'" The
name of William Wollaston (1659–1724) now survives mainly by virtue of this adventitious association with a nineteen-year-old immigrant compositor.
The Religion of Nature Delineated first appeared in
1722 in a small privately printed edition. Presumably this first edition is now rare, but no collector is
impressed thereby, preferring above it that on which
Franklin worked (the third in strict sequence, but
the second published edition), which, happily, is rela-
tively common. It bears the imprint: 'London:
Printed by S. Palmer, and sold by B. Lintott, W. and
J. Innys, J. Osborn, J. Batley, and T. Longman.
1725.' The printer from America pondered over the
copy as he set it, and out of his ruminations came a
pamphlet reply to the recently deceased author: *A
Dissertation on Liberty and Necessity, Pleasure and
Pain* (London, 1725). Franklin printed one hundred
copies, gave a few to friends, and then, repenting of
his materialistic agnosticism, 'burnt the rest except
one copy'; pride of authorship would not wholly
down. That copy may be one of the four known to
survive today, all in institutional collections.

Receiving a better offer from John Watts, who conducted a larger printing establishment, Franklin
went thither, remaining six months, when he accepted the proposal of a Philadelphia merchant then
in London that he return and act 'as his clerk, keep
his books, in which he would instruct me, copy his
letters, and attend the store.' In leaving London,
therefore, Franklin supposed that he thereby 'took
leave of printing forever.'

Man proposes. Franklin and his new employer
reached Philadelphia; the store was duly opened and
its new clerk installed; four months later the em-

ployer died. The establishment was taken over by the executors and Franklin was out of work. Keimer wanted him back as foreman of his new and larger shop, but Franklin, who knew well his Keimer, first sought a place at his new trade of clerk and salesman. Nothing offered, so he reluctantly accepted Keimer's bid. The affiliation did not last long. Franklin and Keimer quarreled over 'a trifle' that represented the culmination of a long series of abuses:

> A great noise happening near the courthouse, I put my head out of the window to see what was the matter. Keimer, being in the street, look'd up and saw me, call'd out to me in a loud voice and angry tone to mind my business, adding some reproachful words, that nettled me the more for their publicity, all the neighbors who were looking out on the same occasion, being witnesses how I was treated. He came up immediately into the printing-house, continu'd the quarrel, high words pass'd on both sides, he gave me the quarter's warning we had stipulated, expressing a wish that he had not been oblig'd to so long a warning. I told him that his wish was unnecessary, for I would leave him that instant; and so, taking my hat, walk'd out of doors.

Had affairs not fallen out thus ludicrously, then some other incident would have 'snapt our connections.' If no 'great noise' had occurred near the courthouse (what, one wonders, was the cause of the disturbance?), there would still have been a subsequent great noise in Keimer's shop, and the hireling would have spoken his piece to the overlord and walked out of the identical door to the fulfillment of his high destiny.

Franklin was of more than half a mind to return to Boston, in which event Philadelphia would one day have been compelled to seek another patron saint. Fortunately for Philadelphia, while working at Keimer's Franklin had struck up a friendship with Hugh Meredith, a fellow craftsman, who suggested a partnership. A secret agreement was drawn up, and, pending the completion of arrangements for launching the venture, Franklin sought temporary work at Bradford's. Keimer meanwhile was negotiating with the provincial government of New Jersey for the printing of an issue of paper money at Burlington, and urged Franklin to accompany him if he was awarded the job. The plan went through, and the pair were in Burlington three months. 'There is not a single piece of this paper money known to exist today,' says Dr. Campbell, 'and of the New Jersey Laws that they printed at the same time there are only two known copies.' The bearing of this excursion on the vexed problem of early New Jersey imprints has been explained in Chapter III.

In the summer of 1728 the new firm of B. Franklin and H. Meredith came into existence. They had scarce 'opened our letters' (their cases, that is, not the morning mail) when a friend 'brought a countryman to us, whom he had met in the street inquiring for a printer.' The identity of this bucolic, casual, but superlatively important patron of the typographic arts is unknown and probably forever unknowable, for he could hardly have been aware that he was the instrument of Providence chosen to motivate the first imprint issued by Franklin as a master printer. Dr. Campbell surmised the job was 'probably stationery, or a small handbill.' Whatever it was, it has probably vanished beyond hope of recall, or at least beyond hope of positive identification.

Almost on the heels of this first customer came another — none other than Samuel Keimer, whose general ineffectualness and chronic state of panic provide much of the comic relief in the history of early American printing. Keimer had been working off and on for three years on William Sewell's *History of the Rise, Increase, and Progress of the Christian People Called Quakers: The Third Edition, Corrected.* The end was not in sight, and Keimer, evidently in a condition of acute mental distress, rushed to the new shop for assistance. Franklin and Meredith composed and printed 'forty sheets,' totaling nearly a third of the seven hundred pages — the first known job to issue from their shop, even though it did not bear their imprint. Sewell's *History* is doubly a Franklin item, as Franklin must have worked on the book while he was still in Keimer's employ.

Thanks to the diligence of its proprietors — or of one of them, for Meredith 'was often seen drunk in the streets, and playing at low games in alehouses' — the new shop prospered. But about the middle of 1730 it encountered a hazard which its sponsors had not foreseen. Meredith's father had advanced one hundred pounds to put the enterprise on its feet and had promised another hundred. When the time came for him to meet his obligation, he could not, and 'the New Printing-Office near the Market' was faced with a creditor's suit. This crisis confirmed young Meredith's conviction that he was not cut out for the printing business; moreover, he was anxious to join a company of fellow Welshmen who were planning a settlement in North Carolina. Two of Franklin's friends offered to come to the aid of the senior partner, and the difficulty was amicably adjusted. Thus was the 'B. Franklin' imprint born. It appeared for the first time not on anything in English, but at the bottom of the title-page of *Mystische und Sehr*

Geheyme Sprueche, by Conrad Beissel, whose religio-communistic Ephrata colony, itself to become one day an important printing center, had been organized only a few years before.

Shortly before the dissolution of the firm of Franklin and Meredith there had been another odd run-in with Keimer. Franklin was already planning a newspaper, and 'foolishly' imparted the secret to a friend who forthwith made it known to Keimer. Toward the end of 1728 the not-to-be-anticipated Keimer issued the first number of *The Universal Instructor in all Arts and Sciences: and Pennsylvania Gazette.* It was Keimer's inescapable genius to start what he could not finish, and he was soon glad to dispose of the paper to Franklin and Meredith, whose control dates from October 2, 1729. One of Franklin's first acts as a newspaper publisher — his memory must have harked back to the old Boston days — was to shorten the too comprehensive title to *The Pennsylvania Gazette.*

Probably some three months after the departure of Meredith, Franklin initiated a new partnership. He married. 'Partnership' is no romantic figure of speech. The name of Deborah Read has an honored place on the roster of women who helped to make American printing. By her husband's own testimony, her share in the work of the establishment included, in some measure, the 'folding and stitching' of pamphlets, and it is not unlikely that her hands had a busy share in the preparation of some of the series of pamphlets with which, more than with any other, Franklin's name is most clearly associated as author-printer-publisher — the *Poor Richard* almanacs.

The importance of the almanac in the colonial scheme has already been stressed. Franklin was naturally alert to this importance; in fact, as soon as the house of Franklin and Meredith was in existence he had commissioned Thomas Godfrey to compile an almanac. Godfrey was 'a self-taught mathematician, great in his way,' but 'he knew little out of his way,' and there was considerable of the prima donna in his make-up. He prepared almanacs for 1730, 1731, and 1732, and then, in an outburst of temperament, transferred his skill to the shelter of Andrew Bradford. The fortunate result, certainly not anticipated by Thomas Godfrey in his dudgeon, was, as Paul Leicester Ford defines it, the birth of American humor. Franklin initiated the *Poor Richard* series, compiling the bulk of the contents himself, but attributing their authorship to Richard Saunder or Saunders, whose almanacs had enjoyed enormous popularity in England and were still enjoying it, though Saunders had been gone this many a year. A *Poor Robin* series of almanacs was also popular in England, and James Franklin a few years earlier had begun a series of Rhode Island almanacs under this title. *Poor Richard* was an immediate success, and though the first number was not advertised in *The Pennsylvania Gazette* until December 19, 1732, which was rather late in the year for a new almanac, three printings were necessary to supply the demand. *Poor Richard* thereafter issued regularly every December under Franklin's own editorship until 1757 (for 1758).

Poor Richard's rich wisdom has become part of common speech wherever English or any other language is spoken. Everyone from China to Peru knows that God helps those that help themselves, that three removes are as bad as a fire, that

> Vessels large may venture more,
> But little boats should keep near shore.

A recent commentator — Carl L. Becker in the *Dictionary of American Biography* — says of the *Poor Richard* almanacs:

Nothing better exhibits the man, or better illustrates his ingenuity as an advertiser.... 'Richard Saunders,' the Philomath of the *Almanack*, was the Sir Roger de Coverley of the masses, pilfering the world's store of aphorisms, and adapting them to the circumstances and the understanding of the poor. 'Necessity never made a good bargain.' 'It is hard for an empty sack to stand upright.' 'Many dishes make diseases.' 'The used key is always bright.' The *Almanack* was immediately successful, and commonly sold about ten thousand copies. 'As poor Richard says' became a current phrase, used to give weight to any counsel of thrift. The work made Franklin's name a household word throughout the colonies.... The introduction to the last *Almanack* (Father Abraham's speech at the auction) spread the fame of Poor Richard in Europe. It was printed in broadsides and posted on walls in England, and, in translation, distributed by the French clergy among their parishioners. It has been translated into fifteen languages, and reprinted at least four hundred times.

Franklin's rise to the position of the most important printer in the colonies after the well-entrenched Bradfords was now rapid. Before long he was official printer to Pennsylvania, New Jersey, and Delaware. Of the bulk of his non-governmental productions, Ford writes that while generally 'of little moment,' still 'there can be no doubt that as a whole they contain more of genuine merit than those of any other printer of the same or previous periods in the colonies, the amount of doctrinal and polemical theology being a minimum, and bearing a less proportion to the whole mass than can be found in the books of contemporary American printers.' In 1735 appeared over Franklin's imprint James Logan's *Cato's Moral Distichs Englished in Couplets.* Nine years later Franklin sponsored Samuel Richardson's *Pamela* — not only the first American edition, but the first novel to be printed in America, 'Price 6 s.' In the same year, 1744, he issued what is generally regarded as the typographical masterpiece of his press, *M. T. Cicero's Cato Major, or His Discourse of Old-Age: With Explanatory Notes* (also Englished by James Logan), referring to it in a four-page foreword of his own composition as 'this first Translation of a Classic in this Western World.' This was a wide error, for George Sandys had translated Ovid on the banks of the James River a life-span earlier, and the translation had been printed in London in 1626; moreover, Franklin forgot those *Moral Distichs* of Cato and James Logan which he himself had issued in 1735.

In 1748, Franklin formed a partnership with an alert young Scotchman whom he had engaged five years before, and the 'Franklin and Hall' imprint thereupon replaced (with a few exceptions) the familiar 'B. Franklin.' A few earlier connections must be mentioned. Franklin's name is found on several German titles in combination with that of Gotthard Armbruester and with that of Johannes Böhm, and, apparently once only, with that of Johannes Wüster, but these seem to have been purely partnerships of convenience, and suggest no such dual affiliations as those with Meredith and Hall. The Hall partnership lasted eighteen years, and during that period Franklin's connection with printing and publishing became less and less important as the crisis in international affairs that was bringing on the American Revolution grew more and more acute. But the printer in him could not wholly be suppressed. When he went to Paris in 1776 as representative of the colonies, he established a little press for his own amusement at his home in Passy, then a suburb, now as much a part of the metropolis as Greenwich Village is of New York. It was not quite such a toy as Robert Louis Stevenson and his stepson Lloyd Osbourne were one day to set up in Switzerland, the main difference being that the Stevenson-Osbourne combination knew nothing about printing and was joyously aware of it, whereas Franklin, with just as joyous awareness, knew as much about it as any man of his time. One factor the two private presses of Passy and Davos-Platz have in common — their productions are excessively rare and costly collectors' playthings. The story of the French venture is authoritatively set forth in Luther S. Livingston's *Franklin and His Press at Passy*, issued by the Grolier Club of New York in 1914. Livingston listed thirty-two entries, and since his monograph was published six others have come to light, according to Will Ransom's *Private Presses and Their Books* (New York, 1929).

The output of Franklin's press from 1729 to the termination of the Hall partnership (1766) is statistically impressive. The following summary is tabulated from the short-title check list of all Franklin imprints known in 1918 which Dr. Campbell appended to the Curtis catalogue (excluding *The Pennsylvania Gazette* and the numerous issues of paper currency printed by Franklin from 1731 to 1764):

1729.... 8	1734.... 15
1730.... 15	1735.... 20
1731.... 8	1736.... 8
1732.... 15	1737.... 13
1733.... 14	1738.... 9

1739....	12	1753....	16
1740....	46	1754....	15
1741....	45	1755....	27
1742....	31	1756....	20
1743....	25	1757....	31
1744....	25	1758....	13
1745....	15	1759....	16
1746....	23	1760....	10
1747....	27	1761....	12
1748....	30	1762....	8
1749....	33	1763....	15
1750....	19	1764....	18
1751....	24	1765....	19
1752....	18	1766....	4

Any book, pamphlet, broadside, or periodical that bears a Franklin imprint, alone or in combination, is worth treasuring on that account alone. In general the scale of desirability is set by scarcity. This scale, one might suppose, should follow the line of chronology with reasonable accuracy, but it happens that it does not. The Sewell *History*, for instance, ought by chronological measurement to be an excessively rare book as the first book on which Franklin worked as an independent printer, and rare it assuredly is, but by no means to the point of utter elusiveness.

Twelve years later the total of Franklin imprints was moving toward two hundred — and in that twelfth year, 1740, there issued from his press the second edition of David Evans's *A Short, Plain Help for Parents and Heads of Families, to Feed Their Babes with the Sincere Milk of God's Word. Being a Short, Plain Catechism, Grounded Upon God's Word, and Agreeable to the Westminster Assembly's Excellent Catechism.* No copy of the first edition is known to be extant — Dr. Campbell quoted the title imperfectly from a contemporary advertisement — and neither Hildeburn nor Campbell knew that a second edition had ever been issued. Neither did anyone else until 1929, when a copy came to light and won its way to a New York bookseller's catalogue. The book is mentioned here, not because it possesses great intrinsic importance (it would be of trivial note if a hundred or two copies of it survived), but as an indication of the fact that unrecorded Franklin imprints are likely to appear at any time, and as indication, further, that the scarcity of Franklin imprints does not altogether parallel the dates of his activity as printer and publisher.

In these notes it has been necessary to neglect Franklin, the author (save as Poor Richard), in favor of Franklin, the printer and publisher. But it would be an effrontery to allude even briefly to Franklin without mention of the Autobiography. Begun in 1771 in the quiet charm of an English countryseat, the first great American classic never was completed. The manuscript first appeared in print, by an odd series of accidents, in French in 1791. Subsequently Franklin's grandson, William Temple Franklin, issued it in a Bowdlerized English version that would have afforded the old man quiet and somewhat indignant laughter. The text was not definitively published until 1868, soon after John Bigelow had come into possession of the original manuscript.

Franklin's epitaph is easily the most familiar in American history, and almost as well-known a document, perhaps, as Lincoln's Gettysburg Address. It is not generally known, however, that the original version of it was composed in 1728, the very year in which its author, a youth of twenty-two, entered into partnership with Meredith. The version written in that year, which differs in minor details from the final draft, was this:

THE BODY OF
B FRANKLIN PRINTER,
(LIKE THE COVER OF AN OLD BOOK
ITS CONTENTS TORN OUT
AND STRIPT OF ITS LETTERING & GILDING)
LIES HERE, FOOD FOR WORMS.
BUT THE WORK SHALL NOT BE LOST;
FOR IT WILL, (AS HE BELIEV'D) APPEAR ONCE MORE,
IN A NEW AND MORE ELEGANT EDITION
REVISED AND CORRECTED,
BY THE AUTHOR.

CHAPTER V

Gentlemen of the Press

MAROON two Americans on a desert island, it
has been said, and before the next sunset
one of them will have started a newspaper. Such
zeal would betoken the operation of one of two impulses — either an innate spirit of national enterprise
or an inherited effort to make up for lost time. For
the earliest English Americans were slow to acquire
the newspaper habit. American journalism was not
born until fifty years after the appearance of the Bay
Psalm Book, and blossomed but to die.

The first newspaper in the colonies was Benjamin
Harris's *Publick Occurrences,* which began and ended
its career on Thursday, September 25, 1690. Harris
holds a double title to immortality, for, as noted in
Chapter II, it was he who inaugurated the *New
England Primer.* All unwittingly he specialized in
fugitive publications. He did not intend to print only
a single issue of *Publick Occurrences,* but the provincial council scanned the three pages of text (the
fourth page of the paper was blank) and bent its
thumbs earthward. There was probably specific
objection to an account of a fight between 'French
Indians' and Mohawks, but behind this presumed
pretext was the affront to authority implicit in the
fact that the paper was not licensed. England itself
was hardly yet a haven of liberalism, but the colonies
were far behind the mother country in this respect.

Against Harris too, perhaps, was the fact that he
was an alert journalist. Not only did he found the

first American newspaper, but he was the first American newspaperman. More successful enterprises were to follow in his train, but many decades were to elapse before American journalism was to reattain the latter-day standards of news-gathering and news-writing which *Publick Occurrences* manifested in its first and last issue. A copyreader on today's Boston *Globe*, *Herald*, *Post*, or *Transcript* could take the following piece of copy and, with only a little editing, a little more information (such as the name of the principal character), turn it into a contemporary news story:

> A very *Tragical Accident* happened at *Water-Town*, the beginning of this Month an *Old man*, that was of somewhat a Silent and Morose Temper, but one that had long Enjoyed the reputation of a *Sober* and a *Pious Man*, having newly buried his Wife, The Devil took advantage of the Melancholly which he thereupon fell into, his Wives discretion and industry had long been the support of his Family, and he seemed hurried with an impertinent fear that he should now come to want before he dyed, though he had very careful friends to look after him who kept a strict eye upon him, least he should do himself any harm. But one evening escaping from them into the Cow-house, they there quickly followed him, found him *hanging by a Rope*, which they had used to tye their *Calves* withal, he was dead with his feet near touching the Ground.

James Melvin Lee, in his *History of American Journalism* (Boston, 1923), quotes the single issue of *Publick Occurrences* entire. It occupies, in transcription, five octavo pages. It is worth reading, as history and as entertainment, and also as a tribute to the memory of Benjamin Harris, who returned to London in 1695, issued more newspapers and books, engaged

Numb. 1,

PUBLICK
OCCURRENCES

Both *FORREIGN* and *DOMESTICK*.

Boston, Thursday Sept. 25th. 1690.

IT is designed, that the Countrey shall be furnished once a moneth (or if any Glut of Occurrences happen, oftener,) with an Account of such considerable things as have arrived unto our Notice.

In order hereunto, the Publisher will take what pains he can to obtain a Faithful Relation of all such things; and will particularly make himself beholden to such Persons in Boston whom he knows to have been for their own use the diligent Observers of such matters.

That which is herein proposed, is, First, That Memorable Occurrents of Divine Providence may not be neglected or forgotten, as they too often are. Secondly, That people every where may better understand the Circumstances of Publique Affairs, both abroad and at home; which may not only direct their Thoughts at all times, but at some times also to assist their Businesses and Negotiations.

Thirdly, That some thing may be done towards the Curing, or at least the Charming of that Spirit of Lying, which prevails amongst us, wherefore nothing shall be entered, but what we have reason to believe is true, repairing to the best fountains for our Information. And when there appears any material mistake in any thing that is collected, it shall be corrected in the next.

Moreover, the Publisher of these Occurrences is willing to engage, that whereas, there are many False Reports, maliciously made, and spread among us, if any well-minded person will be at the pains to trace any such false Report so far as to find out and Convict the First Raiser of it, he will in this Paper (unless just Advice be given to the contrary) expose the Name of such person, as A malicious Raiser of a false Report. It is supposed that none will dislike this Proposal, but such as intend to be guilty of so villanous a Crime.

THE Christianized *Indians* in some parts of *Plimouth*, have newly appointed a day of Thanksgiving to God for his Mercy in supplying their extream and pinching Necessities under their late want of Corn, & for His giving them now a prospect of a very *Comfortable Harvest*. Their Example may be worth Mentioning.

'Tis observed by the Husbandmen, that altho' the With-draw of so great a strength from them, as what is in the Forces lately gone for *Canada*, made them think it almost impossible for them to get well through the Affairs of their Husbandry at this time of the year, yet the Season has been so unusually favourable that they scarce find any want of the many hundreds of hands, that are gone from them; which is looked upon as a Merciful Providence.

While the barbarous *Indians* were lurking about *Chelmsford*, there were missing about the beginning of this month a couple of Children belonging to a man of that Town, one of them aged about eleven, the other aged about nine years, both of them supposed to be fallen into the hands of the *Indians*.

A very *Tragical Accident* happened at *Water-Town*, the beginning of this Month, an Old man, that was of somewhat a Silent and Morose Temper, but one that had long Enjoyed the reputation of a *Sober* and a *Pious Man*, having newly buried his Wife, The Devil took advantage of the Melancholy which he thereupon fell into, his Wives discretion and industry had long been the support of his Family, and he seemed hurried with an impertinent fear that he should now come to want before he dyed, though he had very careful friends to look after him who kept a strict eye upon him, least he should do himself any harm. But one evening escaping from them into the Cow-house, they there quickly followed him found him hanging by a Rope, which they had used to tye their Calves withal, he was dead with his feet near touching the Ground.

Epidemical *Fevers* and *Agues* grow very common, in some parts of the Country, whereof, tho' many dye not, yet they are sorely unfitted for their imployments; but in some parts a more *malignant Fever* seems to prevail in such sort that it usually goes thro' a Family where it comes, and proves *Mortal* unto many.

The *Small-pox* which has been raging in *Boston*, after a manner very Extraordinary, is now very much abated. It is thought that far more have been sick of it then were visited with it, when it raged so much twelve years ago, nevertheless it has not been so Mortal, The number of them that have

527

THE FIRST NATIVE NEWSPAPER

One number was issued, and of this only one copy, now in
the Public Record Office at London, survives

in numerous controversies, and died obscurely about 1716.

The untimely suppression of *Publick Occurrences* evidently instilled 'an impertinent fear' in the heart of any intending newspaper publisher for fourteen years. Then, on April 24, 1704, John Campbell, postmaster of Boston, issued the first number of the *Boston News-Letter*, 'Published by Authority.' Campbell had been accustomed to prepare written intelligence reports — literal news letters — to the New England provincial authorities, a means of news dissemination which had excellent precedent behind it, in England and elsewhere. The *News-Letter* was hardly a signal commercial success. Government subsidies twice transfused a fleeting vitality into it, but in 1709 it was forced to suspend for eight months, at the end of which time the reading public apparently felt the lack of it so greatly that Campbell was heartened to try again. Yet, in 1719, in which year he lost his postmastership, Campbell protested that the circulation of the *News-Letter* was under three hundred.

This first American newspaper proprietor and editor (excluding the unfortunate Harris from a statistical survey on account of the ephemerality of his performance) was no genius, but the lack was compensated by a dogged perseverance to see a thing through that entitles him to an honored place on the scroll of the pioneers of enlightenment.

Campbell edited his paper [says Willard Grosvenor Bleyer in *Main Currents in the History of American Journalism* (Boston, 1927)] in a painstaking but conservative and uninspired manner. He was scrupulously accurate, even to the extent of pointing out in one issue that a comma had been misplaced in a preceding number. On another occasion he explained that, in an account of a fire at Plymouth in the preceding issue, 'whereas it is said Flame covering the Barn, it should be said Smoak.'

Campbell's successor in the postmastership was William Brooker, who expected the transfer of the *News-Letter* to himself as a matter of course, for in that pre-railroad, pre-postage-stamp day the post-office was the logical, inevitable, official, and semi-official news center — far more so than the church and the tavern. But Campbell held fast to his property, declining to have it regarded as one of the perquisites of office (eventually, in 1722, he turned it over to his printer, Bartholomew Green, son of the printer of the Eliot Bible), and Brooker instituted a paper of his own, the *Boston Gazette*, which was issued from the shop of James Franklin. Through a subsequent shift in postmasters James Franklin lost the contract, and forthwith set about the publication of a paper on his own account, the *New-England Courant*, the first number of which appeared on August 7, 1721. The vicissitudes of the *Courant* have been summarized in Chapters II and IV in detailing the transcending importance of the enterprise as a factor in the careers of James and, more notably, Benjamin Franklin.

On December 22, 1719 — the day after the initial appearance of the *Boston Gazette* — there had been issued in Philadelphia the first number of the *American Weekly Mercury*. Its proprietor was Andrew Bradford, postmaster, printer, and son of William Bradford. The *Mercury* throve peaceably for more than a year, and then, in January, 1722, aroused the potent ire of the authorities by publishing this mild editorial comment: 'Our General Assembly are now

94

sitting, and we have great expectations from them, at this juncture, that they will find some effectual remedy to revive the dying credit of this Province, and restore us to our former happy circumstances.' Bradford escaped with a reprimand and a warning after declaring that the offending sentence was written and inserted by a compositor without the proprietor's knowledge. The council may have connived at this arrangement with a view to a joint saving of faces; the thing may actually have happened, neither for the first nor for the last time. Bradford fell into more serious difficulties later and was sent to prison (though his paper continued to appear), but on this occasion he declined to eat humble pie and waged doughty battle for the freedom of the press, establishing thereby a precedent of principle and conduct that had an important bearing on a famous case that will shortly be considered. After Bradford's death in 1742 the *Mercury* was conducted by his widow Cornelia.

Andrew Bradford had the Philadelphia newspaper field to himself (barring official interference) until late in 1728, when Samuel Keimer brought out his *Universal Instructor in all Arts and Sciences: and Pennsylvania Gazette* in order to anticipate a like project that was about to be launched by Benjamin Franklin and Hugh Meredith. But Keimer did the launching and Franklin got the paper, as already related.

Meanwhile William Bradford, father of Andrew, since 1693 a resident of New York and official printer to that colony, had inaugurated, on November 8, 1725, the *New-York Gazette*. The paternal *Gazette* was a much less interesting affair than the filial *Mercury*; the *Gazette's* importance is chiefly chronological — it was New York's first newspaper. Its contents consisted in the main either of official pronouncements or of material taken from the English press; it depended, that is, not so much on reporters as on rewrite men. Benjamin Harris and Andrew Bradford had done better — they had sought, written, and printed the spot news of Boston and of Philadelphia. Frederic Hudson's classic and copious *Journalism in the United States, from 1690 to 1872* (New York, 1873) designates as 'the first effort at reporting in this country' an account of the execution of six pirates on the Charles River on June 30, 1704, which appeared with commendable promptness in the next issue of Campbell's *Boston News-Letter*. 'In describing the scene,' says Hudson, 'the "exhortations of the malefactors," and the prayer made by one of the ministers, after the pirates were on the scaffold, "as near as it could be taken in writing in the great crowd," filled nearly one half of the paper.' But this was hardly 'the first effort at reporting' in America — it was the first big local story.

The younger Bradford was not confronted by a competitor for nine years; the elder had to wait one less. On November 5, 1733, appeared the first number of the *New-York Weekly Journal*, founded by John Peter Zenger, who had left Germany as a boy of thirteen and become an apprentice in the Bradford shop. To the *Journal* belongs the distinction, as Bleyer expresses it, of being 'the first newspaper established in America by a political faction as a means of carrying on a political controversy.' The *Journal's* cause was the cause of the opponents of Governor William Cosby, who, soon after his appointment in 1732, became at odds with an influential provincial group who effected the establishment of the *Journal* as a weapon. The *Dictionary of American Biography* sets Cosby 'among New York's most unenlightened royal governors' and quotes from a famous letter which he wrote to his patron, the Duke of Newcastle: 'I am sorry to inform your Grace, that the example and spirit of the Boston people begins to spread among these colonys in a most prodigious manner. I had more trouble to manage these people than I could have imagined' — and this was written forty years before Lexington and Bunker Hill.

The *Journal* had barely celebrated its first anniversary when its proprietor was arrested on a charge of seditious libel and for a time held incommunicado. For this reason the *Journal* was compelled to skip an issue, but this number was the only one that failed to appear during the eight months of the editor's imprisonment in default of the heavy bail demanded. Zenger was a stalwart champion of the rights which were at issue, and his native courage was heightened by the conviction that not only was a powerful group of colonial leaders arrayed with him, but the populace as well was staunchly on his side.

Cosby's opponents sprang a sensation by engaging for Zenger's defense one of the greatest of colonial lawyers, Andrew Hamilton, of Philadelphia. One reason for going so far afield was that the royal authorities manifested an apparent intention to disbar every New York attorney who might be assigned to the case. Two paramount issues were involved — the question whether evidence tending to prove the alleged libel could be admitted, and the right of the jury to go beyond a simple weighing of the evidence and to determine whether the statements complained of actually were libelous — the right, that is, to pass upon the law as well as upon the fact. The court's position was that it could admit or decline to admit evidence as it chose (for which there was abundant precedent in English procedure) and that the jury must limit itself to finding whether or not Zenger actually published the material complained of (which was conceded by the defense), leaving the determination of the alleged libel to the court. Hamilton attacked both these positions in the first grand forensic ever delivered in America — and won his case. Doubtless the jury was his to begin with, but, equally doubtless, his eloquence heartened them to formulate a verdict which Gouverneur Morris described as 'the morning star of that liberty which subsequently revolutionized America.' The detailed story is available in Livingston Rutherfurd's *John Peter Zenger: His Press, His Trial and a Bibliography of Zenger Imprints* (New York, 1904), which also reprints the first pamphlet edition (1735) of the account of the trial, written by Zenger himself.

Zenger's career, and the *Journal's* as well, continued to an inevitable anticlimax. He died in 1746, and the *Journal* was operated by his widow Catharine until his son John was old enough to take over its management. The *Journal* itself died of inanition in 1752.

By the time the odious Stamp Act went into effect (November 1, 1765), opening the road to revolution and independence, newspapers had been established in Maryland (1727), South Carolina (1731), Rhode Island (1732), Virginia (1736), Connecticut (1755), North Carolina (1755), New Hampshire (1756), Delaware (1762), and Georgia (1763). The roster of the thirteen original colonies was not completed until 1777, when the *New-Jersey Gazette* appeared at Burlington, although late the previous year the alert but momentarily fugitive Hugh Gaine had removed his *New-York Gazette* to Newark and issued it thence until his return to New York and the Tory fold. Vermont and Maine had newspapers in 1781 and 1785 respectively. In the instances of certain colonies, as has previously been noted, the earliest newspapers were also the earliest examples of printing. By the time 'the shot heard 'round the world' was fired at Concord Bridge the colonies boasted thirty-seven newspapers, and it is interesting to note that, checking journalistic casualties against journalistic innovations during the war period itself, a slight net gain in the total had been recorded at the end of hostilities.

Hudson defined the colonial press as one of neutrality and the Revolutionary press as one of action. The story of the Revolutionary press belongs to history in the broader sense rather than to that restricted field which is here being considered. It can perhaps be viewed to best advantage in the present summary through a brief presentation of three careers on whom it exercised a formidable influence and who themselves exercised an impressive degree of influence on the period through the medium of printer's ink.

Born in Belfast and bred a printer, Hugh Gaine came to New York in 1745 at the age of eighteen and entered the shop of that James Parker who ten years later was to print the laws of Yale College at New Haven and to establish the first permanent New Jersey press at Woodbridge. By 1752 he was in business for himself, not alone as printer, but also as newspaper proprietor, bookseller, general storekeeper, and, later, as purveyor of patent medicines. His *New-York Mercury* developed a pro-American bias as the grand crisis approached, despite the fact that

in 1768 Gaine was made official printer of both
colony and city. With the British occupation of New
York, Gaine retreated to Newark, and seven numbers
of his paper were published from there. But he soon
returned to New York, and supported the British
cause until the evacuation of the city, when he abandoned his newspaper and devoted himself to the
printing, publishing, and sale of books until his death
in 1807.

The importance of Gaine's place in the colonial
publishing scheme may be measured from the fact
that the bibliography of the issues of his press from
1752 to 1800, in Paul Leicester Ford's *The Journals
of Hugh Gaine, Printer* (New York, 1902. Volume I:
Biography and Bibliography. Volume II: Journals
and Letters), occupies eighty-eight pages. He devoted special and shrewd attention to the literature
of self-help, witness such titles as *The Complete
Housewife* (1761), *Every Man His Own Lawyer* (1768),
The Young Clerk's Vade Mecum (1776), and *The
American Instructor; Or Young Man's Best Companion* (1785). He also had the foresight to invest
heavily in children's books, and so avidly were most
of his juvenile issues devoured that no copies of
several which he is known to have published (the
proof is in his own advertisements) are known to be
extant. In 1929 — one hundred and fifty-five years
after its publication — a tattered copy of *The Wonderful Life and Surprizing Adventures of Robinson
Crusoe, Who Lived Twenty-eight Years on an Unin-
habited Island Which He Afterwards Colonized*, bearing
the Gaine imprint, came to light, though Ford had
already postulated its existence, assigning it to 1775
instead of to 1774. This severely abridged *Crusoe*
was the first American edition of Defoe's classic;

Gaine himself, as probably the largest book importer in the America of his day, must have brought in many copies of various available English editions. Many of the books which Gaine issued, whether for youthful or adult consumption, were so abundantly consumed that several of them may have vanished forever. But forever, it is worth stressing once more, is a dangerous word to play with in bibliography. The extent of the peril may be gauged roughly from the fact that since the appearance of the meticulous Ford bibliography more than fifty new Gaine titles, according to Paltsits, have been discovered and recorded.

Gaine's career did not lack its romantic elements, but a far more colorful personality was that of his contemporary, fellow-townsman, and fellow-loyalist, James Rivington. Established as a prosperous London bookseller in early manhood, Rivington backed too many horses that were not quite fast enough, and in 1760, when he was thirty-six, he decided to risk all on a greater hazard, and emigrated to America. He followed the path of William Bradford from Philadelphia to New York, where in 1773 he established his *New-York Gazetteer: or Connecticut, New-Jersey, Hudson's-River, and Quebec Weekly Advertiser.* In 1777, with New York securely in British hands, he condensed this inclusive title to the *New-York Loyal Gazette* and soon afterward to the *Royal Gazette.*

The *Royal Gazette* quickly became one of the most notorious dispensers of manufactured news that has ever been disseminated to a credulous and partisan circulation. In Rivington's behalf it must be admitted that he had more than a shadow of a grievance against the colonists. In the lively spring of 1775 a group of patriots had raided his office, smashed his press, seized his types with a view to converting them into a more compelling medium of argument, and forced Rivington to flee to a British warship anchored in the bay. The theory that Rivington was actually a patriot spy, supplying Washington with secret messages bound in book-covers, seems to lack that final seal of documented confirmation which one would like to set upon it. Lorenzo Sabine's *Biographical Sketches of Loyalists of the American Revolution* (Boston, 1864) says of him: 'His tact and ability in conducting a newspaper were much feared, and... his press had more influence over the public mind than any other in the Royal interest in the country.' But tact and ability could not save the *Gazette* at the end of the war. It was discontinued on the last day of 1783, seven weeks after the demise of Gaine's *Mercury*. Rivington survived into the administration of Thomas Jefferson, dying in New York in 1802.

Coincident with every war of men and arms is fought a war of words, and printers thrive no less than munition makers. From Rivington's press issued such exemplars of this truth as Thomas B. Chandler's *What think ye of the Congress Now? or, an Enquiry, how far the Americans are Bound to abide by, and Execute the Decisions of the late Congress?* (1775), Joseph Galloway's *A Candid Examination of the Mutual Claims of Great-Britain, and the Colonies: with a Plan of Accommodation, on Constitutional Principles* (1775), and John Lind's *An Englishman's Answer to the Address, from the Delegates to the People of Great-Britain, in a Letter to the Several Colonies, which were Represented in the late Continental Congress* (1775). And, as the battle clouds gather, satire invariably walks hand in hand with propaganda and argument; witness *The Association of the Delegates of the Colonies, at the Grand Congress, held at Philadelphia, Sept. 1, 1774, Versified, and adapted to Music, calculated for Grave and Gay Dispositions; with a short Introduction. By Bob Jingle, Esq; Poet Laureat to the Congress,* 'Printed in the Year, 1774,' by Rivington, but without imprint, and Jonathan Sewall's *The Americans Roused, in a Cure for the Spleen. Or Amusement for a Winter's Evening,* reprinted by Rivington in 1775 from the Boston edition of the same year.

Special reference is due *The American Querist: or, Some Questions Proposed relative to the Present Disputes between Great Britain, and Her American Colonies. By a North-American. The Tenth Edition,* printed by Rivington in 1774, the authorship of which has been assigned to Myles Cooper, second president of King's College, now Columbia University, who was saved from possible martyrdom in the summer of 1775 only because his anti-British students (young Alexander Hamilton was one of the more obstreperous among them), setting out on an announced lynching bee, tarried too long for stimulants, so that Cooper, forewarned, was able to reach a man-o'-war in the harbor and withdraw in good order to the homeland, never to return. The first edition of *The American Querist* suffered a harsher fate — a fate described by Rivington himself on the title-page of the declared 'Tenth Edition' (which it almost certainly was not, the designation probably being mere ironic bravado): 'This Pamphlet, on the 8th Day of September last, was, in full Conclave of the Sons of Liberty in New-York, committed to the Flames by the Hands of their Common Executioner; as it contains some Queries they cannot, and others

they will not Answer!' The *Gazetteer* tartly remarked, following this incident: 'When you damn
the printer, and burn his pamphlet, he laughs, reprints, triumphs and fills his pocket.'

James Rivington's career and accomplishments
richly merit extensive biographical and bibliographical treatment, and the effort is hereby commended to
any scholar seeking a little-exploited phase of American history wherein an abundance of fascinating
material is available. The task could have been ably
performed by the late George H. Sargent, who offered
a competent and valuable synopsis in his account of
Rivington which appeared in *The American Collector*
for June, 1926 (Volume II, Number 3), accompanied
by a check list of Rivington imprints. Any future
student of Rivington will turn, in his earliest researches, to the remarkably fair appraisal of Rivington
set down by Isaiah Thomas in his *History of Printing
in America* (Worcester, 1810), which concludes with
this paragraph:

It is but justice to add, that Rivington, for some time,
conducted his Gazetteer with such moderation and im-
partiality as did him honor. To the other qualities of a
gentleman he added benevolence, vivacity, and, with
the exceptions already mentioned, punctuality in his
business. Interest often produces a change of opinion,
and the causes which induced Rivington to support the
measures of the British cabinet, were sufficiently apparent. And, the visit made to him by a party of men from
Connecticut, who destroyed his press, &c. as will be
hereafter related, doubtless tended to prejudice his
mind against the American cause; and, prompted him,
after he was appointed printer to the king, and placed
under the protection of the royal army, boldly, and without disguise, to carry his resentment beyond the bounds
of truth and justice.

Thomas's *History* is itself the primary source of information concerning the career of Isaiah Thomas. He was born in Boston in 1749, and six years later was apprenticed to Zechariah Fowle at about the time the latter's brother Daniel, in conflict with the local authorities, was preparing to go to Portsmouth to establish the first New Hampshire press. In 1765, Thomas went to Halifax, planning to make that city a stepping-stone on the road to England, but he 'found typography in a miserable state' in Nova Scotia and had to be content with merely keeping body and soul together by his trade during his exciting two years there, foreign travel being out of the question. He returned to Boston by way of Portsmouth and assisted Daniel Fowle for a few weeks. At Boston an opportunity offered to go to South Carolina, where he remained for two years, chiefly in the employ of Robert Wells at Charleston. In 1770, having just attained his majority, but wise in the ways of printing beyond his years, he was back in Boston.

Zechariah Fowle was still doing business there after a fashion, and he and Thomas established *The Massachusetts Spy*. After three months Fowle withdrew from the partnership, Thomas giving his security for equipment and intangibles. 'Fowle had, during nineteen years, been in possession of his press and types, and had not paid for them. The creditor was a near relation by marriage, and had exacted only the payment of the annual interest of the debt.' For a time Thomas sought to conduct a truly independent press, 'free to both parties which then agitated the country,' but the agitation soon grew too strong to admit of any neutrality, and Thomas cast his lot with the patriots. In the spring of 1775 he withdrew to

Worcester, but before establishing himself there 'he was concerned, with others, in giving the alarm' on the epochal night of the 18th of April, and 'at day break, the next morning, he crossed over to Charlestown, went to Lexington, and joined the provincial militia in opposing the King's troops.'

Thomas's inland migration was the result of no sudden inspiration born of the stimulus of imminent battle. 'A number of gentlemen in the county of Worcester' had waited upon him the preceding year and urged him to establish a press in their chief town, and by February, 1775, he had definitely decided on the move. 'The war commencing sooner than was expected' — war invariably commences sooner than even the most rampant jingo expects — hastened the Worcester establishment, and enabled Thomas, as a participant, to offer his waiting circulation list a first-hand account of the Battle of Lexington.

The story of Thomas's subsequent journalistic career cannot be set forth here; it can be had in detail in the notes of a later contemporary, Joseph T. Buckingham, whose *Specimens of Newspaper Literature: With Personal Memoirs, Anecdotes, and Reminiscences* (Boston, 1850) is a source book worth frequent consultation by the student. Buckingham himself drew heavily on Thomas, and complained that the *History of Printing* 'is not now to be found in the literary market; — *it is entirely out of print*' (the italics and the tautology are Buckingham's). Hudson (assigning a wrong date to Buckingham) paid a similar tribute to both works twenty-two years later; Thomas and Buckingham, he asserted, 'are now out of print, and can rarely be found in a library or at a book-stall.' Buckingham's *Reminis-*

cences is still out of print, and has been since 1850, though copies of the original edition are today by no means so rare as Hudson indicated; Thomas's *History* was reissued in 1874, 'with the author's corrections and additions,' by Joel Munsell, of Albany, himself a competent printer-historian in the Thomas tradition.

Before briefly discussing Thomas as publisher and bookseller, it is essential to present him in another highly important aspect of his vigorous and abundantly useful career. 'I have been, perhaps,' he says in the preface to his *History*, 'too easily, led to engage in a task which has proved more arduous than I had previously apprehended, and which has been attended by much expense.' An asterisk after the last word conducts the eye to this significant footnote:

> Few persons would form an idea of the cost which has attended the collection of the information I have found it necessary to procure, from various parts of the continent. An entire sale of the edition of this work would barely defray it. The purchase of volumes of old newspapers alone, has required a sum amounting to upwards of a thousand dollars. It is true, however, these volumes are valuable; and, together with the collection previously owned by the author, probably, constitute the largest library of ancient public journals, printed in America, which can be found in the United States.

These 'volumes of old newspapers,' plus the accessions of a century and a quarter, still 'constitute the largest library of ancient public journals, printed in America, which can be found in the United States.' They are housed in the American Antiquarian Society at Worcester, founded and endowed by Thomas — itself a monument more than sufficient to immortalize his memory even if he had no other claim to the grateful consideration of his countrymen. Out of this noble repository has fittingly issued, among numerous other contributions to history and scholarship, a monumental *Bibliography of American Newspapers, 1690–1820*, compiled by the present director, Clarence S. Brigham, now available in the *Proceedings* of the Society from October, 1913, to April, 1927, and planned to appear in book form. An indication of the development and growth of American journalism from Benjamin Harris to the Era of Good Feeling may be found in the fact that the Brigham compilation embraces nearly two thousand titles.

Thomas's alertness and acumen made Worcester a book-publishing center of an importance that has never been approached by any American city except for the obvious metropolitan survivals into our own day. From his press, competently and often finely printed, issued inevitably the familiar run of almanacs, political tracts, sermons, theological treatises, and murderers' scaffold addresses (the latter generally in the fugitive form of broadsides), and much more. Like Gaine, he was thoroughly alive to the potentialities of how-to literature: *The Writing Scholar's Assistant, Containing Alphabetical Copies of Plain Running Hand. Necessary to be learned by all who would wish to write neat, easy, and fit for all Purposes, and have not opportunity to practice a Variety of Hands* (1785), Samuel Deane's *The New-England Farmer; or, Georgical Dictionary* (1790), *A Complete Guide for the Management of Bees* (1790), *The Family Female Physician* (1793), ready reckoners, manuals of etiquette, spellers, and every other variety of collective and individual textbook. He issued Blackstone's *Commentaries* in four volumes, and in as decorous and convenient an edition as has been printed wheresoever and whensoever, a *Robinson Crusoe*, a *Pilgrim's Progress*, the Bible in four sizes. And he issued in addition *Be Merry and Wise; or, the Cream of the Jests, and the Marrow of Maxims, For the Conduct of Life. Published for the Use of all good Little Boys and Girls. By Tommy Trapwit, Esq.* (1786), *The Brother's Gift: or the Naughty Girl Reformed*, twinned with *The Sister's Gift: or, the Naughty Boy Reformed* (both 1786), and *A Bag of Nuts, Ready cracked; or Instructive Fables, Ingenious Riddles, and Merry Conundrums. By the Celebrated and Facetious Thomas Thumb, Esq. Published for the Benefit of all little Masters and Misses Who love Reading before Playing* (1787).

Most famous of all in this group, he issued *Mother Goose's Melody; or Sonnets for the Cradle. In Two Parts. Part I. Contains the most celebrated Songs, and Lullabies of the good old Nurses, calculated to amuse children and to excite them to Sleep. Part II. those of that sweet Songster and Nurse of Wit and Humour, Master William Shakespeare. Embellished with Cuts, and illustrated with Notes and Maxims, Historical, Philosophical, and Critical* (1786). Of this edition of *Mother Goose* but a single tattered copy remains, which copy, fitly, is in the American Antiquarian Society. A pamphlet issued by the Society in 1928 to accompany its *Exhibit of American Children's Books Printed Before 1800* calls Thomas 'the most noted printer of children's books of his time, as well as the first successfully to occupy this field.' He was shrewd enough to see that the trail blazed by John Newbery, of London, was a beneficent and profitable one, and republished an abundance of Newbery juveniles by special arrangement — 'yet he apparently did not deem them worthy of preservation in his library,' according to the 1928 manual. 'Except for eight titles, not a copy did he present or bequeath to the American Antiquarian Society. Practically our entire collection has been subsequently acquired, and most of the titles in the last twenty years, largely through the interest and generosity of Dr. Charles L. Nichols.' Dr. Nichols died the year after this tribute was published, but he had compiled, seventeen years earlier, a bibliography of Thomas imprints which is appended to his *Isaiah Thomas: Printer, Writer and Collector* (Boston: The Club of Odd Volumes, 1912).

Early newspapers, in their very nature, are attractive collectors' items. Almost any copy of a colonial weekly, semi-weekly, or tri-weekly — the first American daily, the *Pennsylvania Packet and Daily Advertiser*, appeared at Philadelphia September 21, 1784, under the joint proprietorship of David C. Claypoole and John Dunlop — has a flavor about it that makes an intimate and sentimental appeal even to the most consistent scoffer at antiquarian survivals, and this is especially true of those papers which printed the minor happenings of their own localities. Here is source material of unimpeachable richness, and of a social and historical value that is obvious to any beholder.

Yet, somewhat paradoxically, old newspapers are not commonly absorbed by individual collectors. Occasionally one or two copies are handed down from grandfather to father to son, are preserved religiously at trunk bottoms, and safeguarded as the years go by with greater care and tenderness than many inheritances of far greater potentiality. An economic emergency, private or general, arises; the treasured relics are reluctantly sent to market; dismay and abandonment of faith in human nature ensue when word comes back that the heirlooms are not actually worth their weight in gold leaf.

The classic example of this recurring tragedy is the *Ulster County Gazette*, published at Kingston, New York, by Samuel Freer and his son Samuel S., particularly the issue for January 4, 1800, which chronicled the death of George Washington. The *Gazette*, of course, was far from being the sole American newspaper to record that event, but it was one of the first American newspapers to be reprinted in approximate facsimile — possibly, but by no means probably, as early as 1825, certainly as early as the 1850's and as late as 1923, when Goad-Ballinger Post of the American Legion of Springfield, Missouri, published a reproduction for distribution both to the public and to other Legion posts. The first reprint, presumably, was copied by somebody else, and the re-reprint by still other somebodies, and an inevitable geometric progression of reprints has made the Washington obituary issue of the *Gazette* the most widely copied of early American newspapers.

Meanwhile every trace of the original had vanished — it must once have existed, everyone logically surmised (for copies of earlier and later issues were familiar), but no expert had ever seen one. The thing became ludicrous, with a tragic overtone, and the story was at last set down, with due appreciation of both of its contrasting emotional elements, by R. W. G. Vail in *The Ulster County Gazette and Its Illegitimate Offspring* (New York: The New York Public Library, 1930). Then, marvel of marvels, a copy of the original issue for January 4, 1800, came to light — a copy now carefully enshrined in the Library of Congress, as unique as the original of the Declaration of Independence. Mr. Vail's pamphlet was reprinted in 1931 with the triumphant sequel: 'The *Ulster County Gazette* Found at Last.' The impossible had happened, the unfindable had been found. It is ever so in bibliography.

The *Ulster County Gazette* is by no means the only old newspaper which has been many times reissued — it is simply the most abundantly reissued, sixty times and more. The practice of reprinting old papers is so common, in fact, that it has its own check list — *A List of American Newspaper Reprints*, by Joseph Gavit, senior librarian of the New York State Library (New York: The New York Public Library, 1931). Surviving newspapers have frequently published facsimiles of their original issues by way of observing centenaries or semi-centenaries; time dulls the ink and tones the paper, and before many years have passed the reproduction wears an air of antiquity that might well be envied by its all-rag prototype. But there will always be some mark, deliberate or accidental, whereby the original is identifiable.

CHAPTER VI

The Rise of the Magazine

TO Andrew Bradford, of Philadelphia, son of the
pioneer William, appertains the distinction not
alone of establishing the first American magazine,
but of being the first American magazine proprietor
to steal an editor. The editor was John Webbe, a
lawyer, whom Benjamin Franklin had already engaged to conduct a similar venture. Webbe paid
dearly, one trusts, for his perfidy. The periodical to
which he transferred his devotions, *The American
Magazine: or A Monthly View of The Political State
of the British Colonies*, survived through a third issue
(January–March, 1741), and then was seen no more.

Thereby Andrew Bradford achieved another primacy in the history of the native periodical. He was
the first American publisher to bury a magazine.
The graveyard which he thus dedicated has become
abundantly tenanted in the nearly two centuries that
have intervened; hope springs eternal, but no hope
springs so blindly as that which impels a new periodical into being. And the supreme tragedy lies in
the fact that while an epic may perish unprinted with
only a single name on the casualty list (to wit, one
starved poet), while a play may fall short of Broad-
way only to the dramatist's hurt (and perhaps not
even to his), while a novel may remain permanently
in manuscript solely to the novelist's disillusionment
and despair, a magazine seldom founders without
carrying down a whole crew.

The Bradford enterprise was too primitive an

undertaking to wreak such extensive havoc. Webbe was probably the solitary victim, and he, presumably, recovered and lived to regret his treachery; Andrew Bradford pocketed his probably inconsequential loss and went back to his newspaper, *The American Mercury*, and to his general printing and publishing business. He died in November, 1742, not as a result of his magazine's collapse, and the *Mercury* turned its rules for six weeks by way of mourning — not for *The American Magazine*, but for Andrew Bradford.

Franklin's *General Magazine and Historical Chronicle, For all the British Plantations in America*, enjoyed a career only a little less undistinguished than that of its rival. The *General* was the first American periodical to be projected; the first issue appeared in January, 1741, three days after the earliest number of the *American*, the last issue in June of that year. The *General*, therefore, endured twice as long as the *American*, but a complete run will still fit the pocket.

The editorial program for the first colonial magazine was thus set forth in the initial issue of the *American*:

> It is proposed to publish Monthly, *An Account of the publick Affairs transacted in His Majesty's Colonies, as well on the Continent of* America *as in the* West-India *Islands:* Under this Head will be comprehended, Abstracts of the Speeches of the several Governors, the Addresses and Answers of the Assemblies, their Votes, Resolutions and Debates. So that this Part of the Work will contain Journals of the *most important* Proceedings of each particular Assembly. Moreover, at the End of every Sessions, we shall give an Extract of any remarkable Laws therein passed, with the Reasons on which they were founded, the *Grievances* intended to be remedied by them, and the *Benefits* expected from them.

That the Reader may be the better enabled to form a Judgment of the various Transactions intended to be set in View; Succinct Accounts will be given, *in the Course of the Work*, of the Situation, Climate, Soil, Productions, Trade and Manufactures of all the *British* Plantations; the Constitutions of those several Colonies, with their respective Views and Interests, will be opened and explained; and the Nature and Extent of the various Jurisdictions exercised in each Government particularly described.

There was more, but this is enough by way of indication. The emergent fact is that the magazine in America began as an extension of the newspaper. It had not been wholly so in England; there were the glorious examples of Joseph Addison and Richard Steele, to whom (particularly to Addison) the earliest American periodicals often frankly acknowledged an indebtedness which was not always apparent in the performance. In America the Magazine became at the outset, and remained for a considerable time thereafter, a topical review, a summary, a digest. 'We are to be considered,' wrote Editor Jeremiah Gridley of *The American Magazine and Historical Chronicle* of Boston (September, 1743–December, 1746), 'as mere reporters of facts'; William Bradford's *American Magazine and Monthly Chronicle for the British Colonies* (October, 1757–October, 1758) discussed in a single number 'European Affairs,' 'English Militia Law,' and 'Proposal for a Militia in Pennsylvania,' offered an essay 'On the uses and abuses of Militias' in order that the militia question might not be wholly ignored, and concluded with a 'Monthly Chronicle of American Affairs.'

With the approach of the Revolution the native magazine began to parallel the change that has previously been noted in the development of the native newspaper. Despite its title, Isaiah Thomas's *Royal American Magazine, or Universal Repository of Instruction and Amusement* (Boston, January, 1774–March, 1775) was a doughty vehicle of patriotic propaganda. But already, in the midst of alarums, a significant infiltration was taking place. More and more the factor of entertainment was coming to be appreciated as an important element in the editorial scheme. Before the end of the century William Biglow, speaking out of an editorial experience gained on *The Massachusetts Magazine* (Boston, 1789–96), was able to offer this sardonic 'Receipt for a Magazine':

> A plate, of art and meaning void,
> To explain it a whole page employed:
> Two tales prolonged of maids deluded;
> Two more begun, and one concluded;
> Life of a fool to fortune risen;
> The death of a starved bard in prison;
> On woman, beauty-spot of nature,
> A panegyric and a satire;
> Cook's voyages, in continuation;
> On taste a tasteless dissertation;
> Description of two fouls aquatic:
> A list of ladies, enigmatic;
> A story *true* from French translated,
> Which, with a *lie* might well be mated;
> A mangled slice of English history;
> Essays on miracles and mystery;
> An unknown character attacked,
> In story founded upon fact:
> Advice to jilts, coquets, and prudes:
> And thus the pompous Prose concludes.

Biglow devoted almost as many couplets to an equally detailed and equally unflattering examination of the periodical poetry of his era. He ended with the following lines as proof of the fact that while much had changed, much remained as it had been a half-century and more earlier:

> Next, from the public prints, display
> The news and lyings of the day;
> Paint bloody Mars & Co. surrounded
> By thousands slain, ten thousand wounded:
> Steer your sly politics between
> The Aristocrat and Jacobin;
> Then end the whole, both prose and rhyme, in
> The ravages of Death and Hymen.

Magazine editing was only an incident (and evidently not a pleasant one) in Biglow's career; his 'Receipt' was written, Buckingham surmises, in his twenties. He may have lived to regret it; — he lived, at any rate, until 1844, by which time *The North American Review* (an outgrowth of *The Monthly Anthology*), *Godey's Lady's Book*, *Graham's Magazine*, *Southern Literary Messenger*, *The Knickerbocker Magazine*, and other notable contemporaries were earning a merited immortality in social and literary history. It will be well, however, before abandoning Biglow and his causticity, to consider for a moment his initiatory couplet. He did not put 'a plate' first without reason. Magazine proprietors were quick to sense the importance of illustration — Bradford had adorned his *American* with a representation of Philadelphia from the Delaware River. Isaiah Thomas's *Royal American* was designed to carry two copperplate engravings in each issue, and Thomas prevailed on his friend Paul Revere to execute several of these. Had Revere never mounted horse, these reproductions would now be of rather bloodless historical significance; but ride he did, and who today can look at his

timely *Royal American* cartoons unmoved? An ante-
cedent Bostonian, John Foster, had been the first en-
graver in British America as well as the first printer
in Boston; his crude portrait of Richard Mather,
principal translator of the Bay Psalm Book, done in
1670 or 1671, was the earliest engraving to be
executed in what is now the United States.

Thomas himself could engrave at a pinch — at
least he had done so occasionally in the grindstone
days of his youth — but he knew well where his more
assured talents lay. One of his Philadelphia contemporaries, however, who also owned a magazine,
was more of an adept at the graphic arts, though if he
had enjoyed no other claim to subsequent recognition
his memory would hardly survive today outside of a
few technical monographs. His career, and a portion
of that of his more famous editorial collaborator, are
worth tracing in some detail because the periodical
and publishing history of their time finds in them so
clear a reflection.

Born in Scotland in 1734, Robert Aitken was
established in Philadelphia in 1771 as bookseller and
bookbinder. In 1773 he added book publishing to
these activities, and two years later (January, 1775)
established *The Pennsylvania Magazine: or, American
Monthly Museum*, the final issue of which appeared
about the time that Thomas Jefferson, in modest
lodgings hard by, was sweating over the stylistic
niceties of 'a "Declaration" which I was lately
directed to draw.' The *Pennsylvania* might have become the first conspicuously successful American
magazine if Aitken had been more publisher than
patriot, and if he had not engaged the services of another Thomas, certainly the next most famous after
Jefferson in the annals of the Revolution, as his editor.

PAUL REVERE, CARTOONIST

England lording it over America in the frontispiece of Edes
and Gill's *North American Almanack for 1769* (Boston, 1768)

Thomas Paine, Aitken's junior by three years, out-
lived him by seven, and Aitken died at sixty-eight.
Paine, therefore, is an unfortunate example for cita-
tion by those who assert that longevity is not compat-
ible with an addiction to alcohol. He emigrated from
England in 1774 under the high sponsorship of Benjamin Franklin, and a few weeks after his arrival in-
formed Franklin, then the colonies' agent in the mother country, that Aitken had engaged him. Isaiah
Thomas records a famous incident of this partnership:

> On one of the occasions, when Paine had neglected
> to supply the materials for the Magazine, within a short
> time of the day of publication, Aitken went to his
> lodgings, and complained of his neglecting to fulfil his
> contract. Paine heard him patiently, and coolly answered,
> 'You shall have them in time.' Aitken expressed some
> doubts on the subject, and insisted on Paine's accompa-
> nying him and proceeding immediately to business, as the
> workmen were waiting for copy. He accordingly went
> home with Aitken, and was soon seated at the table with
> the necessary apparatus, which always included a glass,
> and a decanter of brandy. Aitken observed [that is, to
> Isaiah Thomas], 'he would never write without *that*.'
> The first glass put him in a train of thinking; Aitken feared
> the second would disqualify him, or render him untract-
> able; but it only illuminated his intellectual system; and
> when he had swallowed the third glass, he wrote with
> great rapidity, intelligence and precision; and his ideas
> appeared to flow faster than he could commit them to
> paper. What he penned from the inspiration of the
> brandy, was perfectly fit for the press without any
> alteration, or correction.

Thomas felt it essential to bulwark the account with
this footnote:

> Aitken was a man of truth, and of an irreproachable

character. This anecdote came from him some years before his death.

Early in 1776, while Paine was still editor of the *Pennsylvania*, he published, over the imprint of Robert Bell, his *Common Sense*, the first American bestseller. He established thereby his reputation as the most cogent penman of the Revolution — not excepting the adroit Jefferson. *Common Sense*, a well-considered, well-grounded, well-presented, forthright statement of the case for independence, was reprinted with such zeal that every literate inhabitant of the colonies may well have read it and every illiterate have had it read to him — at any rate everybody knew about it. It enjoyed a wide distribution in England, and was quickly translated into several foreign languages. Its authorship was frequently assigned to Franklin, who did see it in manuscript, just as he saw the *magnum opus* of that other and more effulgent Thomas.

Aitken's fame did not suffer eclipse with the extinction of *The Pennsylvania Magazine*. He was soon busy about a project that was to lend his name an undiminishable luster on the scroll of the pioneers of American printing. The colonists believed in the sanctity of their cause; theirs was a holy war, but when they required soul stimulus for its prosecution, they had to get it from Bibles of hostile origin. If they read German, as many of them did, they could find comfort in an indigenous product — the Bible printed by Christoph Sauer in his native tongue at Germantown in 1743.

The Continental Congress had already been memorialized to import twenty thousand Bibles, and the petition stirred Aitken to action. In 1777 he published a New Testament, which went into a fourth edition in 1781. Then, in 1782, he brought out a complete Bible. It was a chunky and unlovely volume, too nearly cubic to fit any breast pocket, else it had indubitably stopped dozens of Hanoverian bullets in later fable, but it helped to stimulate the new sensation of independence by proving tangibly that God dwelt at Philadelphia as well as at Oxford. The Aitken Bible is today a rare and valuable collector's item, and most of the surviving examples of it show signs of having been put to rugged and earnest use.

Robert Aitken was succeeded on his death in 1802 by his daughter Jane, who, Isaiah Thomas wrote while she still lived, 'has obtained much reputation by the productions which have issued from her press.'

By the end of the eighteenth century the roster of American periodicals had swollen to what would have been formidable proportions if every name enrolled had represented a then still flourishing vehicle of expression. Frank Luther Mott, as an appendix to his indispensable *History of American Magazines, 1741–1850* (New York, 1930), compiled a chronological list of 'such periodicals as have seemed important enough in some respect for treatment (or at least enumeration) in the text.' The list, here reduced for brevity's sake to a simple statistical compilation of original appearances, through 1800, is as follows:

1741.... 2	1775.... 1	1793.... 5
1743.... 3	1779.... 1	1794.... 2
1752.... 1	1783.... 1	1795.... 6
1753.... 1	1784.... 1	1796.... 8
1755.... 2	1785.... 1	1797.... 11
1757.... 1	1786.... 5	1798.... 11
1758.... 2	1787.... 2	1799.... 3
1769.... 1	1789.... 5	1800.... 10
1771.... 2	1790.... 1	
1774.... 1	1792.... 2	

The summary is even more striking when recapitulated by decades:

$$
\begin{array}{ll}
1741-1750. & 5 \\
1751-1760. & 7 \\
1761-1770. & 1 \\
1771-1780. & 5 \\
1781-1790. & 16 \\
1791-1800. & \underline{58} \\
& 92
\end{array}
$$

But if the Union News Company had been operating stands in the metropolitan centers of Philadelphia, Boston, and New York during the adult life of George Washington (the inventory of whose library recorded files of several contemporary periodicals), it could hardly have offered the public an abundant and impressive variety of native wares at any given time. Dr. Mott compiled charts of the chronological relationships of American magazines during the century and more covered by his survey, and the gaps evident therein provide melancholy testimony to the reluctance of the colonists to achieve magazine-mindedness. *The American Magazine and Historical Chronicle* of Boston expired, as has been noted, in December, 1746, to be succeeded by a magazineless night which no alleviating ray pierced until the first number of *The Independent Reflector* was issued at New York at the end of November, 1752. Following the demise of *The New American Magazine* (printed at Woodbridge, New Jersey, for urban consumption) in March, 1760 — the changes rung on the name *American* in the chronicle of the early American periodical, plus the frequent custom of not troubling to ring any changes at all, make its history as confusing as that of the Kingdom of Prussia and the German Empire with their successive Williams, Fredericks, and Frederick Williams — came an even longer interval before the appearance of the first number (Philadelphia, January, 1769) of *The American Magazine, or General Repository*. There were four other *lacunæ* up to October, 1783, when *The Boston Magazine* initiated its triennium. Since then no American has had to go without an issue of a current periodical.

The statistics cited above are impressive. They are too impressive. 'The sparsely settled new States were decidedly over-exploited,' wrote Algernon Tassin in *The Magazine in America* (New York, 1916). 'However barren were some departments of literature in the early days,' he added, 'magazines indicated at the outset their eternal disposition to multiply faster than the traffic will stand.' Tassin quotes from a letter which Jeremy Belknap, Congregational clergyman and one of the earliest contributors to the important *Columbian* of Philadelphia, wrote to Mathew Carey (of whom there will be more to say in a later chapter) in 1787 when Carey sought some of that commodity which the most meagerly endowed of mortals is always willing to dispense — advice:

> Several attempts have been made within my memory both here and at the Southward to establish such a repository of literature, but after a year or two they have uniformly failed. To what other causes the failure may be ascribed I will not say, but this appears to me to be one, viz: the too frequent publication of them. We are fond of imitating our European Brethren in their monthly productions without considering the difference between our Circumstances and theirs. Such a country as this is not yet arrived at such a pass of improvement to keep up one or two monthly vehicles of importance.

Dr. Mott, examining the situation in detail, quotes another contemporary authority — the Noah Webster who has come down to posterity as compiler of a dictionary, but who, forty years before, was the first and sole editor of New York's first monthly, another *American*: 'The expectation of failure is connected with the very name of a Magazine.'

Belknap and Webster spoke with an accuracy which the passage of a century and a half has not impugned. America finally accepted the magazine because there was no way out of accepting it. The choice was sound if Hobsonian. From tenuous seedlings struggling for rootage in overcrowded and exiguous soil sprang the noble trees that were to flourish mightily in the century that lay ahead. By the end of that other century, perhaps, inbreeding and overfertilization would begin to exact a toll of hardihood — but the conclusion can best be left to the examination and dissection of some yet unborn commentator.

What was said earlier of the newspaper as a province for the private collector can be substantially repeated here of the magazine. Files of eighteenth-century American magazines are rare — their circulations in general were much smaller than those of the newspapers, and the newspaper circulations of that day were nothing to send their proprietors into ecstasies or to keep counting-room staffs engaged after hours unless in futile efforts to balance the books. Even less than the newspapers, fortunately for these same business offices, did the magazines involve a ponderous financial outlay. Begun on a shoestring, often as the by-product of a tolerably successful printing shop, they ran to the end of that tenuous tether and expired. Like the newspapers, they were fragile in format, and were quickly consumed under the rigors of a sturdy era. The fortunate survivors among them are to be found for the most part in public collections.

CHAPTER VII

Tools of the Trade

To transmute a fragment of handwritten copy into a specimen of printing requires type, ink, paper, a press, and a printer. The earliest examples of printing in what is now the United States inevitably depended for their execution on imported materials handled by imported practitioners. Printing had been established in British North America considerably more than a century before it became possible to issue a finished product whereto the five essential contributing factors were themselves indigenous.

In one sense the human equation offered the least difficulty. To impart the rudiments of typography to a fellow-being was a comparatively simple matter, even in primitive Cambridge; to conjure a press into existence was another affair altogether. The printing press itself, indeed, was the last of the five elements to emerge as an all-American production, and it was born virtually hand in hand with a native type. Ink and paper, particularly ink, offered far less difficulty, though both, particularly paper, remained inferior to the imported product until a period too late to lend a powerful sentimental interest to their attainment of equality with it.

But Yankee ingenuity began to flourish in the field of printing well before the term Yankee itself was incorporated in English speech, and makeshift mechanical aids were frequently improvised. Excluding certain machined parts of the press itself which would

126

have to come from abroad, the printing process, in a pinch (and there were frequent pinches), could and did depend on the ready adaptability of American craftsmen, immigrant or native, for the solution of the emergencies of the moment.

The priority of a native paper among the physical essentials of printing is attested by the fact, noted in Chapter III, that William Bradford was instrumental in the establishment of a paper mill in Pennsylvania in 1690, only five years after the appearance of the first Pennsylvania imprint. Moreover, the passage from John Holme's *Flourishing State of Pennsylvania* which has been cited, noting that Bradford 'wants not paper, ink, nor skill,' might possibly be interpreted to mean that he was making, or could make, his own ink as well. Ink certainly offered the lesser difficulty; given a sufficient quantity of lampblack and flaxseed (linseed) oil, its fabrication was elementary. Now lampblack, as a discovery of Prometheus, was no mystery to the earliest settlers, and by 1640 both Massachusetts and Connecticut had enacted legislation to foster the cultivation of flax. To be sure, the immediate concern of the founding fathers in adopting this legislation was the manufacture of linen, but flaxseed oil was a natural by-product, and an 'oil-mill' was functioning in Pennsylvania by 1691, more than a century and a half before a muddier and murkier kind of oil was brought into the light of day in the same State to initiate a memorable epoch in the history of American industrialism and financial manipulation.

The early American printer, then, began fairly quickly to taste the fruits of commercial independence in the detail of ink. His home-made paper, however, was for long more of a makeshift.

It must be understood [writes Lawrence C. Wroth in *The Colonial Printer* (New York: The Grolier Club, 1931), from which fine monograph the factual material in this chapter is largely summarized] that the paper made in colonial America, especially in the early days, was not the finest in quality. The word 'handmade' has a connotation in these days that dazzles the intelligence even of persons ordinarily unimpressed by shibboleths. The American paper of the seventeenth and early eighteenth centuries, handmade, of course, from rags, was an honest paper, tough and durable in general, but as variable in quality as one would expect from indifferent materials handled by provincial workmen in rude manufactories. It is idle to think of the bulk of it as more than this. Like most things 'early American' in origin, it was that or nothing for its users, and if the printer could have imported European paper at a reasonable cost he would have been no more content with the local product than the man of taste of the period with furniture from the village carpenter if Chippendale and Sheraton had been within his means.

By the eve of the Revolution there were papermills in Massachusetts, Connecticut, Rhode Island, New York, Virginia, and North Carolina — a fact not without a highly specific bearing on the crisis just ahead. For the law that taxed tea and thus set that innocent beverage well to the fore among the notable *casus belli* of history also taxed paper, and taxed it to more purpose if with less popular hullabaloo.

It is quite likely that paper was more emphatically an immediate cause for the outbreak of the spirit of revolt than the insipid herb of which so much has been written [writes Mr. Wroth]. Certainly one would like to think this true. Tea as the father of the Eagle has always been something of an embarrassment to the American with a sense of humor. Paper is a much more dignified and spiritually important commodity. A tax on paper struck a vital blow at the business of the American printer, and this provincial craftsman was likewise the newspaper editor and a political influence in his community. United, he and his fellows formed a powerful factor in opposition, and they could be counted on to unite against the law that included paper among the taxable articles. They succeeded, too, in directing the indignation of their readers against the act without letting the element of self-interest appear too prominently. We hear little of the illegality of taxing paper, but there seems to have been a furious pother about tea. The air was full of tea, and one suspects the printers of having thrown it about to screen their real grievance.

The scarcity and expense of type was perhaps the major annoyance suffered by the colonial printer. The strict circumscription of the type-founders' craft in England, dating from a Decree of Star Chamber of 1637, wrought a hardship even on the English craftsman, but the effect was far more galling on the American. Necessity became the mother of invention, but there was a limit to her fecundity, and while many printers were able to fashion stop-gap letters, whole fonts were a problem of baffling magnitude, involving, as their manufacture did, the contriving of matrices, punches, and moulds. Not until 1768 did Abel Buell of Killingworth, Connecticut, begin to conduct experiments in type-founding that led him the following year to petition the provincial government for financial assistance to establish a foundry. A committee investigated and recommended that the public treasury advance Buell one hundred pounds, to be followed by a like bestowal a year later if he fulfilled certain conditions and, of course, proved his competence as a type-founder. The high hopes entertained for the project proved vain, however; defects in Buell's temperament, plus honest hard luck, conspired to nullify the grand program, although by 1781 he was supplying letter to the printing Greens — Thomas and Samuel, of New Haven, and Timothy, of New London.

In 1771, Christoph Sauer (or Christopher Sower), of Germantown, Pennsylvania, son of that other Christoph Sauer who printed, in German, the first Bible to be issued in America in a European language, cast in his own shop a quantity of German letter which was apparently sufficient for the bulky spiritual needs of his devout neighbors. He used imported matrices, a consideration that deprives his achievement of much of its pioneer luster, but two of the journeymen employed in the casting, Jacob Bay and Justus Fox, within a few years were performing the entire operation of type-founding. Thus, by 1775, type that was wholly a native product was being produced in Germantown on a sound commercial basis.

The Sauer dynasty presents one of the most interesting sets of phenomena in the history of colonial printing. The elder Christoph was born near Marburg, Hesse, in 1693, received an excellent education which included training in medicine, and emigrated to Philadelphia in 1724. With him came his three-year-old son, also Christoph. Setting up as a farmer in Lancaster, Sauer in 1731 established himself in Germantown, where he began supplying his numerous co-nationals with imported theological treatises in their native tongue. For one of Sauer's acumen and executive flair the transition from the vending of print to its manufacture on his own account involved few difficulties, and in 1735 he issued the first German almanac to be published in the colonies. A religious quarterly, *Der Hoch-Deutsch Pensylvanische*

Geschicts-Schreiben, approached the phenomenal circulation of ten thousand copies. In 1743 was issued
his famous Bible, the most ambitious undertaking yet
ventured by an American printer. Isaiah Thomas
called Sauer 'a man of good information, and a well-
instructed printer.' Under Christoph the younger,
the Sauer enterprise flourished and expanded; there
were two later issues of the large Bible in German,
one of two thousand copies in 1762 and another of
three thousand in 1776. Indeed, the plant became,
according to Thomas, 'by far the most extensive book
manufactory then, and for many years afterward, in
the British American colonies.'

The Sauer establishment suffered severely during
the battle of Germantown (1777), and the younger
Christoph (the elder had died in 1758) withdrew to
Philadelphia in the hope of preserving thereby what
was left of his property, since the British were bound
to win anyway. But the tide turned; Sauer's goods
were confiscated, and the sheets of much of the 1776
issue of the Bible were converted into gun-wadding.
A third Christoph, born in 1754, migrated to St. John,
New Brunswick, established a newspaper, and returned to the United States in 1799, settling in Baltimore, where he died the same year.

More than a century elapsed following the establishment of Stephen Daye's Cambridge shop before any
colonial artificer felt the urge to attempt to duplicate
the cumbersome apparatus on which the final test of
the printer's competence must be met. By 1750 the
versatile elder Sauer was constructing his own presses,
but 'there is no reason to believe,' declares Mr. Wroth,
'that he made presses for other printers or took up to
any extent the manufacture of printing machinery as
a commercial enterprise.' Not until 1769 — the year

of Abel Buell's ambitious but abortive effort to set himself up as a type-founder — did Isaac Doolittle, 'Clock & Watch-maker, of New Haven,' construct the first American press designed for sale. More than that, he sold it — to William Goddard of Philadelphia.

William Goddard has already appeared in these notes as the founder of printing in Providence thirty-five years after James Franklin had introduced the art into Rhode Island at Newport. Printing has always been among the most motionable of enterprises (provided the printer need cart only a minimum of paraphernalia with him); its very diffusion throughout Europe in the latter half of the fifteenth century was largely the result of the wanderlust (or wander-impulsion) of its earliest exponents, and their New World descendants were loyal to the tradition. Stephen Daye stands by way of a rule-proving exception; against him can be set whole families — the Greens, the Spooners, the Fowles, the Franklins. Goddard himself was a native of New London (1740), and learned his trade in New York under James Parker, whose pioneership in two localities has been made matter of record. He was only twenty-two when he set up shop in Providence, and only twenty-five when he left it in charge of his mother and returned to New York. A few weeks later he was back in Providence, but in 1766 he undertook his most ambitious venture to date by entering into partnership with Joseph Galloway and Thomas Wharton at Philadelphia. Their *Pennsylvania Chronicle, and Universal Advertiser*, initiated in January, 1767, was printed on one of Benjamin Franklin's worn presses — presumably it was in order to replace this senescent apparatus that Goddard bought a new press from

Doolittle in 1769. The Galloway-Wharton-Goddard partnership split on the rock of political dissension; the incident is described in unusually elaborate detail by Isaiah Thomas, and Goddard is beyond peradventure the hero of the episode. In 1773, Goddard established the *Maryland Journal; and the Baltimore Advertiser* in that city, which two years later he turned over to his sister Mary Katherine, who conducted it for nine years. In 1785, at the age of forty-five, this alert and controversial tourist took time out to get married, and it was to his wife's Rhode Island farm that he repaired, in 1793, to live in the calm retirement earned by one who had become a part of all that he had met, and who had met much.

The best compendium of information on the life of the journeyman printer in colonial times (and of the development of the chrysalis out of which the journeyman emerged — the apprentice printer) is Benjamin Franklin's Autobiography. Lacking that grand piece of documentation, we should have to depend largely on casual allusions. A compilation of the latter, such as Mr. Wroth assembles, offers a consistent if unflattering portrait of the man who held the stick and stood before the cases — and performed all the other operations between blank paper and finished product. Not in that day — not, at least, at its dawning — were the processes of a printing shop divided into specialties; the journeyman was a man of all work, as skilled in taking an impression as in justifying a line.

A few generalizations regarding the employed printer and his condition may, however, be safely made. He was as much a wanderer as Ulysses — occasionally he began to wander before his apprenticeship was served, and his employer often heralded his delinquency in a frantic advertisement. He could afford to wander, certainly if he were a skilled journeyman. For his calling was somewhat of a mystery, as Andrew Bradford had denominated it; it demanded then, as it demands today, that which sets it midway between the trades and the professions. Men who knew what it was all about were as scarce as many of the surviving examples of their handiwork, and if they found themselves in uncongenial surroundings, they had no need to stand upon the order of their going, but went at once, certain of a situation in the next important center. These two generalizations — the mobility of the practitioners of colonial printing, and the shortage of the supply — are probably safe. So, unfortunately, is a third: their fondness for the cup that cheers, but drives proofrooms frantic. Wroth cites numerous instances: William Goddard appealing in his newly established *Maryland Journal* for 'one or two sober Journeymen Printers who *can* and will work' (and they were 'wanted Immediately'); Hugh Gaine seeking a refugee 'pretty much pitted with the Small-Pox, wears his own hair and is much bloated by Drinking, to which he is most uncommonly addicted'; Joseph Royle of Williamsburg, Virginia, setting up a hue and cry for an indentured servant who had been trained as a bookbinder, but who certainly could lend a hand at cases or press, for whose return Royle was eager, despite the fact that the delinquent was 'very thick, stoops much, and has a down look; he is a little Pock-pitted, has a Scar on one of his Temples, is much addicted to Liquor, very talkative when drunk and remarkably stupid.'

The journeyman printer of colonial times was well paid, at least by comparison with the common laborer, who received only about a quarter as much.

Employed printers were slow to organize, but in 1776 there existed in New York an organization sufficiently powerful to initiate a strike for higher wages and to carry it through to a successful conclusion.

The diffusion of printing throughout the colonies is the more remarkable when one takes into account the amount of dunnage which the pioneer was forced to move with him. Virtually none of his equipment or material could be replaced *en route* or at his destination; the era of standardization, with the ready availability of spare parts, lay in the distant future. Difficulties of transport were to persist for generations after the colonial era, as will be seen when the time comes to discuss the introduction of printing to the Pacific Coast. Not quite half a century after the birth of independence, and in staid and settled New England, Samuel Bowles in 1824 loaded his wife, infant daughter, household goods, and hired printing press on a flatboat at Hartford, whence it was poled twenty-six miles up the Connecticut River to Springfield in order that Bowles might initiate the *Springfield Republican*. Every tentative thrust north, south, west of an established center was at the most modest computation a doubtful enterprise; often it was a desperate gamble. It will soon be essential to consider the spread of printing into the interior of a country which was for the most part less familiar to the average resident of the seaboard and the hinterland than Labrador or the Mackenzie basin is today.

CHAPTER VIII

Muses Ten to Twelve

GEORGE SANDYS traveled widely for his day (the day of Elizabeth, James, and Charles), journeying to Turkey, Egypt, and the Holy Land in his early thirties, and to the New World a little more than ten years later following his selection as treasurer of the Virginian Company. He remained in America until some time after 1631, bearing an important share in the occasionally acrimonious give-and-take of early colonial politics.

He had set down the chronicle of the earlier tour in his *Relation of a Journey begun an. Dom. 1610* (London, 1615), to which Izaak Walton alluded favorably in the second (1655) edition of *The Compleat Angler* and which led Edward Gibbon, a century and a quarter later, to characterize Sandys as 'that judicious traveller.' Sandys had translated the first five books of Ovid's *Metamorphoses*, and the work had been licensed in 1621, but no copy of the first, or even of a reasonably presumed second, edition now seems to be extant.

In Virginia he made time to devote to the remaining ten books (or, more strictly, eight, for he accomplished the translation of two on the high seas), and the complete version was issued at London in 1626, three years after the publication of the Shakespeare first Folio, as *Ovid's Metamorphosis Englished by G. S.* The dedicatory preface to Charles I made it quite clear that the work had not been prosecuted to the detriment of the King's business; rather had it been achieved in moments 'snatcht from the howers of night and repose, for the day was not mine, but dedicated to the service of your Great Father, and yourselfe.' Sandys returned home to survive his doomed sovereign by two years, unaware that a later age would hail him as the first exponent of a literature other than utilitarian, and with a certain claim to durability that was not utterly due to geographical accident, to be produced in what was to become the United States.

Probably not many months before Sandys sailed for home, Anne Bradstreet, born Anne Dudley in 1612, arrived in New England with her husband and her father.

> Although the mother of eight children [records Dr. Samuel Marion Tucker in the *Cambridge History of American Literature*], she found time to write over seven thousand lines of verse in what must have been, to her, peculiarly uncongenial surroundings.... But Anne Bradstreet was not a poet; she was a winsome personality in an unlovely age. That she should have written verse at all was phenomenal, but that it should have been poor verse was inevitable.

Her lyric candle, feeble as it was, might have been extinguished without posterity's knowing that it had ever been lighted had not a genially officious brother-in-law taken a collection of her manuscripts to England, where they were published by Stephen Bowtell in 1650 as *The Tenth Muse Lately sprung up in America. Or Severall Poems, compiled with great variety of Wit and Learning, full of delight. Wherein especially is contained a compleat discourse and description of The Four Elements, Constitutions, Ages of man, Seasons of the Year. Together with an Exact Epitomie of the Four Monarchies, viz. The Assyrian, Persian, Grecian,*

Roman. Also a Dialogue between Old England and New, concerning the late troubles. With divers other pleasant and serious Poems. By a Gentlewoman in those parts. Twenty-eight years later, and six years after Anne Bradstreet's death at the age of sixty, there appeared at Boston, with the imprint of John Foster, *Several Poems Compiled with great Variety of Wit and Learning.... By a Gentlewoman in New-England. The second Edition, Corrected by the Author, and enlarged by an Addition of several other Poems found amongst her papers after her Death.*

Cotton Mather, who himself strummed an occasional lyre, eulogized Anne Bradstreet fulsomely; her poems, he declared, 'divers times printed, have afforded a grateful entertainment unto the ingenious, and a monument to her memory beyond the stateliest marbles.' 'Divers times' was a somewhat lavish overstatement. A third edition of Anne Bradstreet's works was not issued until 1758, thirty years after Mather's death. More than a century elapsed before her prose and verse were edited definitively by John Harvard Ellis (Charlestown, 1867), itself a scarce book which is now available in a photographic reprint (New York, 1931).

Anne Bradstreet may legitimately be denominated an American because she crossed the Atlantic to stay — at any rate she never again saw England. Sundry earlier arrivals who wrote verse and had it published on their return were tourists rather than sojourners, but their usually awkward couplets are important if they had anything to do with America. There was the clerical William Morrell, who attained the Massachusetts shore in 1623, left it, probably, in 1624, and issued in London, in 1625, his *New-England. Or a Briefe Enarration of the Ayre, Earth, Water, Fish and*

Fowles of that Country. With a Description of the Natures, Orders, Habits, and Religion of the Natives; in Latine and English Verse. Morrell observed, or at least listened, to good advantage during his short stay, witness this passage from his factual account of Indian life:

They may not marry nor Tobacco use,
Tell certaine yeares, least they themselves abuse.
At which yeares to each one is granted leave,
A wife, or two, or more, for to receive;
By having many wives, two things they have,
First, children, which before all things to save
They covet, 'cause by them their Kingdomes fild,
When as by fate or Armes their lives are spild.
Whose death as all that dye they sore lament
And fill the skies with cryes: impatient
Of nothing more than pale and fearefull death,
Which old and young bereaves of vitall breath;
Their dead wrapt up in Mats to th' grave they give,
Upright from th' knees, with goods whilst they did live,
Which they best lov'd: their eyes turn'd to the East,
To which after much time, to be releast
They all must March, where all shall all things have
That heart can wish, or they themselves can crave.
A second profit which by many wives
They have, is Corne, the staffe of all their lives.

More widely known than Morrell's descriptive treatise, Nathaniel Ward's *The Simple Cobler of Aggawam* (not the Agawam of today on the west bank of the Connecticut River, but Ipswich) was the work of a divine far more conversant with New England affairs. Ward remained in America for twelve years (1634–46), publishing his contemporaneously popular rhymed contribution to the political and theological philosophy of the day in London in 1647. Its first appearance in America, where it was almost certainly written, was at Boston in 1713.

An American poem by a native American which, in the words of J. F. Hunnewell, who edited a one-hundred copy reprint for the Club of Odd Volumes in 1894, 'may be called our first Epic,' was Benjamin Tompson's *New Englands Crisis. Or a Brief Narrative, of New-Englands Lamentable Estate at present, Compar'd with the former years of Prosperity....* (Boston: John Foster, 1676), the London edition of which, issued the same year, has this much more circumstantial title: *New Englands Tears for her Present Memories: or, A Late and True Relation of the Calamities of New-England since April last past. With an Account of the Battel between the English and Indians upon Seaconk Plain: and of the Indians Burning and Destroying of Marlbury, Rehoboth, Chelmsford, Sudbury, and Providence. With the Death of Antonnies the Grand Indian Sachem; and a Relation of a Fortification begun by Women upon Boston Neck.... Written by an Inhabitant of Boston in New England to his Friend in London.* This seven-hundred-line account of King Philip's War is unfortunately too full of classical allusions and misplaced humor to be as important a contribution to American literature and history as it well could have been. Tompson's works are available in a scholarly edition compiled by Howard Judson Holt (Boston, 1924).

But easily most popular and (Anne Bradstreet aside) most productive among the verse-makers of his day was the Reverend Michael Wigglesworth. This 'little feeble shadow of a man,' in Cotton Mather's phrase, a native of England, and a graduate of Harvard in 1651, preached *viva voce* when he could and with his pen when, as frequently happened, ill health drove him from his pulpit. During one of his longer respites he took up the study of medicine and became an efficient practitioner. His *The Day of Doom* may have passed through four editions (two in America and two in England) before 1700, and certainly was printed frequently during the following century. Oscar Wegelin's *Early American Poetry* (second edition, revised and enlarged, New York, 1930) calls the London edition of 1666, a copy of which is in the British Museum, 'without doubt the third edition of this famous poem.' No copy of an earlier edition is known to exist. Wegelin concludes that, 'as nearly as can be ascertained,' these are the editions which were published before 1800: First, Cambridge, 1662 or 1663; second, Cambridge, probably 1666; third, London, also 1666; fourth, London, 1673; fifth, Boston, 1701; sixth, Newcastle-upon-Tyne, 1711; seventh, Boston, 1715; eighth, Boston, 1751; ninth, Norwich, Connecticut, 1774 (abridged); tenth, Norwich, 1777 (abridged). It is worthy of special note that, according to Wegelin, the Boston edition of 1701 (the fifth in sequence, the third American, and the first Boston) is the earliest American edition of which a complete copy survives today.

Of Wigglesworth's *Meat out of the Eater or Meditations Concerning the Necessity, End, and Usefulness of Afflictions unto God's Children, All tending to Prepare them For, and Comfort them Under the Cross*, no copy of any edition earlier than the declared fourth (Boston, 1689) is now known to be in existence. The first edition was presumably printed at Cambridge in 1670. Of the fifth edition, published at Boston in 1717, there are known 'at least five issues... each bearing the name of a different bookseller.' A sixth edition was issued at New London in 1770.

This detailed summary merits presentation here not so much for the value of the borrowed bibliographical minutiæ as because these minutiæ offer an admirable indication of the difficulties that confront the seeker after the earliest volumes of American-composed, American-inspired, or American-printed verse. The field is not one to attract the new or the advanced collector — rather, it is a field definitely to attract both, but one in which their forerunners appear already to have reaped the sparse harvest. Most of the existing copies of the earliest native verse, in any editions except for recent reprints (and recent is here intended to embrace the last century), have been absorbed into public collections. It is within the bounds of possibility that other copies will yet turn up — copies, perhaps, of earlier editions than have been recorded. But the repositories in which they are most likely, even most unlikely, to lie have already been diligently ransacked. And if they should turn up, the miracle might just as easily occur in Bruges or Pernambuco or Helsingfors as in Salem or Quincy or Leominster.

Their scarcity is due to two factors. They were thin productions physically as well as æsthetically, lacking that bulk which would have better tended to preserve them if their authors had extended them into thousands of lines instead of reining in their Pegasuses at hundreds or dozens. And they were read avidly by a print-hungry population eager for a story or its nearest poor equivalent.

They are rare, whoever wrote them and wherever they were published: *A Looking Glass for the Times* (Boston, 1677), by Peter Folger, maternal grandfather of Benjamin Franklin and ten generations removed in direct line from Henry Clay Folger, who was one day to form the most superb collection of Shakespeareana ever assembled and bequeath it to the nation on his death in 1930; Jacob Steendam's *Klacht van Nieuw-Amsterdam, in Nieuw-Nederlandt, tot haar Moeder* (Complaint of New-Amsterdam, in New-Netherland, to her Mother), printed as a broadside in Old Amsterdam in 1659, the first poem to be written in New York (or at least the first poem written in New York to have itself published); Edward Winslow's *Good Newes from New England* (London, 1624); Roger Wolcott's *Poetical Meditations, Being the Improvement of Some Vacant Hours* (New London, 1725), of transcendent importance, despite its uninformative title, not only for its being the first book of verse to be printed in Connecticut, but because of the historical value of its contents; the slender elegies of Mather Byles and his *Conflagration, applied to that grand Period or Catastrophe of our World, when the Face of Nature is to be changed by a Deluge of Fire, as formerly it was by that of Water* (Boston, 1744); the topical satires of Byles's particular *bête-noire*, Joseph Green, notably his *Entertainment for a Winter's Evening: Being a full and true Account of a very Strange and Wonderful Sight Seen in Boston on the Twenty-seventh of December, 1749, at Noon-Day* (Boston, 1750), describing the antics of a gaily bibulous clergyman (not the Reverend Mr. Byles); the poems of the slave girl Phillis Wheatley; and, later, the more ambitious and more readily discoverable performances of the 'Hartford Wits,' most notable among them Jonathan Trumbull and Joel Barlow, the former's *McFingal* (Philadelphia, 1775) being the most gleefully read as it was the most significant example of the satiric poetry inspired by the imminent Revolution, the latter's *Vision of*

Columbus (Hartford, 1787), later lengthened into *The Columbiad* (Philadelphia, 1807), remaining to this day the most ambitious attempt at an American epic, and achieving, at any rate, the epic length of more than seven thousand lines.

No consideration of early American verse can omit mention of a particularly fugitive type of composition issued in a format by no means peculiar to America. The occasional poet has always had his day — a day that has often lengthened into an eternity of fame. He had it in post-aboriginal New England and elsewhere in the colonies — indeed, many if not most of the labored ventures in rhyme that have already been considered in this chapter were the work of members of the occasional school, and many of those which were not would have been of more enduring interest if they had been occasional as well.

Sometimes the poet makes the occasion, but far oftener the occasion makes the poet. The numerous broadsides of the period were virtually without exception the work of occasion-made poets (and anonymous ones into the bargain) — poets inspired in many instances by a printer or bookseller who saw a legitimate opportunity to seize the day to his own golden advantage. Broadside is the mildly technical bibliographical term for what we of today would denominate a handbill. Once the made-to-order text had been composed (and it invariably bore the marks of haste, though most of the authors could not have improved on their work no matter how long they might have taken about it), the task of setting the type, and embellishing it with stock borders or ornaments or with crude wood-blocks that had been turned out as quickly as the copy itself, required little additional time. The product would be ready to hawk about the streets, if not quite so speedily as an election-day extra of this century, at least while the subject was still the absorbing topic of local discussion and thought. A week later it might have been difficult for anyone except the printer (and perhaps even for him) to lay hands on a copy, and the search has become no easier with the passage of one hundred and fifty years and more.

Ola Elizabeth Winslow, in *American Broadside Verse from Imprints of the 17th and 18th Centuries* (New Haven, 1930), a highly diverting anthology of facsimiles, divides the poetic ephemera of the period comprised into seven groups: funeral verses and memorials, usually more pious than informative, but occasionally both; meditations upon portentous events, as earthquakes, fires, hurricanes, and the memorable 'Dark Day' of 1780; dying confessions and warnings, always immensely popular; war-time ballads and marching songs, whereof the Revolution produced an abundance; comment on local incidents; admonitions and timely preachments; New Year's greetings or 'carriers' addresses.' The last-named group has survived to our own day, and units in it have occasionally become pearls of special price when the authors have subsequently won renown. The youthful Hawthorne wrote two (in prose) for the Salem *Gazette*, his home-town paper: *Time's Portraiture* (1838) and *The Sister Years* (1839), the earlier a broadside, the later an eight-page pamphlet. Of the first of these, three copies are known to exist, of the second, six. The wonder is not that so few but that so many survive; one can conjecture, from this census, the scarcity of many of the predecessors of the Hawthorne addresses. Scores, of course, have vanished beyond recall; others are immortalized in unique copies.

The greatest of Revolutionary poets — 'the most significant poetic figure in America before Bryant,' as Fred Lewis Pattee has characterized him — was himself moderately prolific of carriers' addresses. Victor Hugo Paltsits's bibliography of Philip Freneau (New York, 1903) lists nine from his versatile and swiftly moving pen, and of this total, four can only be presumed to have existed, for no copies are known.

Philip Freneau was a native of New York City (1752), the son of a prosperous wine-merchant of Huguenot extraction. Educated at the College of New Jersey (not yet Princeton), he was a classmate of Hugh Henry Brackenridge, destined like himself to a career of letters, and James Madison, who might reasonably be set in the same category through his share in the drafting of the Constitution and his co-authorship of the *Federalist*. Freneau began to write verse when he was sixteen, and composed, in collaboration with Brackenridge, *A Poem, on the Rising Glory of America* for the Commencement exercises of his class — this was when Commencement really meant Commencement — on September 25, 1771. It was published at Philadelphia the following year. *The American Village, a Poem. To which are added, Several other original Pieces in Verse. By Philip Freneau, A.B.* (New York, 1772) may have preceded it. Paltsits located but one copy of the latter, and that (now in the Library of Congress) turned up just as he was completing his bibliography.

The dawn of the Revolution brought Freneau's talents into full play, and he waged doughty satiric war against the opposition, including in his onslaughts, ultimately, the timorous Gaine and the arch-propagandist Rivington. Some time after the opening of hostilities he found ample personal cause for disliking the enemy. He had gone to the West Indies, remaining three years as secretary to a Santa Cruz planter, and on his return, sea-salt having got into his blood, he shipped as a supercargo. His brig was pursued by British warships, but managed to elude them. On her second trip she was not so fortunate. Freneau was held prisoner aboard a British man-o'-war in New York Harbor, whence, after a period of genuine suffering, he was finally exchanged. The story of his experiences is graphically set forth in *The British Prison-Ship: A Poem, in Four Cantoes* (Philadelphia, 1781). The printer was Francis Bailey, who five years later issued *The Poems of Philip Freneau. Written Chiefly During the Late War*, the bulkiest as it was the best collection of one poet's verse yet produced in America.

Nine years later, in the year of 'American Independence XIX' (1795), Freneau issued from a press which he had established at his home, Mount Pleasant, at Monmouth, *Poems Written between the years 1768 & 1794, by Philip Freneau, of New Jersey: A New Edition, Revised and Corrected by the Author; Including a considerable number of Pieces never before Published*. It was a compact volume of 456 pages, indifferently printed. The pagination was erratic; in one observed copy, page 61 lacks the folio, page 159 is folioed at the left, page 267 has become 243, 286 is 287, 287 is 286, 330 is 320, 420 is 420, but with the 4 upside down, and 427 is 407. There is an erratum notice on page xv, at the end of the table of contents, and a list of nineteen additional errata (of which one contains itself an error) on page 455. The Monmouth edition of Freneau's poems is his most important book; it was certainly edited by him, whereas the 1786 edition, according to Paltsits, was not; moreover, it is not excessively rare.

Pamphleteer, journalist, fierce champion of democracy (Jefferson credited him with having 'saved our Constitution, which was galloping fast into monarchy' beneath the spurs, of course, of Alexander Hamilton), mariner, printer, gentleman farmer as well as true poet, Freneau lived a full life (and a long one, surviving until 1832) in a momentous era — an era for which he was definitely born if man ever was. But he would have been a poet none the less — perhaps even a better poet — if there had never been a War for Independence.

Only a single poem by Freneau was included in *American Poems, Selected and Original*, published at Litchfield, Connecticut, in 1793. The compiler, Elihu Hubbard Smith, was a Connecticut man and, perhaps without altogether intending it, exhibited a strong bias in favor of local celebrities. The collection is designated 'Vol. I' on the title-page, but a second volume never appeared — a fact for which the editor's early and heroic death during the New York yellow-fever epidemic of 1798 may have been partly responsible. *American Poems*, however, will always be an important and sought-for book, for it is the first anthology of strictly native verse.

Of much deeper significance and importance, the factor of priority aside, was Samuel Kettell's three-volume *Specimens of American Poetry, With Critical and Biographical Notices*, published at Boston in 1829. Kettell was a self-taught scholar and an early associate of S. G. Goodrich, 'Peter Parley,' whose *Recollections of a Lifetime* (New York and Auburn, 1857) is a

valuable source book by the most prolific publisher
of his generation. Kettell was not only the first important American anthologist — he was the first
bibliographer of American verse. Following the text
of the third volume of the *Specimens* is a 28-page
'Catalogue of American Poetry' comprising 'a list of
all the poetical works of American origin which have
come under notice in the course of this undertaking...
arranged in the chronological order of their publication.' Beginning, properly, with the Bay Psalm
Book, Kettell listed 7 titles to 1701, 22 from 1701 to
1751, 157 from 1751 to 1801, and 300-odd from 1801
to 1829. If one include broadsides, Kettell's census
is probably a thousand titles short of the total that
later research has brought to light, but his pioneer
effort in the field can be lauded without patronage,
for he undoubtedly worked with great diligence and
intelligence, but was seriously handicapped by a general lack of antiquarian interest.

A long road stretches from 1829 to 1930, from Kettell's 'Catalogue' to the revised edition of Oscar
Wegelin's *Early American Poetry*, embracing nearly
1400 titles through 1820. In the 27-year interval that
separated the first from the second edition 'hundreds
of new titles,' Mr. Wegelin declared, were discovered,
and more will as certainly come to light. Serviceable
check-lists of American poetry are appended to
William Bradley Otis's *American Verse, 1625–1807*
(New York, 1909) and (more extensive) to the first
volume of the *Cambridge History of American Literature*.

If Samuel Kettell had undertaken a 'catalogue' of
American fiction, the result would have required less
space in the listing, but would have been at least as
difficult to assemble as was his chronological sum-

mary of American poetry. Verse is visibly identifi-
able (the tightly corseted verse of colonial days, at all
events). Fiction is not. John Dunlap published at
Philadelphia in 1774 Francis Hopkinson's *A Pretty
Story written in the Year of Our Lord 2774. By Peter
Grievous, Esq.*, of which the invaluable *Cyclopædia of
American Literature* (New York, 1855), compiled by
Evert A. and George L. Duyckinck, offered this
synopsis:

> It represents England as a nobleman, possessed of a
> valuable farm, and with a great number of children and
> grandchildren, for the government of whom he had
> entered into various compacts. Parliament is represented
> as his wife, chosen for him every seven years by the
> family. The fortunes of the American settlers are
> depicted, and the encroachments of parliament none the
> less forcibly represented in the humorous description.

Can this allegory reasonably be denominated the
first American novel? If so, then *The Power of Sympathy: or, the Triumph of Nature. Founded in Truth*
(Boston: Isaiah Thomas and Company, 1789) must
yield pioneer honors. But *A Pretty Story* was a pretty
short story as well as a tract, whereas the two volumes
of *The Power of Sympathy* contained nearly three
hundred pages of text — honest dimensions for a
novel. But may not the qualification 'Founded in
Truth' disqualify it from consideration and set it in
the category either of biography or of history? Apparently it may. *The Power of Sympathy* had long
been attributed to Sarah Wentworth Morton, but
one of those romantic bits of detective work that forever maintain the fascination of bibliography tended
to prove, no longer ago than 1932, that Mrs. Morton,
far from writing so much as a line of *The Power of
Sympathy*, did everything in her own power of

The STORY of *OPHELIA*.

"*O Fatal! Fatal Poison!*"

FRONTISPIECE OF 'THE POWER OF SYMPATHY' (1789)
This was the only illustration (the engraving was by
Samuel Hill) in the first edition of the first American novel

antipathy to suppress the work. The evidence is submitted in *Philenia: The Life and Works of Sarah Wentworth Morton* (Orono, Maine: University Press, 1932), by Emily Pendleton and Milton Ellis. Miss Pendleton set about assembling data for a monograph on Mrs. Morton mainly because the latter was credited with being the first American novelist, but investigation quickly indicated that the claim was based on the most meager and casual testimony. *The Power of Sympathy* was rooted in a scandal involving Mrs. Morton's husband (his first name was Perez) and her twenty-year-old sister, Frances Apthorp, who poisoned herself in 1788 as a climax to the lurid episode. The Pendleton-Ellis study attributes authorship of the narrative to a neighbor, William Hill Brown (1765–93). Either because it was eagerly read, or because Mrs. Morton's attempts at suppression were partly successful (or by reason of a combination of these factors), *The Power of Sympathy* in its original edition is today an exceedingly rare book.

Whoever wrote it, *The Power of Sympathy* was indubitably 'Founded in Truth.' The next novel to see the light in New England, *The Coquette, or the History of Eliza Wharton* (Boston, 1797), was likewise proclaimed on the title-page to have been 'Founded on Fact.' It was somewhat less anonymous, authorship being assigned to 'A Lady of Massachusetts.' Hannah Webster Foster (1759–1840) chose for her plot the tragic history of Elizabeth Whitman, who had died unwed in childbirth some ten years earlier, the incident involving, perhaps unjustly, the name of a subsequently prominent jurist.

Seduction, too, had been the theme of Susannah Rowson's *Charlotte* (Philadelphia, 1794), which boldly emblazoned its author's name on the title-page.

Charlotte was designated 'A Tale of Truth,' and sur-
mise, or better, persists that it was based on the authentic incident of a British colonel who prevailed on
a young woman of aristocratic connections to journey
with him to America, where he promptly abandoned
her. Mrs. Rowson was herself a native of England,
emigrating to America with her father, a naval officer,
in childhood, returning home several years later, and
settling in the New World permanently in 1793.
She wrote eight novels and a volume of verse, and
she wrote plays and acted them professionally. On
her retirement she opened a school for girls — one
wonders whether *Charlotte* was required reading.
Her pupils were doubtless acquainted with the book,
for *Charlotte* was enormously popular. Mrs. Rowson
left the manuscript of a sequel which was published
four years after her death — *Charlotte's Daughter: or,
The Three Orphans* (Boston, 1828).

The sacred ark of fiction, however, had not been
tended exclusively by feminine hands during the first
Presidency. Hugh Henry Brackenridge, Freneau's
classmate and collaborator, was a native of Scotland
who reached America at the impressionable age of
five and grew up in York County, Pennsylvania, in
circumstances that anticipated the career of the
youthful Lincoln. Following his graduation from
Princeton in 1771, Brackenridge continued the study
of divinity as well as of letters, combining his accomplishments during the Revolution by serving as chaplain and by inditing patriotic compositions. In 1781
he went to Pittsburgh, then the gateway to a Middle
West that was virtually a Far West — a frontier town
the beginning of whose history as a permanent settlement predated his arrival only by some fifteen years.

Brackenridge entered the field of fiction with the

first two volumes of a picaresque satire, *Modern Chivalry: Containing the Adventures of Captain John Farrago, and Teague O. Regan, his servant... Philadelphia: Printed and sold by John M'Culloch. No. 1, North Third-street. M.DCC.XCII.* On the title-page of the second volume the date appeared as 'M.DCC.-XII,' which, if it had been accurate, would have given Brackenridge the clearest possible title to the honor of being the first American novelist. Volume III was issued at Pittsburgh in 1793, though the pioneer trans-Allegheny printer, John Scull, made the date 'M.DCC.XIII.' Wegelin, in his *Early American Fiction, 1774–1830* (third edition, corrected and enlarged, New York, 1931), believes that the error was due to the Pittsburgh printer's using Volume II as a model, mechanically copying the wrong date, and adding one instead of eighty-one. Volume IV appeared in Philadelphia in 1797, and there was more to come. Volume I of Part II was issued at Carlisle, Pennsylvania, in 1804, and Volume II in 1805. What with changes of imprint, errors in dates, abundant textual errors, fantastic foliations, *Modern Chivalry* is as physically intricate a production as one could well want. He who would explore the labyrinth further may do so in Wegelin, in the bibliography appended to the first volume of the *Cambridge History of American Literature*, and in Charles F. Heartman's bibliography of Brackenridge. Brackenridge himself, who had gone over from divinity to law, became a justice of the Supreme Court of Pennsylvania, and lived until 1816. *Modern Chivalry* in first edition is an excessively rare book.

No one of these early exponents of the craft of fiction in America was a professional writer; some of them, had they been so characterized, would have replied with robust and sincere indignation. Others may have had the will but appreciated the lack of a way. The period under consideration did, however, produce one writer who made letters his trade by deliberate choice. Charles Brockden Brown was born in Philadelphia in 1771, and began his literary career by contributing to the *Columbian Magazine* in 1789. He had been apprenticed to a lawyer, but in 1793 he severed this string to his bow, providing thereby an interesting contrast to Brackenridge. He forswore law for literature, declares Carl Van Doren in the *Dictionary of American Biography*, 'against the advice of his parents and his elder brothers who presumably saw themselves obliged to support him in his adventure.'

The family doubtless breathed easier when Brown forsook Philadelphia for New York, although his return journeys to his birthplace were frequent. In 1794, Brown came under the spell of the eccentric William Godwin's *Caleb Williams*, and the Godwin influence was thereafter operative on almost everything he wrote. In 1798 appeared *Alcuin: A Dialogue*, one of the earliest American treatises on women's rights, part of which had appeared in the *Weekly Magazine* of Philadelphia. During the same year, and in one month, he wrote *Wieland*, a fantastic forecast of Poe and Hawthorne, and this was followed by *Ormond* (New York, 1799), *Arthur Mervyn* (Part I, Philadelphia, 1799; Part II, New York, 1800), *Edgar Huntly* (Philadelphia, 1799), *Jane Talbot* (Philadelphia, 1801), and *Clara Howard* (Philadelphia, 1801). Appended to a *Life* of Brown by Paul Allen and William Dunlap published at Philadelphia in 1815, five years after Brown's death, was a fragment, *Memoirs of Carwin, the Biloquist*. Brown's later years were given up to editorial and hack work. He married, and fathered four children — a fact which explains in part the assiduity with which he drove his pen.

Did Brown make writing pay? The answer is supplied in the fact that he existed for seventeen years after abandoning the law and that during six of those years he raised and supported a family. True, he found the struggle for existence bitter — he laid up no such store as would the successful fictioneer of a later day, bulwarked by first and second American serial rights, motion-picture rights, dramatic rights, radio rights, syndicate rights, foreign rights, and initial book printings of fifty thousand copies. But Brown had at least a slight foretaste of the economic potentialities of letters. Much of his copy appeared originally in serial form, and he was the first American writer to envisage the possibilities of this legitimate dual exploitation.

None of his novels went into a second edition during his lifetime, but English editions were issued (most of them after his death), and a collected edition in six volumes was published at Boston in 1827. It is significant of the scarcity of Brown's novels that the Allen-Dunlap *Life* of 1815 (only Dunlap's name appeared on the title-page) was announced as including 'Selections from the Rarest of His Printed Works.' The rarity of these printed works has not lessened since the year of Waterloo.

This condition inevitably applies to the whole field of early American fiction. While the first native novels, with a few exceptions, did not go into many editions, and in most instances stopped at the first, they contrived to get themselves read, and read to such purpose that their hopes of abundant survival were speedily compromised. This factor, of course, adds vastly to their desirability from the collector's point of view, whether the collector be an individual or an institution. The scarcity continues well beyond the date of the birth of an authentic native fiction with the appearance of James Fenimore Cooper, who must be left for later consideration.

A statistical summary of Wegelin's *Early American Fiction* (omitting a handful of foreign imprints and reprints of foreign originals and accepting certain conjectural dates as definitive) shows that between 1774 and the end of 1795 some 17 'novels' were published in America; from 1796 to 1801, 25; from 1801 to 1806, 17; from 1809 to 1811, 15; from 1811 to 1816, 12; from 1816 to 1821, 16; from 1821 to 1826, 49, and from 1826 to the beginning of 1831, 59. The fiction output of the decade from 1821 to 1831, therefore, exceeded that of the whole preceding half-century (or, for that matter, the preceding century and a half), and the ratio holds even if one include in the earlier period the few scattered reprints of British novels that were issued from colonial and early national presses.

Just as Charles Brockden Brown was the first professional novelist, so does the name of his biographer, William Dunlap, stand out as that of the first professional playwright worthy the designation. The history of the American drama has no part in this series of notes save in so far as published plays are concerned. That history offers a bewildering abundance of plays that were written but never printed and never acted, of plays (mainly amateur) which were acted but never published, and of dialogues which were at least semi-dramatic compositions but were not intended to be acted. Wegelin's *Early American Plays*,

1714–1830 (second edition, revised, New York, 1905)
lists, at the end of his tabulation of printed plays, one
hundred and fifty additional pieces in manuscript,
the work of an imposing variety of dramatists, including Dunlap himself, and explains that 'many
more titles could be added.'

More than half a century before Dunlap's birth,
Governor Robert Hunter's *Androborus*, a satire on a
pre-Tammany administration by a colonial executive
with a sense of humor, was issued at New York from
the press of William Bradford (1714) — the first
dramatic composition to be written, as well as the
first to be printed, in America. One copy survives,
now in the Huntington Library.

Royall Tyler's *The Contrast*, published at Philadelphia in 1790 (and reprinted by the Dunlap Society
at New York in 1887), has hardly approached the
vanishing point of *Androborus*, although it is excessively rare. *The Contrast*, 'written by a Citizen of
the United States,' and declared also on its title-page
to have been 'performed with applause at the
theatres in New York, Philadelphia, and Maryland,'
ranks as the first native play acted professionally on
an American stage. Tyler, born in 1757, became a
justice of the Supreme Court of Vermont in 1794 and
chief justice in 1800, holding this office until his death
in 1826. His later career thus offers an interesting
parallel to that of Hugh Henry Brackenridge, who
himself dabbled in the dramatic arts.

Dunlap's own career presents an admirable example
of cultural versatility. He was educated as a painter,
despite the loss of an eye in his boyhood, and it was
by way of the door of the fine arts that he entered the
three-walled room of the drama. In 1784, when he
was eighteen, he was sent to London to become a

pupil of Benjamin West, and soon forgot all (or much) about painting in a rationally acquired zest for the theater. Returning to New York, he found *The Contrast* the talk of the town, and wrote a play. It was not produced (what a collection one could form of plays like that!) so he tried again. *The Father; or, American Shandy-ism*, both produced and published at New York in 1789, was enough of a success to cause him to adopt dramatic writing as a profession, and some sixty-four plays were the result. Through his own fault or the theater's (or the audiences'), he did not find a road to wealth in this productivity, and died in moderate poverty in 1839. In his later years he had found time to write a *History of the American Theatre* (New York, 1832), a *History of the Rise and Progress of the Arts of Design in the United States* (New York, 1834), and a *History of New Netherlands, Province of New York, and State of New York, to the Adoption of the Federal Constitution* (New York, 1839). He left, too, the manuscript of a diary of the first importance which was published nearly a century after his death by the New York Historical Society (New York, 1931).

Any summary of the published drama in America must include mention of a compilation of plays which were not the work of a playwright who was born in America, or who died in America, or who ever set foot on any soil beyond that of

> This precious stone set in the silver sea,
> Which serves it in the office of a wall
> Or as a moat defensive to a house,
> Against the envy of less happier lands,
> This blessed plot, this earth, this realm, this England —

a playwright who found all the world a stage, and the drama a mirror to hold up to universal nature, but who, so far as the evidence shows, never ventured a hundred miles out of London. His magic has wrought so potent a spell on the hearts and minds of men everywhere that America may take proper pride in the knowledge that the first edition of his writings in whatever form to be published outside his native island was issued on her shores: *The Plays and Poems of William Shakespeare. Corrected from the Latest and Best London Editions, With Notes by Samuel Johnson, L.L.D. To Which Are Added, A Glossary and the Life of the Author. Embellished With a Striking Likeness From the Collection of His Grace the Duke of Chandos. First American Edition. Philadelphia: Printed and Sold by Bioren & Madan. MDCCXCV* (for Volumes I–III, *MDCCXCVI* for Volumes IV–VIII). The sponsors of the enterprise were aware of the importance of their undertaking, and concluded their ten-page preface (dated July 1, 1795) with these words: 'In preparing this work for publication, the editors have exerted themselves as much as possible, by an elegant type and good paper, to do credit to the American press.' And a credit to the American press it was, printed in comfortably readable type (though not, thank Heaven, 'elegant') and on a size of page adapted to hand or pocket. The engraved portrait by Robert Field which serves as frontispiece to the first volume is, of course, the first likeness (if hardly a 'striking' one) of Shakespeare to be executed in America. It belongs, therefore, in that unfortunate category of embellishments which melancholy cataloguers are frequently forced to describe as 'wanting,' which simply means that a print-collector saw the book ahead of a book-collector. With portrait or without, this first American edition of Shakespeare is rarely met with. A dozen or so copies are known, of which at least a third are imperfect. But humanity itself, as Shakespeare often noted, likewise has its imperfections.

CHAPTER IX

Over the Hills and Far Away

THERE is now a press at St. Louis, in Upper Louisiana, at the confluence of the Missouri and Missisippi rivers, at which a newspaper is printed.'

So declared Isaiah Thomas in 1810, employing an accepted contemporary spelling of Mississippi, and bringing the notes for his *History of Printing in America* down to a date which, taken from the moment at which he wrote, was barely the day before yesterday. For it was not until the middle of 1808 that the first number of the *Missouri Gazette* was given to the world to signalize the typographical passage of the Father of Waters.

Military experts have said that if a hostile force ever landed on the northern New England coast and began a march on New York City, the fate of the metropolis would be decided at the Wilbraham Mountains, some ten miles east of Springfield, Massachusetts, and next (assuming the defenders lost) along the Redding Ridge, fifteen miles northwest of Bridgeport, Connecticut. Similarly, the Alleghenies acted as a doughtier barrier to the westward sweep of printing than any of the rivers that lay beyond. The rivers, indeed, occasionally proved a convenience.

The rapidity of the westward spread of printing once the Alleghenies had been hurdled is readily demonstrable by the application of a combined chronological-geographical yardstick: It required one hundred and forty-six years for printing to cover the four-hundred-and-eighty-mile crow-flight between Cambridge and Pittsburgh; it required only twenty-two years for printing to span the five hundred and sixty miles that separate Pittsburgh from St. Louis.

The Pittsburgh of 1786 was a settlement of fewer than forty log houses and not over three hundred souls —vital statistics which indicate a degree of overcrowding that the frontiersman's axe was doing its best to alleviate. Thither in the tenth year of American independence John Scull transported a press and equipment, making use, doubtless, of the turnpike from Philadelphia that had been opened only a few months before, for Scull, according to Reuben Gold Thwaites in *The Ohio Valley Press Before the War of 1812–15* (Worcester, 1909), came 'apparently from Eastern Pennsylvania.' He established himself in the trading post at the forks of the Ohio and issued there, on July 29, 1786, the first number of the *Pittsburgh Gazette*. Printing had arrived 'west of the Mountains.'

The following year John Bradford and his brother Fielding, native Virginians, followed in Scull's wake, and then floated their paraphernalia down the Ohio from Pittsburgh and transported it overland by packhorse to Lexington, in the heart of the bluegrass country, where they offered to a scanty clientèle on August 11, 1787, the first issue of the *Kentucke* (later *Kentucky*) *Gazette*. Fielding's son, Thomas G., was one day to become proprietor of the *Madison Gazette* at Huntsville, Alabama, but pioneer honors in the latter state were to go to Samuel Miller and John B. Hood, who initiated the *Mobile Centinel* on May 23, 1811. No press was established at Louisville until the new century was born, when, on January 12, 1801, Matthew Lyon, Judah P. Spooner, and Samuel Vail, Vermonters all (Spooner, it will be recalled, had introduced the art to his home state twenty-one years earlier), began publication of the *Farmer's Library, or Ohio Intelligencer*. It was another hardy spirit out of the East, William Maxwell, of New Jersey, later of Kentucky, who brought printing to authentic Ohio by issuing at Cincinnati, on November 9, 1793, the first number of the *Centinel of the North-Western Territory*. The same year saw the establishment at Knoxville, Tennessee, of another *Gazette*. Printing found a local habitation in Indiana at the end of July, 1804, with the appearance at Vincennes of the *Indiana Gazette*, produced by Elihu Stout, freshly transplanted from Kentucky. Vincennes was then the capital of the recently created (1800) Territory of Indiana (Indianapolis was still undreamed of), just as Kaskaskia, the eventual birthplace of printing in the adjacent western commonwealth, and two full days' journey distant, was soon (1809) to become the capital of the Territory of Illinois.

Meanwhile, in 1790, Nathaniel Willis, grandfather of that Nathaniel Parker Willis who was to be one of the literary Pooh-Bahs of his day, had disposed of his Boston *Independent Chronicle* and migrated to Winchester, Virginia, considerably more than twenty miles away. Finding competition in that neighborhood somewhat keen, he soon journeyed on to Shepherdstown, where, in November, he issued the first number of the *Potowmac Guardian and Berkeley Advertiser*. Willis could hardly know it, but he had introduced printing to soil which, seventy-three years later, would be part of the State of West Virginia. Sometime before April 3, 1792, the *Guardian* moved to Martinsburg. The only examples of early numbers which survive are in the Harvard College Library, according to Boyd B. Stutler's summary of the state's news-paper history in *The West Virginia Encyclopedia* (Phil Conley, Editor in Chief: Charleston, West Virginia, 1929).

Printing had been introduced into Florida, still Spanish territory, at St. Augustine in 1783 with the appearance of the *East-Florida Gazette*. The earliest known surviving number is the fifth, for the week ending March 1, and Douglas C. McMurtrie (*The First Printing in Florida*, Atlanta, 1931) reasonably assumes from this fact that the *Gazette* was first issued on February 1. Its sponsors were John and Charles William Wells.

Nearly twenty years earlier, however, a press had been established in New Orleans in territory that had not yet become Spanish. In 1764, the French governor had requested permission from Paris for Denis Braud to set up a printing office. 'One learns from the petition,' says Lawrence C. Wroth in his compact account of printing in English-speaking North America in *Printing: A Short History of the Art*, edited by R. A. Peddie (London, 1927), 'that Braud was awaiting the arrival of type and other articles of equipment he had ordered from France, though in the meantime he had already set up a press and had been usefully employed in printing paper money from an engraved plate.' New Orleans had to wait until March, 1794, for a newspaper of its own; in March of that year the *Moniteur de la Louisiane* ap-peared. Fourteen years later a press was established farther up the Mississippi at Natchez, and Isaiah Thomas learned of it just in time to include mention of it in his *History*.

The one wide river had thus twice been reached, but it still remained to be crossed. The passage was triumphantly effected by Joseph Charless, who in 1796 had emigrated from Ireland to Philadelphia and had begun to learn printing at the hands of an erstwhile compatriot and highly competent tutor, Mathew Carey.

Carey, to whom reference has been made previously in these notes, was a striking and significant figure in the post-colonial period of American printing and publishing history. He had reached America in 1784, a fugitive from Ireland, where he had been born twenty-four years earlier. On an earlier flight from the scene of his nativity, this time to France, he had met Benjamin Franklin and, already a skilled printer, had worked for a time on Franklin's toy press at Passy. A devout Catholic from boyhood to the end of his days (he died at Philadelphia in 1839), and lame from infancy, he had written at seventeen a tractate against dueling — and in 1786, as proprietor of the *Pennsylvania Herald*, was himself painfully wounded in a duel with a rival Philadelphia editor, Eleazer Oswald, of the *Independent Gazetteer*. His *Columbian Magazine*, already referred to, yielded to the *American Museum*, the first noteworthy indigenous scrapbook (but containing considerable original material), which was not a financial success, although it became of genuine historical importance — a fact which would have pleased Carey. With borrowed capital he then embarked in the general publishing business, and while there were times when it seemed that this enterprise might explode with an even more resonant bang than his earlier ventures had done, it finally emerged into a triumphant success. Carey was a voluminous writer, a keen and incisive student of affairs and of economic and social trends, a brave and tireless worker in any cause that attracted him.

He was a fighting Irishman of the type who enjoys war above everything in the world except peace. His zeal for the closing of wounds ancient or fresh was exemplified in an attempt at a reconciliation with Oswald which alienated even some among his own adherents. His story is available in a monograph prepared by E. L. Bradsher: *Mathew Carey, Editor, Author, and Publisher* (New York: Columbia University Press, 1912).

Carey was fully alert to the potentialities of advertising, and eleven of his wares are listed on a leaf preceding the title of *The Beauties of Poetry, British and American*, which he issued in 1791. Among the eleven are Hugh Blair's *Sermons* in two volumes, price two dollars ('the British edition sells in London for nineteen shillings and six pence sterling'); *The American Jest Book — and Merry Fellow's Companion* ('price of each a quarter dollar — price of the two bound together, three fifths of a dollar'); 'the Doway Translation of the vulgate bible... price neatly bound, six dollars — elegantly bound and gilt, £.2 10s 2d'; *Select Poems, Chiefly American; Information to Europeans, disposed to migrate to America*; and *Think Well On't — or, reflexions for every day in the month. By the rev. R. Chaloner*. The down (or lower-case) style of this advertisement leaf is manifest in 'the Doway Translation of the vulgate bible'; it is more strikingly evidenced in the notice of 'the constitutions of the several united states, according to the latest amendments — with the declaration of independence — the federal constitution, and the amendments thereto.' Not the least successful commercially of Carey's activities was his affiliation with the Reverend Mason Locke Weems — author, book-racketeer, and super-salesman. Weems's *Life of George Washing-*

ton, originally published in 1800, was reprinted again and again even after author and publisher alike had gone to their rest. This is the 'biography' which gave to the world the whole-cloth fiction of the cherry-tree episode; it is significant to note that this incident did not appear until the fifth (1810) edition. Weems has had his own far more competent biographer in Lawrence C. Wroth (*Parson Weems*, Baltimore, 1911); all in addition to this that one need know about him and his productions is contained in *Mason Locke Weems, His Works and Ways* (New York, 1929), the three volumes of which comprise a bibliography left incomplete by the untimely death of Paul Leicester Ford plus Mr. Weems's bulky correspondence, the whole edited by Mr. Ford's sister, Emily Ellsworth Ford Skeel.

The present concern of this narrative, however, is not with the wily Weems or the broad-visioned Carey, but with the latter's pioneering pupil, Joseph Charless. Having served his novitiate as a printer with Carey, Charless, in the early 1800's, headed west, tarried a while in Lexington and Louisville, decided that if any more printers congregated in Kentucky it would indeed become a dark and bloody ground, and pushed on to the Mississippi. Traversing his bridgeless Rubicon, he established the *Missouri Gazette*, of which the first number appeared July 12, 1808 — the year preceding the incorporation of St. Louis. The general westward migration had already given the community a preponderant English-speaking population, but the circumambient red man still outnumbered the white infiltration. Thwaites records that John Bradbury, the English naturalist, noted how 'Indian chiefs would stalk into the office of the *Gazette* and gravely seat themselves there, holding a newspaper before their faces for hours at a time, in imitation of the actions of white men. When Bradbury was on the upper Missouri river... he met a chieftain who at once lifted his buffalo robe before his face, and pretended to scan it, as though it were a newspaper. He recognized in Bradbury one of the white men whom he had seen peruse newspapers in the office of the St. Louis *Gazette*, and took this means of indicating his recognition.'

Visions of a gasoline age did not motivate the exodus of James M. Miller from Utica, New York, to Detroit, where, on August 31, 1809, he established the *Michigan Essay; or, The Impartial Observer*. The *Essay* was emphatically tentative; Ralph Leslie Rusk, in *The Literature of the Middle Western Frontier* (New York, 1925), notes that only examples of the first two issues are extant, though he records evidence to indicate that two more numbers were published. Miller's failure may have deterred others from following quickly in his steps; not until 1817 did John P. Sheldon and Ebenezer Reed initiate the *Detroit Gazette*. They fared better than Miller, though they soon abandoned the scheme of printing part of the text in French and part in English.

When Matthew Duncan came out of Kentucky to establish a newspaper at Kaskaskia, he had the originality to call it something other than *Gazette* — it blossomed in 1814 as the *Illinois Herald*. Nearly a score of years were to elapse before printing reached Chicago, from the east rather than from the south, and even then there was very little Chicago for it to reach. At about the time Duncan arrived at Kaskaskia, the United States Government was rebuilding Fort Dearborn following the massacre of its garrison and the destruction of the post by Indians two years before. The Chicago to which printing was introduced a few months after the beginning of Andrew Jackson's second term was a settlement of much less impressive stature than the St. Louis of 1808 or even the Pittsburgh of 1786.

But the right of way of empire would not be denied. On the last day of the summer of 1833, John Calhoun left Watertown, New York (where he had found the going hard for his *Eagle*) *en route* to Chicago, of which village his fellow-townsman Harlow Kimball had brought enthusiastic reports. Calhoun's was an inauspicious argosy, for severe lake storms, which were doubtless attributed to the equinox, vexed the passage of the steamer by which he proceeded from Buffalo to Detroit. Arrived in Chicago, he set up his equipment (which, with admirable foresight, he had shipped ahead of him), and issued, on November 26, 1833, the first number of the *Chicago Democrat*, thus flinging the banner of Jacksonian adherence to the breezes of Lake Michigan.

The initial *Democrat*, however, was not the first fruit of Calhoun's press. Fortunately his account book survives as the property of the Chicago Historical Society, and an entry for November 13 shows that the printer charged (and certainly delivered) to 'C. Ingersol' of the Travellers' Home 'one pack of cards' (business, not pleasure). The best proof that the cards were actually produced lies in the documentary testimony that Ingersol paid for them, unaware of the fact that the successful completion of the transaction made him the first sponsor of typography in the dawning metropolis of mid-America.

Calhoun had the field to himself until the spring of 1835, when the *Chicago American* appeared under the proprietorship of T. O. Davis, 'a printer of whose antecedents we know nothing,' declares McMurtrie in *The First Printers of Chicago* (Chicago: The Cuneo Press, 1927). The *American* changed hands in 1837, and, with the transfer, T. O. Davis made as inconspicuous an exit from as he had made an incursion into the recorded history of printing in the United States.

The scarcity of the earliest Chicago imprints is attested by data which McMurtrie submits in the bibliography of items other than newspapers for the period 1836 to 1850 which he appends to his monograph. In the spring of 1836, Calhoun printed '100 pamphlets for charter' for the Chicago Fire Insurance Company, receiving ten dollars therefor. No copy is known. In 1837 he printed *An Act to Incorporate the City of Chicago,* of which only one copy, now owned by the Chicago Historical Society, appears to have survived. The McMurtrie bibliography lists fewer than seventy-five entries, but it would have been more extensive if the superb library of George W. Paullin had been available for inspection. The Paullin library, unfortunately, was in packing cases at the time McMurtrie was making his compilation, although its owner was able to give McMurtrie, from memory, several important details which the latter wisely declined to employ as definitive data. In the spring of 1929 the Paullin library was dispersed at auction in New York, and McMurtrie was enabled to make several important additions to his earlier findings from the Paullin collection and from other sources. His *Notes in Supplement to 'The First Printers of Chicago,'* issued at Chicago in 1931, lists eighteen additional titles, which still leaves the recorded total through 1850 under one hundred. The Paullin collection included, in addition to many

Chicago imprints of the first half of the nineteenth century, more than one hundred units (exclusive of newspapers and magazines) printed in Chicago before the great fire of October 8–10, 1871.

It is in order at this point, when early seems to be becoming pretty late, to pause a moment to consider the implications of these two adjectives as they are applicable to the progress of printing in America or anywhere else. Early and late are purely relative modifiers. What might be two centuries late for Cambridge would be early indeed for San Francisco. But a first printing is by that fact an early printing, be it dated 1640 or 1840 or 1940. Let us assume that when Captain Robert E. Peary attained the North Pole in 1909, he paused there long enough to un-sledge a pair of type cases and a small hand press and composed and printed a four-page leaflet, or even a broadside, detailing the story of his epochal achievement. One need not even imagine his having employed the press for the perpetuation of such momentous intelligence — let us assume merely that a day or two earlier Peary had learned from an Eskimo about a particularly succulent manner of preparing blubber, and, having his press with him, had put the recipe into type before his observations disclosed the tremendous fact that he had reached full ninety degrees north. Assume further that by some meteorological freak or by the application of some fabulous scientific discovery, the region centering on the Pole should become not only habitable but inhabited — that a great city should come to flourish there, a surpassing summer and winter resort of fireproof crystal palaces whereof the sole competitor would be a whole earth distant (for what was sauce for the Arctic would indubitably be sauce for the Antarctic),

and that out of this physical and cultural acclima-
tization should be evolved a Polar journalism, a
Polar literature, a Polar drama. In the wake of this
productivity would trail a host of collectors of Pole-
ana, and great endowed libraries in the temperate
zone as well as in Polaria itself would vie with wealthy
private accumulators for early septentrional imprints.
And competition would attain its fiercest heights
when a copy of the blubber recipe of 1909 — the
veritable cornerstone of a boreal collection — came
into the auction room.

C. Ingersol's 'pack of cards' is an instance in
point. The history of the origins of printing in
Wisconsin offers another example. The first number
of the *Green Bay Intelligencer* appeared December 11,
1833, fifteen days after the publication of the initial
Chicago Democrat. But the art had been practiced in
Wisconsin before the end of 1830, and by the pioneer
who was one day to establish the *Intelligencer* —
Albert G. Ellis, in partnership with John V. Sydenham (or Suydam). Ellis, relating his reminiscences
before a meeting of the Wisconsin Editorial Association in 1859 (as quoted by Hudson from the *Proceedings* published at Madison the same year), said:

> Among the various pursuits that engaged my atten-
> tion at Green Bay, that of printing, and newspaper pub-
> lishing, was never forgotten; but always thought of as
> my legitimate business, as soon as circumstances would
> allow. In 1826, Dr. Philleo, of Galena, volunteered a
> correspondence with me, proposing a co-partnership for
> publishing two papers — one at Green Bay, and the
> other at Galena; a meeting was agreed upon between us,
> to be had at Fort Winnebago in May of that year. I
> kept my appointment, but the Doctor failed of his,
> which ended the affair with him. I did nothing further

in my profession for several years, except to print a thousand lottery tickets, on a scheme for the benefit of sufferers by fire. John P. Arndt, of Green Bay, had lost a store and its contents by fire. He conceived the plan of selling lottery tickets, to reimburse; there was a singular genius in the place who, among a thousand other notions, had a handful of old Brevier, and an ounce or two of printer's ink. On examination, I found sufficient letter to set the necessary matter for a ticket. A bit of pewter furnished the means of a kind of border for the bill; an oak log, sawed off and made smooth of an end, furnished the stone; and by means of a planer instead of a platten, I worked off 1,000 of these tickets, which was, on the whole, a rather fair job, and the first printing ever executed in the State. Latterly I have offered a premium of $20 for one of them; but in vain.

It was a romantic enterprise, this ceaseless westward migration of type, and those who directed it and fashioned the product were frequently alive to the romantic element in the venture — far more so, probably, than Stephen Daye had been nearly two centuries before. Further evidence of this fact is provided by another incident in the typographical history of Wisconsin, as related in the *Boston Post* and quoted in the *American Publishers' Circular and Literary Gazette*, the official organ of the Book Publishers' Association, for February 16, 1856:

The first copy of the *Newport Mirror*, a paper recently started at Newport, Wisconsin, was sold at auction for sixty-five dollars, the second for ten dollars, and the third for five dollars. These papers were purchased and paid for by men who intend to preserve them as records of the beginning of a city which they expect to see spring up about the spot — now a wilderness — where the papers were struck off. The *Mirror* says, in an editorial article: 'We are doing what, perhaps, has never been

done in the United States before — we are printing the
Wisconsin *Mirror* in the woods! — not a dwelling, except
our own, within half a mile of us, and only one within a
mile of us!! The forest oak hangs over our office and
dwelling, the deer and rabbits shy around us, the prairie
hens, partridges and quails, seek our acquaintance by
venturing nearer and nearer our doors.... But much of
this romance is soon to be spoiled. Already several dwell-
ings are in progress near us, and before many weeks they
are to be occupied by enterprising neighbors; and when
Spring and Summer shall come, we expect such a clatter
of axes and spades, and trowels and hammers, that we
shall hardly be able to write our editorials without in-
troducing more or less of the confusion. The fact is, we
expect a large village — yes, a city — to grow up rapidly
around us; and that is why we are — PRINTING IN
THE WOODS!'

Northwestward, southwestward, due west the
course of typography took its way. The story is
largely available, state by state, in the monographs
of Douglas C. McMurtrie, several of which have
already been heavily drawn upon here.

By the time printing was well established in the
Mississippi Valley, nearly two centuries had elapsed
since the Widow Glover's paraphernalia had been
set down on the Atlantic seaboard. Before that
second century was quite complete, the art would
span the continent. The forging of this ultimate link,
however, involves elements of so distinctive a character — social, historical, economic, geographic — that
the story of its fashioning must be postponed while
this narrative returns momentarily eastward.

CHAPTER X

Enter the Professional Author

WITH the exception of a few editors of magazines and reviews, Mr. Irving is almost the only American who has attempted to support himself by literary labors.'

Thus wrote Richard Henry Dana, the elder, in 1819 in an extended notice in the *North American Review* of the first two numbers of *The Sketch Book of Geoffrey Crayon, Gent.* Since Washington Irving was the first professional writer in America to become a classic author, and since his attempt 'to support himself by literary labors' necessarily involved him in the economics of publishing and the mechanics of printing, his career up to the moment at which Dana was discussing it has some pertinence here. Fortunately many of the statistical details are available in the four-volume *Life and Letters* by his nephew, Pierre M. Irving (New York, 1862–64), and it is now possible to supplement these with data from the Irving bibliography compiled by William R. Langfeld with the assistance of Philip C. Blackburn which was published serially in the *Bulletin of the New York Public Library* (June–December, 1932) and subsequently issued in book form.

During the first one hundred and fifty years and more of printing in America, the professional author was generally an inconspicuous, often a somewhat furtive, figure. There is the example, already cited, of Samuel Atkins, compiler of that *Kalendarium Pennsilvaniense* which is the earliest imprint in the

Middle Colonies. Whatever else he may have written none may say, but he remains the earliest identifiable hack-writer in British America. The great Mather copy-factory, extending from Richard (1596–1669) to Moses (1719–1806), produced six hundred and twenty-one published works, according to a tabulation by Thomas J. Holmes which appears in his account of the William G. Mather collection at Cleveland published in Part XIV (June, 1933) of the *Colophon*. Mr. Mather owned three hundred and forty-two of these at the time the article appeared. Increase and Cotton Mather account for five hundred and forty-six of the total, and Cotton alone for four hundred and forty-four — more than two thirds of the whole output of fourteen writers. These figures, moreover, Mr. Holmes points out, 'do not include fragmentary writings, such as Prefaces, To the Reader, etc.' But Cotton Mather would have scorned (and who ever better at scorning?) the imputation that he was a professional writer in the sense that he wrote for profit — any further profit, that is, than the regeneration of an unregenerable human race.

The spread of printing among the colonies and, later, into trans-Allegheny territory, was often effected, as has been noted, by printers who were also editors, or, to put the emphasis a little differently, by editors who were also printers. The mechanization of printing has well-nigh ended the era when the newspaper proprietor composed his fulminations stick in hand and disseminated them abroad without benefit of manuscript. But pioneers must needs be handy men, jacks of all trades. The southward and westward sweep of printing would have moved at glacier pace if the enterprise had had to be conducted as a dual alliance consisting of a practical printer on the one hand and a compiler of almanacs, a newspaper editor, or — save the mark! — a poet on the other. This explains in part why the professional author was so slow in arriving. Of at least equal importance was the lack of leisure for reading and for writing alike — the inevitable accompaniment of the opening-up of virgin territory. Neither was the factor of literacy negligible; books were for such as needed them in their businesses, just as the woodsman needed his axe in his, and those who needed books could get them from the mother country. A London representative of Rhode Island College (now Brown University) was authorized in 1768 to buy in Great Britain 'such Books as he may think necessary at this Time not exceeding Twenty Pounds value,' and no further appropriation for books for the college library, according to Dr. Walter C. Bronson in *The History of Brown University, 1764–1914* (Providence, 1914), was made thereafter until 1784, when some fourteen hundred volumes were ordered — from London. Eight years later Nicholas Brown presented the college with a law library of three hundred and fifty volumes — imported from London.

But by 1819 the picture was changing, or had already changed. Certainly the New York of that year was, for all practical and sentimental purposes, as staid and settled a community as the New York of today — even more staid and more settled. Men and women who could recall the British occupation were becoming fewer and fewer; certainly Washington Irving could not.

When he was nineteen years old, Irving had begun contributing to the *Morning Chronicle* of New York the *Letters of Jonathan Oldstyle,* of which he was later not overproud, and which were not assembled into book form until 1824 — New York and London, both pirated. Since Irving's brother Peter conducted the *Morning Chronicle,* it is possible that Irving was not compensated specifically for these contributions, of which nine appeared between November 15, 1802, and April 23, 1803 — and even if he were compensated, the profits, in the circumstances, can legitimately be deducted from his eventual returns as a professional author. The *Oldstyle* letters attracted the attention of Charles Brockden Brown, who was then editing the *Literary Magazine and American Register,* and he attempted to interest Irving in contributing to it — 'without success,' declares Pierre Irving, who assigns no reasons for the declination and gives no details of the offer.

Pierre Irving's biography abounds in citations of his uncle's impecuniosity at this early stage of his career. Irving's father, to be sure, had left his widow in comfortable circumstances, and it would be absurd to assume that the youngest of his eleven children (three of eight sons had died in infancy, so that Washington was indeed a dearly loved baby brother) would ever suffer actual want. But Washington was too independent a youth to regard any drafts on his mother's or brothers' competences as a satisfactory substitute for earning his own living. His half-humorous (and only half-humorous) disapproval of his situation as one wilfully starving in the midst of plenty became itself something of a family joke. His sister Catharine (Mrs. Daniel Paris) wrote him, in 1808: 'I am sorry for the lowness of your purse, and might possibly bestow a sixpence in charity, but I fear you are not a deserving object.'

Pierre Irving, citing this passage from Catharine's letter, continues:

> In this stage of his finances, he was induced to accept an offer of Isaac Riley, the bookseller, to translate from the French a work in two volumes, of which he could not in after years recall the title. Despatch was an object, and one volume was assigned to George Caines, counsellor at law and author of a Book of Practice, while the other was allotted to Washington, who associated his brother Peter with him. One hundred dollars was to be paid per volume, which was afterwards increased to one hundred and fifty; the translators finding the labor greater than was anticipated, from the multitude, I believe, of technical terms.

Along with its vagueness, this quotation embodies one definite inaccuracy, for the Riley offer was certainly not made 'in this stage of his finances,' because the book under discussion had been published two years before Catharine's letter was written. Pierre Irving, better biographer than bibliographer, might have troubled to look up the 'work in two volumes' (to appear in English in three) whose title his uncle could not in after years remember. It is pleasantly significant of Washington's determination to make his own way in the world that he definitely did remember the amount he received for the task — but did he have to divide with Peter? The book, as translated, was François Raymond Joseph de Pon's *Voyage to the Eastern Part of Terra Firma, or the Spanish Main, in South-America, during the Years 1801, 1802, 1803, and 1804,* and it was published by Riley at New York in 1806. The title-page declares it to have been 'translated by an American gentleman.'

Irving's first important literary venture was his

collaboration with his brother William and with William's brother-in-law, James Kirke Paulding, in *Salmagundi*, the twenty numbers of which appeared from January 24, 1807, to January 25, 1808. Some numbers at least went to a third edition, and an edition in book form was issued at New York in 1814, but this was anticipated by a London edition in two volumes (1811). A subsequent early New York edition (1820) is outside the scope of the immediate discussion, which is limited to Irving's status as a professional writer up to the time of the appearance of the Dana notice in the *North American Review*.

Salmagundi, declares Pierre Irving, 'was undertaken for their [the three compilers'] own amusement,' and David Longworth, who published it, appears to have embarked on the venture in the same carefree spirit. But the whim succeeded magnificently; of one number (perhaps the fourth — February 27, 1807) eight hundred copies were sold in a day, which was a phenomenal figure for a contemporary periodical. David Longworth — 'dusky Davie' — had fallen into that most embarrassing of predicaments, for a publisher or for anybody — he was making money in spite of himself. 'All they ever received from him,' says Pierre Irving, 'was a hundred dollars a piece, although at the time the original copyright expired in 1822, Paulding conjectures, in a letter to Ebenezer Irving, that he [Longworth] had made by all accounts ten or perhaps fifteen thousand dollars out of it.' Pierre Irving regarded this as 'probably an extravagant estimate,' and adds in fairness: 'Longworth had at first suggested a copyright to them, but they did not think it worth while, and he thereupon took it out himself.'

Irving's next enduring literary venture was more

profitable alike to himself and to posterity. Of the first edition of *A History of New York, from the Beginning of the World to the End of the Dutch Dynasty ... By Diedrich Knickerbocker* (New York, 1809) the 'avails,' in Pierre Irving's phrase, 'amounted to about three thousand dollars.' For the revised edition of 1812, Irving received twelve hundred dollars. The third American (1819) and the first English (1820) edition need not concern us.

There is no evidence to show that Irving was himself remunerated for his share in the preparation for the press in 1810 of *The Poetical Works of Thomas Campbell* ('including several pieces from the original manuscript, never before published in this country') with a 'biographical sketch of the author, by a gentleman of New-York' — and this time the gentleman was indubitably Washington Irving, *solo*. The book was a joint publishing enterprise, 'printed for Philip H. Nicklin & Co., Baltimore. Also, for D. W. Ferrand and Green, Albany; D. Mallory and Co., Boston; Lyman and Hall, Portland; and E. Earle, Philadelphia.' Irving prepared the biographical sketch at the request of the poet's brother, then a resident of New York.

'The biographical sketch of Campbell,' says Pierre Irving, 'was the only thing which came from his pen this year, and his literary pursuits would seem now to have been brought to a stand.' What follows is of significant interest in a study of this all but 'only American who has attempted to support himself by literary labors' as viewed in 1819 by Dana:

> The success of Knickerbocker had been far beyond his expectations, but it did not quicken his zeal for literature as a profession. He liked the exercise of his pen as

an amusement, or a source of occasional profit, but to be tied down to a literary career as his destiny, to be under bonds to write for a livelihood, this presented no enviable prospect to him. Indeed, his whole soul recoiled from the idea of a dependence upon literature for his daily bread. Such a career was beset with too many trials and vexations, was too precarious, too fitful, too much exposed to caprice, vicissitude, and failure. His happiness was at stake in obtaining some employment that would insure a steady income; and disappointed, as we have seen, in some hopes of an office, for which his friends had urged his claims, and shut out apparently from every other avenue to a modest competence — he seems at this period to have pondered the future with a boding heart.

Nevertheless, toward the end of 1812 Irving accepted the editorship of *Select Reviews*, the title of which periodical was forthwith altered to the *Analectic Magazine*. His salary was fixed at fifteen hundred dollars a year. Irving characterized this as 'an amusing occupation, without any mental responsibility of consequence.' But disillusionment lay just ahead for this naïve Daniel on the threshold of a den of lions whom he apparently took for a mere cluster of overgrown tabby-cats. It could have been worse; his tenure of the *Analectic's* chair was a casual and largely absentee affair; inevitably, it soon proved 'an irksome business.' Washington's editorship lasted almost precisely two years; on January 15, 1815, exactly a week after the post-peace battle of New Orleans, he wrote his brother William from Philadelphia: 'Bradford and Innskeep have failed and ruined poor Moses Thomas, the bookseller, who publishes the *Analectic*.' Thomas picked himself out of the ruins, became one of the proprietors of *The Sketch Book*, and survived to a hale and prosperous old age, his friendship with Irving enduring above all the hazards of the book business. Following the *Analectic's* collapse (or more properly Thomas's, for the *Analectic* managed to last a few years), Irving, according to his nephew, 'signed off what was owing to him' — perhaps a month's pay, perhaps much more.

Irving's *Analectic* contributions included a series of brief biographies of American naval heroes, and one of these (appearing originally in the issue for August, 1813) was issued separately soon afterward: *Biography of James Lawrence, Esq. Late a Captain in the Navy of the United States: together with a Collection of the Most Interesting Papers, Relative to the Action Between the Chesepeake and Shannon, and the Death of Captain Lawrence, &c. &c. Embellished with a Likeness. New-Brunswick: Printed and Published by L. Deare, at Washington's Head. 1813.* This vest-pocket volume has become one of the rarest of Irving titles; in preparing his bibliography Mr. Langfeld inspected such copies as were available, but was unable to give accurate data regarding the page size; each of the copies examined measured five and three-eighths by three and seven-sixteenths inches; all were bound in sheep, but the bindings were not uniform, so that Mr. Langfeld could not 'state with certainty that they were not trimmed.' Then, almost a century and a quarter after its publication, there came to light a copy of the *Biography of James Lawrence* in the original boards with the edges of the leaves uncut — that is, untouched by the binder's knife. The page size was six and one-sixteenth by three and thirteen-sixteenths inches — nearly half an inch both taller and wider than any of the copies bound in sheep. The uncut copy had been reposing in the James Lawrence collection of Mrs. Michael Gavin, the finest in existence devoted to the brief career of the too gallant captain. Harry MacNeill Bland, a leading authority on early American art and Currier and Ives prints and owner of one of the finest Lincoln collections in existence, and the largest pictorially, chanced to recall this copy in reading the June, 1932, installment of the Irving bibliography. The discovery was triumphantly proclaimed to the world by Philip C. Blackburn in the November, 1932, issue of the *Bulletin of the New York Public Library*.

The fact that Mrs. Gavin's copy was untrimmed may be of only remote technical interest to the layman; it is perhaps unnecessary to point out that the term untrimmed (or uncut) denotes another condition altogether than unopened (or unreadable without recourse to a paper-knife). But the matter is of definite interest as exhibiting the size in which the book was originally issued. More important still, however, Mrs. Gavin's copy was in the original printed boards, 'though size cannot be differentiated from binding,' as Mr. Blackburn points out in his description of the Gavin copy. The publisher, Mr. Blackburn continues, 'evidently rushed the copies through his presses [Lawrence had died June 4th from wounds received in the action with the *Shannon*]; it is probable that he cased up a few at once for immediate circulation, and that these were the copies in the "publisher's binding."'... The majority of owners, however, preferred them bound in something more durable than paper; this is evidenced by the scarcity of copies in boards. The issue would not seem in any case to have been a large one; and of a comparatively small issue there survives at

ENTER THE PROFESSIONAL AUTHOR

least this single copy in its original condition.' The cover is identical with the title-page save for a slight opening-up of the type and the addition of an ornamental border. The back, however, offers the interesting information that Lewis Deare stood ready to execute 'printing, in all its variety, plain and ornamental, on moderate terms' and to carry out binding commissions (the fewer the copies of the *Biography of James Lawrence* that left his shop in printed boards uncut, the better for Mr. Deare), and that he carried 'a general assortment of classical, theological, miscellaneous, and school-books.' Having two usable inches left at the bottom, Deare listed six 'books recently published,' to wit: 'Watts' Psalms and Hymns, large print; Washington's Legacy; New-Jersey Preacher, Vol. I; Songs in the Night; Blair's Lectures on Rhetoric; Watts' Improvement of the Mind.' If Irving himself profited from the book publication of the Lawrence sketch, the return was certainly negligible.

This is not the place to review Irving's own share in the War of 1812–15 or the circumstances under which he embarked on the epochal visit to the Old World which was to extend over seventeen years. He had not been long in England before he was discussing plans for the American republication by Moses Thomas of English books, Irving to make the arrangements with British publishers. For this work — literary, to be sure, but converting Irving from a producer of literature into a literary agent — 'he was to receive an annual compensation of one thousand dollars.' But the project 'continued only a year, when it was terminated by Mr. Irving's request; he finding it not so productive to Thomas as he had anticipated.'

185

The manuscript of the first number of *The Sketch Book* (which number included *Rip Van Winkle*) was dispatched from London to Irving's brother Ebenezer early in 1819; the second part soon followed. Before discussing the bibliographic entanglements of this most important contribution to American literature that had yet been made, it is essential to recapitulate Irving's status as a professional author, an American attempting 'to support himself by literary labors,' at the instant at which Richard Henry Dana was considering it. Assuming that Pierre Irving has supplied all the figures that were available (and his omissions are certainly trivial), Irving's total literary income, from his twentieth to his thirty-sixth year, can with reasonable accuracy be set at close to eighty-five hundred dollars — an average of roughly five hundred dollars a year. With the great accrual of fame that came with the publication of *The Sketch Book*, Irving was definitely embarked on a career that became as profitable as it was distinguished. At the conclusion of the *Life and Letters*, Pierre Irving tabulates the returns in detail. The 'whole amount realized on his Works during his life' was $205,383.34, and payments to his estate between his death (November 28, 1859) and September 30, 1863, were $34,237.03. Pierre Irving's recapitulation, meticulous as it is, inevitably omits some minor amounts and definitely does not include the pre-*Sketch Book* earnings.

The bibliography of *The Sketch Book* is an amazingly involved affair. Whosoever wishes to read the full story of its intricacies will find them in the Langfeld compilation, where they occupy nearly seven pages, five of which are devoted to a comparison of textual variations between the issues of the first (serial) edition. The work was issued in seven parts between May, 1819, and September, 1820. It was the first great book to be so issued, but in the years that followed, the book in parts was to be a significant phenomenon of the publishing panorama in England and, to a less degree, in the United States. *The Posthumous Papers of the Pickwick Club*, *Vanity Fair* (most of Dickens and much of Thackeray), were given to the world in paper-covered numbers that are today among the crown jewels of the collector's kingdom; Dickens was similarly exploited by American publishers; even Edgar Allan Poe was to toy ineffectually with a project in parts which stopped with a single number.

To give some idea of the mass of minute detail involved in a technical bibliographic appraisal of *The Sketch Book*, a description of Part I may here be summarized from Langfeld:

Title-page: Imprint reads 'Greenwich-street,' changed in second issue to 'Greenwich Street'; eleven dots in rule above date, later ten.

Text: Page iv, line three, 'that' (later 'which'); page 30, lines one and two, 'but which few men exercise, or this world would be' (changed to 'and which, if generally exercised, would convert this world into' and, later still, to 'but which not many exercise, or this world'); page 30, line nine, 'or' (changed to 'nor'); page 41, line fourteen, 'love' (also in the second issue, but with 'at home' added in the third issue); page 45, line nine, 'but feels' (altered to 'but will feel'); page 45, line ten, 'when even' (later 'if even,' subsequently changed back to 'when even'); page 80, line three, 'not one' (later 'none'); page 80, line four, 'for his old' in first and second issues (altered to 'for an old' in third issue); page 94, 'Charles V' (corrected to 'Emperor Frederick'), also in second issue page 94

is blank and the text of the note which previously occupied page 94 has been transferred to page 95 —
which is still designated 94.

If these complexities indicate a painstaking attention to minutiæ, a word-by-word collation of texts in
as many copies as the investigators could lay hands
on (which, in the instance of *The Sketch Book*, would
not be an abundance), let it be added that Part II exhibits four times as many distinctive points as Part I,
Part III twice as many, Parts IV to VI about the same
number each as Part I, and Part VII not quite twice
as many. Altogether there are about one hundred
textual variations in the seven parts. Add to this the
fact that the wrappers present a separate problem
and that the assembling of the separate signatures
(the units, usually today of sixteen pages, which are
gathered in sequence to make a book) sometimes re-
sulted in a single part's containing peculiarities of
both first and second issues within a single pair of
covers, and some conception of the task involved in
dissecting *The Sketch Book* may be gained.

Most of the copies of the original numbers which
survive are bound in sheep or calf, the original
wrappers having been removed by the binder. Such
preservative measures are regrettable from one point
of view, but let it not be forgotten that the measures
definitely were preservative. If a few early readers of
the parts had not had the foresight thus to protect
their copies, not many sets of the earliest dates
would be available to the student — and there are
few enough as it is. The collector, however, usually
wants his treasures 'as issued,' which means, in this
case, with the fragile brown wrappers intact, and
with the edges of the leaves untrimmed. Attired
thus, in the modest but now regal investiture in

which it was given to the world, *The Sketch Book*, with all seven parts in first state, is one of the scarcest of American books — probably actually the scarcest American book of its stature as literature.

Some two years after the appearance of Diedrich Knickerbocker's *History of New York* in 1809, a copy of that engaging chronicle came to the hands of a youth of seventeen who was half-heartedly applying himself to the study of law in an office in Worthington, Massachusetts. Inevitably that copy was an exemplar of the first edition; therefore, if it still exists, it is valuable in its own right; it is much more desirable if it carries, as it almost certainly does, the signature of William Cullen Bryant. Bryant had been born in 1794 in the neighboring village of Cummington, which even today is a dozen miles from a railroad and which up to the coming of the automobile remained virtually as inaccessible as it had been during the first Presidency. For all that, it boasted as long ago as 1820 a library of seventy-two volumes, but this public collection was heavily overshadowed by the seven hundred books which graced the shelves of Dr. Peter Bryant.

Dr. Bryant, as a loyal Federalist, had viewed with alarm in 1804 the initiation of the earliest New Deal in American statesmanship — the rise to power of Thomas Jefferson — and the antics of the dangerous radical and Francophile (which were the least among the epithets his opponents flung at him) had been lengthily and heatedly discussed in the Cummington farmstead. Cullen absorbed this partisan delineation whole. With the adoption of the Embargo of 1807 in an effort to avoid recourse to war with England, New England fairly seethed with indignation against the monster in the White House, and Cullen's personal

allotment of ire exploded in ink. The resulting composition was exhibited to a proud parent, who demanded more and got it, for it paralleled his own
sentiments in heroic couplets that matched Pope for
vitriolic content. Dr. Bryant forthwith carried the
manuscript with him to Boston (he was a member of
the General Court — that is, the State Legislature),
and had it printed at his own expense and doubtless
to the author's immediate delight. The author's maturity grew to be extensive enough to permit him
plenty of leisure wherein to repent this juvenile in-
discretion. Bryant's long-time associate on the staff
of the New York *Evening Post*, executor of his will, and
author of the sketch of his life in the American Men
of Letters Series (1890) — John Bigelow — says that
the diatribe took on in later years 'a notoriety which
it never would have acquired but for the fact that
Mr. Bryant lived to become one of the most influential champions of the so-called Jeffersonian democracy, and for the lack of more effective weapons,
it delighted the Federal press occasionally to quote
these lines about Jefferson, omitting the fact that
they were written when the author was a schoolboy in
roundabouts.'

*The Embargo, or Sketches of the Times; a Satire.
By a Youth of Thirteen. Boston: Printed for the Purchasers. 1808* was a stitched, unwrapped, homely
pamphlet of which most copies must have been scuffed
into tattered disreputability within a week. There is
no way of knowing how many Dr. Bryant ordered
to be printed; putting oneself in his place, one can
hardly picture him suggesting fewer than one hundred, and it is almost equally difficult to picture him
suggesting more. Two hundred, five hundred — who
knows? But he might have commanded a hundred

thousand and, had these actually been distributed, the first edition of *The Embargo* might be equally rare today. That the original edition definitely was distributed is proved by the statement of Bigelow (and others) that it 'sold promptly'—Bigelow doubtless had the information direct from Bryant himself —and by the fact that a second edition was issued at Boston the following year. Important testimony to the scarcity of the original issue within twenty-one years of its appearance is offered in the fact that Samuel Kettell did not list it in the 'Catalogue of American Poetry' which he appended to the third and final volume of his *Specimens of American Poetry* in 1829. Kettell did, however, list the second edition, 'corrected and enlarged,' and with Bryant's name for the first time on a title-page, printed 'for the author' by E. G. House. This second edition, a pamphlet of thirty-five text pages originally dignified with marble wrappers, is common by comparison with the first, but only by comparison. Only some half-dozen copies of the 1808 *Embargo* survive.

Bryant duly completed his legal studies, was admitted to the bar, and began to practice law. Meanwhile he continued to write verse, selecting subjects more congenial to his temperament than the ostentatiously democratic executive whom he had urged to 'go, wretch, resign the Presidential chair.' He tucked at least three of the manuscripts into a desk, where his bustling father, who probably had never got over the thrill of *The Embargo*, chanced upon them. Two of the three remain, and will forever remain, among the most familiar and moving of American compositions: 'Thanatopsis' and 'To a Waterfowl.' Dr. Bryant turned the verses over to Willard Phillips of the staff of the *North American Review*, and Phillips showed them to Richard Henry Dana. Dana's comment is famous: 'Ah, Phillips, you have been imposed upon. No one on this side of the Atlantic is capable of writing such verses.' Poor Dana's memory has endured its share of abuse for this seeming piece of casual superciliousness. But when he uttered it, it was not supercilious at all. Substitute, for 'no one,' 'no American writer with whose work I am acquainted,' which was, of course, what Dana meant, and his declaration was strictly true. So interpreted, it must remain a remarkably accurate and shrewd appraisal. The poems were accepted, and 'Thanatopsis' appeared (anonymously, in accordance with the periodical practice of the time) in the *Review* for September, 1817. But it was not wholly the 'Thanatopsis' that the world knows today. It lacked the first seventeen lines and the final fifteen, beginning, instead, with 'Yet a few days, and thee' and ending with 'And make their bed with thee.' Sundry other additions and repairs were made in the definitive version; the line

Where rolls the Oregon, and hears no sound

originally read

That veil Oregan, where he hears no sound.

East was east and the Far West was very far west in 1817, and the twain seldom encountered each other in pronouncing gazetteers.

The course of Bryant's life was now definitely pointed. Other contributions to the *Review* followed. In 1821 Bryant was invited to deliver the Phi Beta Kappa poem at Harvard; he read 'The Ages,' and poem and poet were so well received that he was asked to make a selection of his work for book publication. The outcome was a *volumette*, as Bigelow inelegantly calls it, which, despite its homely dress, its unpretentious typography, and the physical slenderness of its contents, was the most important book of indigenous poetry that had yet appeared in America.

The simplicity of the title-page could hardly have been exceeded: *Poems by William Cullen Bryant. Cambridge: Printed by Hilliard and Metcalf. 1821.* The front cover read identically, with the type enclosed in a severe double-ruled border. Copies in printed boards are rare, copies in printed wrappers approach the vanishing point — and copies in sheep are not to be held lightly. Issuance of the unassuming collection (the seven units of its contents occupied only forty-four pages) closely followed Bryant's delivery of the Harvard address, for in 1836 he wrote B. B. Thatcher that his Cambridge visit of 1821 'led to the publication of my poems and in consequence my stay was protracted two or three weeks.' The original of this letter accompanied a copy of the *Poems* in the Stephen H. Wakeman collection of the works of New England authors which was sold at auction at New York in 1924.

Bryant had spent a year at Williams College (1810–11) and at the end of it begged leave to be excused from further attendance. Another and a sadder story must be told regarding the termination of the academic career of the next figure to receive special consideration in these notes.

The power of a good deed to enlighten a naughty world is not nearly so impressive as the power of a naughty deed to enlighten any kind of world. Thousands of upstanding Americans go to college and are graduated, if not invariably *cum laude*, at least with decency. A handful emerge in time as men of talent or even genius, but only a thin red line of loyal alumni are willing to give dear old alma mater a tithe of the credit, and an unheeding public is not likely to remember the names of the schools that may have nurtured the company of the elect or even whether they had any schooling at all.

But let a recalcitrant student be uncloistered, for whatever good and sufficient reason, and let him subsequently put on the apparel of immortality — then presto! a chorus of chuckles starts echoing down the centuries at the expense of the uneasy seat of learning which would have none of him. The shades of Edgar Allan Poe and James Abbott McNeill Whistler, according to popular view, will forever be thumbing their noses at the United States Military Academy. Harvard had the wit or the luck not to close the door utterly against James Russell Lowell — she merely exiled him for a few weeks. But the third institution of higher education to be established in the American colonies found nothing to palliate the offense of James Fenimore Cooper, ex-1806. 'The faculty expelled him,' concedes a co-collegian, William Lyon Phelps, 'unaware of the fact that he was to be the most important man of letters ever connected with Yale.'

What had he done? Various commentators have dismissed the episode that motivated his departure as 'a frolic' or 'an escapade,' and have thereby merely whetted curiosity. Henry Walcott Boynton, Cooper's latest biographer (and no eminent American man of letters has had fewer), goes into the fullest available detail, but wisely admits his inability to peer beyond family legend and rumor. Whatever the offense, it was one, doubtless, that would now be looked upon as trivial enough, but it was ample for that rigorous day. In James Cooper's behalf it might have been advanced that he was barely sixteen at the time. Even though his was an academic era in which a graduate of twenty-one was regarded as teetering on the edge of senility, Cooper was a somewhat youthful junior. He was, in fact, the second youngest man in his class, yielding first honors by only eleven days to James A. Hillhouse, who wrote poetry that failed to survive him.

Cooper had been born in 1789 at Burlington, New Jersey, but when he was little more than a year old the family had migrated to central New York to grow up with the country. His father, William Cooper, saw a future in that wooded wilderness — not only saw it, but aided his own dream to fruition. As a result, James Cooper (the Fenimore was a tribute to the maternal stock) came to manhood as the off-spring of a prosperous country squire. There were numerous older brothers and sisters — James was the eleventh of twelve children — but William Cooper was well able to provide for the seven who survived infancy. Perhaps the most imposing measure of the parent's importance in the post-Revolutionary scheme is the fact that Gilbert Stuart painted a portrait of him.

Father William is reputed to have taken James's side in the dispute with the Nutmeg pundits and offered no objection to James's desire to go to sea. Accordingly, in 1806, James joined the crew of the ship *Sterling*, voyaged to England and the Mediterranean, and spent not quite one year before the mast. On his return he received a commission as ensign in a not particularly formidable United States Navy. In the spring of 1811 he resigned.

He did not resign simply because a war was due the

following year. Cooper loved an argument, friendly or otherwise, and he was no coward. The insane little rumpus in which America engaged from 1812 to 1814 can hardly be dignified by the name of war, and whatever dignity does appertain to it in historical perspective was certainly not noticeable at the time. Cooper had fallen in love with Susan De Lancey, and their marriage on New Year's Day of 1811 was no slacker wedding.

The marriage did, however, remove Cooper from the parental acres. He and his bride went down into Westchester, where the De Lanceys were already a famous county family — so famous, in fact, and so respectable that they had taken what had proved to be the wrong side in the horrid old Revolution. The De Lanceys were also well-to-do — Mr. and Mrs. Cooper seemed destined to a life of landed ease.

Books came up from New York — among them the latest English importations. Cooper would read some of them aloud — Walter Scott, Maria Edgeworth, Jane Austen. One day he was reading a recent arrival — possibly, thought his daughter Susan, who became the authority for the historic incident, a novel of Mrs. Opie's 'or one of that school.' Mainly by this tenuous link, though she received three ample columns in S. Austin Allibone's *Dictionary of Authors*, does Amelia Opie adhere to immortality. Born twenty years before Cooper and surviving him by two, she produced *The Dangers of Coquetry*, *The Father and The Daughter*, *Adeline Mowbray, or The Mother and Daughter*, *Temper, or Domestic Scenes, Illustrations of Lying in All Its Branches*, and much more, but these titles seem to be enough to put her where she belongs. According to Miss Susan, Cooper read a chapter or two of the book and then tossed it

aside, saying, 'I could write you a better book myself.' Mrs. Cooper laughed — the one thing needful
to drive her impetuous husband to pen and paper and
the composition of *Precaution*.

The defect of this incident, with all due respect to
Miss Susan, is that it is a little too pat. Even grant-
ing that this was the spark that set off the mine, still
the mine had to be there to be set off. Somewhere in
Cooper's nature had lurked that itch to be doing something besides taking his ease at his genteel hearth —
something of that zest for getting somewhere that had
sent the first William Cooper out from England and the
latest William Cooper up into the forests roundabout
Otsego Lake. Linked to this quality was a passionate
love for the upstart young country which had come
into official existence only six months before his own
birth. The great sign of Cooper's genius was that he
was able to see the forest in spite of the trees.

There was, of course, no hint of this visibility in
Precaution. For *Precaution* was quite as poor a thing
as Mrs. Opie's worst, and quite as English, setting and
all. Somehow it managed to get itself published in
two volumes in New York at the end of 1820 with
the imprint of A. T. Goodrich & Co., which firm immediately reverts to obscurity. It was the work, according to its title-page, of 'A Gentleman of New
York.'

Professor Phelps calls *Precaution* 'one of the worst
novels in history.' But he adds: 'If this book had
been a success, it is possible that he might never have
written another. His temperament was encouraged
by success, but inspired by failure.'

Cooper was already at work on something else. It
was to be an American tale, dealing with that still
little-understood struggle that had won for the

colonies an independence that they had not been at all certain what to do with. It is interesting to note that Cooper, who wrote the great Revolutionary novel, was born at almost the same distance from his war as was Stephen Crane, who wrote the great Civil War story, from Appomattox. Cooper had the advantage of a thorough acquaintance with his chosen locale — the 'neutral ground' of Westchester, where friend and foe had met in inextricable confusion, and where three young men sitting by the roadside playing cards had taken André and saved a nation.

Charles Wiley, of Wiley & Halsted, was prevailed upon to sponsor the book, but would not assume the copyright, which turned out to be a good piece of business for Cooper. As proof of the somewhat haphazard relations existing between Cooper and his publisher, it may be cited that Volume I was in type before Volume II was written, and that the final chapter of Volume II (and of the book) was written and put in type before the rest of that volume was ready. This was not so hard a trick as it sounds, since the final chapter is concerned with events occurring thirty-three years after those immediately preceding them in the text.

The Spy; a Tale of the Neutral Ground. By the Author of 'Precaution' was issued at the end of 1821. On the following January 7, Wiley wrote Cooper a letter recounting the early career of the book which Mr. Boynton reproduces — a letter of considerable bibliographical importance. *The Spy* had already succeeded 'over and beyond' Mr. Wiley's expectations, which apparently were of the most modest. Carey and Lee of Philadelphia, whose name, or a derivative of it, was to appear on virtually every Cooper book beginning with *The Last of the Mohicans* in 1826, took a hundred copies; altogether 'we have sold and sent off on commission about 600 copies, and think it very probable that the whole edition will be sold in three months.' Wiley's conservatism was exaggerated. A second edition of three thousand copies appeared two months later, and a third of five thousand after another two-month interval. It seems reasonable to assume from these data that the first edition did not consist, at the outside, of more than two thousand copies; indeed, taking into account Wiley's caution, fifteen hundred or even a thousand seems a more likely figure.

The Spy in first edition is unquestionably one of the rarest books in American literature. Only two copies, neither in the printed boards in which it was undoubtedly originally issued (as *Precaution* had been), have appeared in the auction room since 1903. *The Spy* was read, re-read, and read again in a day when the young republic had not come to appreciate the potentialities of first editions of American novelists.

Cooper, despite his importance, had to wait an unconscionably long time before a bibliography of his work was available, but when one did ultimately appear it was an admirable compilation: *A Descriptive Bibliography of the Writings of James Fenimore Cooper*, by Robert E. Spiller and Philip C. Blackburn (New York, 1934).

But the young republic was a growing republic, and despite the truly phenomenal sales of *The Spy*, there were plenty of persons who merely heard at second and third hand of *The Sketch Book*, and who survived to old age without having their attention drawn to 'Thanatopsis.' Mr. Wiley was doing famously, but he was one among a host, and altogether a publisher's lot in the 1820's was not a happy one.

The general impression was that we had not, could not have a literature [wrote in after years one of the greatest entrepreneurs of books in all his country's publishing history]. The successful publishers of the country — Carey, Small, Thomas, Warner, of Philadelphia; Campbell, Duyckinck, Reed, Kirk & Mercein, Whiting & Watson, of New York; Beers & Howe, of New Haven; O. D. Cooke, of Hartford; West & Richardson, Cummings and Hilliard, R. P. & C. Williams, S. T. Armstrong, of Boston — were for the most part the mere reproducers and sellers of English books. It was positively injurious to the commercial credit of a bookseller to undertake American works, unless they might be [Jedidiah] Morse's Geographies, classical books, schoolbooks, devotional books, or other utilitarian works.

So wrote Samuel Griswold Goodrich in his *Recollections of a Lifetime* (1857), viewing his own eager twenties from the satisfying viewpoint of his complacent sixties. Goodrich initiated his publishing career by bringing out an elaborate two-volume edition of the poetical works of John Trumbull (Hartford, 1820). A race had sprung up (including, apparently, many good Hartfordians) who knew not the Hartford Wits. Trumbull, according to Goodrich, 'had sought a publisher, in vain, for several years previous.' But Goodrich boldly, and doubtless to the veteran satirist's astonished delight, offered him a thousand dollars and a hundred copies of the projected book for the copyright.

For so considerable an enterprise [says Goodrich] I took the precaution to get a subscription, in which I was tolerably successful. The work was at last produced, but it did not come up to public expectation, or the patriotic zeal had cooled, and more than half the subscribers declined taking the work. I did not press it, but putting a good face upon the affair, I let it pass, and —

while the public supposed I had made money by my enterprise, and even the author looked askance at me in the jealous apprehension that I had made too good a bargain out of him — I quietly pocketed a loss of about a thousand dollars.

It was not until 1827 that Goodrich adopted the mantle of Peter Parley and set out on the career that would make him famous as author, editor, compiler, and purveyor of entertaining and edifying children's books. Of the one hundred and seventy titles which he issued (whereof one hundred and sixteen were Parley books), some seven million volumes had been sold when he wrote his memoirs, according to his own computation, and 'about three hundred thousand volumes are now sold annually.' The most celebrated and valuable among them today is *Peter Parley's Universal History, on the Basis of Geography* (two volumes, Boston, 1837), for which he engaged the services of Nathaniel Hawthorne. Hawthorne's *Fanshawe, a Tale* had been published anonymously nine years earlier at the author's expense and to his severe discomfiture once he saw it in type. He promptly destroyed every copy he could lay hands on, which undoubtedly meant most of the edition, for *Fanshawe* is today a precious rarity. Goodrich seems never to have tried to avail himself of the services of another anonymous author who had published his first book the year before *Fanshawe* appeared, also at his own expense: *Tamerlane, and Other Poems. By a Bostonian.* The author was Edgar Allan Poe, and he did not long remain a Bostonian. *Tamerlane* has become the very touchstone of rarity among American books, although nine or ten examples are known today. It is about as abundant as the Bay Psalm Book, but that hardly means abundance with a big, big A.

It was Goodrich himself who happily christened the period that began with the late 1820's the 'Age of Annuals.' He credited Germany with the invention of the annual, but by 1823 the vogue had spread to England (the *Forget-me-not*), and in 1826 it reached the United States, where it began to thrive with the vitality that was one day to be manifested by the English sparrow. Carey and Lea's *Atlantic Souvenir* initiated the fad (Henry Wadsworth Longfellow contributed to the first and second numbers), and in 1828 came Goodrich's own *Token*. Some of the annuals were annuals indeed; others became hardy perennials, and the *Token* was of these, lasting until 1842. Its contents tables listed a host of nonentities, judged by a twentieth-century appraisal, but Hawthorne contributed thirty-five sketches and stories, including much of the material subsequently assembled in *Twice-Told Tales* (1837). Goodrich gives a partial list of titles of annuals, which indicates the degree to which the plague spread: *Diadem, Bijou, Pearl, Gem, Amethyst, Opal, Amaranth, Bouquet, Hyacinth, Amulet, Talisman, Forget-me-not, Remember-me, Gift, Keepsake, Souvenir, Literary Souvenir, Boudoir, Floral Offering, Friendship's Offering, Iris, Laurel, Wreath, Jewel, Cabinet, Drawing-room, Pictorial, Continental, Picturesque, Fancy, Court, Anniversary, Pearls of the East, Pearls of the West, Favorite, Rhododendron, Waif, Gleaner, Rose.*

The annual was merely a phenomenon of the times, but hardly a dominating influence. It quickly deteriorated into something to keep on the parlor table alongside the stand of wax flowers under a glass bell, and was handled about as frequently. Meanwhile American literature was coming of age, moving toward a noble fruition that was becoming manifest before the annuals were born. When the final part of *The Sketch Book* was issued, Ralph Waldo Emerson was seventeen, Nathaniel Hawthorne was sixteen, Henry Wadsworth Longfellow and John Greenleaf Whittier were thirteen, Edgar Allan Poe and Oliver Wendell Holmes were eleven, Henry David Thoreau was two, and James Russell Lowell, Herman Melville, and Walt Whitman were a year old. What an auspicious moment it would have been for a far-sighted book-collector to choose to be born!

CHAPTER XI

Once More Westward Ho!

ON January 25, 1835, the brig *Pilgrim*, one hundred and sixty-one days out of Boston, dropped anchor in the harbor of Monterey, in the Mexican province of New (otherwise Alta, or Upper) California. Monterey was then quite the most important settlement in those parts — much more important than Yerba Buena (or, as the Anglo-Saxon element were perversely calling it, San Francisco), the most northerly port in the territory. The Californians, take them altogether, were 'an idle, thriftless people, and can make nothing for themselves.' Not even wine. 'The country abounds in grapes, yet they buy bad wine made in Boston and brought round by us, at an immense price, and retail it among themselves at a *real* (12½ cents) by the small wine-glass.' The outspoken critic was a mere member of the *Pilgrim's* crew, and he set down his impressions in a journal which a few years later he made into a book — *Two Years Before the Mast: a Personal Narrative of Life at Sea* (Harper & Brothers, New York, 1840). He was Richard Henry Dana, and he was doubtless identifiable to most of his fellow-Cantabrigians and Bostonians as the son of *the* Richard Henry Dana — the *North American Review* Dana who had noticed *The Sketch Book* and helped discover William Cullen Bryant. Young Dana had not run away to sea — a measles-ridden pair of eyes had driven him thither out of Harvard. Never was such a beneficent ophthalmia, for it gave the world the classic chronicle of a life on the ocean wave under canvas, and the most widely read example of factual Californiana ever written.

Monterey, according to young Dana (he was not yet twenty), was

decidedly the pleasantest and most civilized-looking place in California. In the centre of it is an open square, surrounded by four lines of one-story plastered buildings, with half a dozen cannon in the centre; some mounted, and others not. This is the 'Presidio,' or fort. Every town has a presidio in its centre; or rather, every presidio has a town built around it; for the forts were built first by the Mexican government, and then the people built near them for protection. The presidio here was entirely open and unfortified. There were several officers with long titles, and about eighty soldiers, but they were poorly paid, fed, clothed and disciplined. The governor-general, or, as he is commonly called, the 'general,' lives here; which makes it the seat of government. He is appointed by the central government at Mexico, and is the chief civil and military officer.

Dana's account of Monterey is available in detail in the thirteenth chapter of his narrative; it is a graphic picture of a too placid civilization that was doomed to early supplanting by a breed of Californians who were decidedly not 'an idle, thriftless people.' It is regrettable, however, that Seaman Dana found neither time to visit nor space to mention the local printing shop. Perhaps it escaped his eye altogether; it could hardly have been a conspicuous element in the scenery. The governor-general, likewise, seems to have blushed unseen so far as the sea-going Harvard undergraduate was concerned. This, too, for the purposes of the present discussion, is regrettable. For the local printing shop and the governor-general had much in common.

205

The governor-general of the province of Alta California at the moment of Dana's visit was José Figueroa. Assuming office at the beginning of 1833, he had had the wisdom to see that it might be well to set up a small printing establishment to turn out some of his official pronouncements. He had accordingly brought up with him from Mexico some types rather the worse for wear plus, apparently, a printer who could have done no better with the newest types in the world. A single specimen of this bungler's efforts survives. Dated Monterey, January 16, 1833, it announces, over Figueroa's signature, the fact that the central government had entrusted 'to my insufficiency' political and military authority over the territory.

A few scraps of printed paper — official forms of which some have been filled out and some remain blank — which were executed at Monterey date back to 1831. They were discovered exactly a century later by John Howell, of San Francisco, and are obviously the product of a hand apparatus of little more pretensions than a child's printing set. This fact, however, does not detract from their importance as representing the earliest fumbling typographical essay of the California that was to be.

Several attempts have been made to remove the namelessness of the printer of the 1833 *Anuncia*, but Robert Ernest Cowan, in his *Bibliography of the Spanish Press of California* (San Francisco, 1919), does not venture to unseal this doubtless unsought anonymity, and where Californiana is concerned it is safe to follow Cowan. His monumental *Bibliography of the History of California and the Pacific West, 1510–1906*, first issued at San Francisco in 1914, has since (1933) reappeared in a sumptuous three-volume edition prepared in collaboration with Robert Orannis

Cowan and bearing the imprint of John Henry Nash, and with the terminal date extended to 1930.

The unknown printer was succeeded in 1834 by Agustin Vicente Zamorano, who had come north in 1825 as secretary to a predecessor of Governor Figueroa, and who served the latter in the same capacity, having meantime attained a position of prominence in the political, military, and social life of the province. There is no evidence to show where he learned about printing — possibly he studied under the unknown and went him several better. The first surviving specimen of typography issued under his direction (bearing the date 1834 and the notice 'Imprenta de Zamorano y Ca') is, pleasantly, an *Aviso al Publico* describing the establishment of his plant and listing the prices at which he was prepared to do work. Soon afterward appeared a sixteen-page pamphlet, the first book to issue from his press — the first book, therefore, to be printed in California: *Reglamento Provicional para el Gubierno... de la Alta California* — the provisional regulations for the government of the province. Cowan locates twelve books printed in California during the twilight of Spanish dominion, nine in Monterey and three in Sonoma — four political or military, one medical, one devotional, and six school texts.

When Monterey fell into American hands in the summer of 1846, Commander Robert Field Stockton, in charge of the victorious naval force, appointed Chaplain Walter Colton *alcalde* of the city. Colton, a native of Vermont and a graduate of Yale, forthwith set about the establishment of a newspaper in collaboration with Dr. Robert Semple, and on August 15, 1846, appeared the first number of the *Californian*. Nine months later (May 22, 1847) the *Californian*

207

began to be issued in San Francisco, 'a newly begun settlement,' Dana had reported in 1835, 'mostly of Yankee Californians, which promises well.' Dana believed that 'if California ever becomes a prosperous country, this bay will be the centre of its prosperity.' He praised 'the excellence of its climate, which is as near to being perfect as any in the world' — and it is not a native son speaking, but a New Englander whose visit to the Pacific Coast was all but sheer accident. The printer of the *Californian*, according to Henry R. Wagner's *California Imprints, August 1846 – June 1851* (Berkeley, 1922), was Joseph Dockrill, a sailor in Stockton's command who had been a printer 'on the outside,' and who was forthwith given his discharge in order that he might become the first exponent of typography in English in the great commonwealth that was to be.

The establishment of the *California Star* at Yerba Buena on January 9, 1847, by Samuel Brannan, late of Brooklyn, had already signalized the birth of journalism in San Francisco. Late in 1848 the *Star* and the *Californian* were consolidated, and in January, 1849, the amalgamation was christened the *Alta California*. The staff did not yet include Samuel Langhorne Clemens. No complete file of the *Californian* exists, according to Wagner, although that in the California State Library lacks only the extras, the prospectus (issued six months after the first number), and one fly sheet.

The difficulties which confronted the pioneer printer in California are set forth in engrossing detail by George L. Harding in his history of the *Pacific News*, in Part VI (June, 1931) of the *Colophon*. On January 25, 1849, William Faulkner and his two sons left Mystic, Connecticut, aboard the *Trescott*. The elder Faulkner had operated the *News* at Norwich, and so was familiar with the mechanics and economics of newspaper publishing. His baggage included a No. 3 Washington press, type and other equipment, twenty reams of newsprint, and the lumber for a two-story building. The eighteen-thousand-mile journey around Cape Horn came to an end on August 6. A few days later, the ready-cut building had been set up, and on August 25 appeared the first number of the *Pacific News*, San Francisco's second newspaper (bearing in mind the fact that the *Star* and the *Californian* had already been made one). The *News* made an excellent impression and its job plant also was soon tremendously busy. Mr. Harding says that additional help had to be engaged almost immediately, and that the wages were 'sixteen dollars a day with a bunk in the office at night.' The No. 3 Washington was quickly overwhelmed, and Faulkner asked William Dunn, a local handy man, if he could make a press. Dunn set to work and constructed the first printing press built in California.

Paper quickly ran low, despite Faulkner's foresight, and the *News* often had to be issued on odd sizes, depending on what the proprietor could pick up. According to Mr. Harding, on one occasion 'the proprietors were glad to avail themselves of a few reams of tea-paper, which was procured from a physician who had brought out a small quantity to use as wrapping paper for his drugs.'

For reasons which Mr. Harding is unable to determine, William Faulkner returned East at the end of 1849, leaving one son, George L., in San Francisco. It is not essential here to go into the subsequent history of the *News*, which Mr. Harding sets forth in full.

Mr. Harding reproduces the first page of the issue for September 15, 1849, devoted exclusively to advertisements, mainly of commission merchants. Nearly a column, however, is given over to a recital of the cargo of the brig *Georgiana*, here offered for sale, including dry goods, hardware, groceries and provisions, ready-made clothing, crockery and glassware, looking-glasses, India-rubber goods, medicines, boots and shoes, stationery, fancy goods, and a miscellany which specified, among other commodities, one Irish jaunting car with harness complete. The *Georgiana* also brought from New York the following books: 'Ure's Dictionary of Arts and Sciences, Parnell's Chemistry, Spanish Grammars, Moore's, Byron's, Burn's [*sic*], Campbell's [,] Cooper's, Scott's, Milton's, Heman's [also *sic*], and Pope's Works, Lamartine's Holy Land, U.S. Exploring Expedition, Comprehensive Commentary, and a great variety of Religious, Historical, Geographical, and Biographical Works, Novels, school books.'

William Faulkner had not undertaken the perilous and tedious jaunt around the Horn merely because the Golden Gate was now a strictly American channel. In 1848 a group of workmen in the employ of the great landowner of the Sacramento district — a native of Switzerland named John Augustus Sutter (properly Suter) — were opening a mill flume when they came upon a quantity of shining particles the sight of which all but drove them into a frenzy, and the finding of which did, by a tragic irony, eventually drive Sutter into poverty. The actual discovery seems to have been made by Sutter's construction superintendent, James Wilson Marshall — the rock-bottom truth is not likely ever to be known. But whoever found it, and however it was found, there was much fine gold in California. The great romantic hegira was about to begin. When Stockton had made the conquest of Upper California certain in 1846 by the capture of Los Angeles, the population of the province — that portion of it, that is, of other than Spanish extraction, and not including the uncounted Indians — numbered perhaps fifteen thousand souls. Within less than three years the total had doubled; in the months immediately following the announcement of Marshall's discovery, it grew to a hundred thousand. The gold-production figures of the period provide even more striking statistics. In 1847, the gold yield for the whole United States was well under a million dollars; in 1848, it was ten million; in 1849, fifty million.

Some ten years after the World War, a native daughter of California whose entrance into that delectable land occurred during the Presidency of Abraham Lincoln experienced an impelling urge to reverse the Greeley dictum and to visit a married daughter in New York. An imposing and familiar obstacle intervened — what was she to use for money? Suddenly it occurred to her that in a trunk in the attic (this incident is not an improvisation) was the identical little overland guide-book which her father had used in his Pacificward trek from the Middle West nearly eighty years before. It had been preserved as an intimate family relic rather than as a scarce example of Western Americana.

The lady had read somewhere that such apparently trivial manuals often had a value far in excess of that of the customary old family Bible. To part with the relic seemed at first in the nature of a sacrilege — a flouting of the Lares and a scoffing at the Penates. On the other hand, the ancestral gods might well beam propitiously at any commercialization of sentiment aimed at bringing the old generation into touch with the new. The book was sent to New York and sold at an amount sufficient to bring the lady East and return her West with a degree of speed and convenience that her father had never dreamed of. Only two other copies of the guide were known.

There is a romantic appeal in Western Americana, particularly the early emigrant guides and the narratives of pre-railroad travel, which must quicken the pulses even of him who can gaze unmoved at a Columbus letter or a Waldseemüller *Cosmographiæ Introductio.* The dusty pall of pseudo-antiquity covers these latter, and while no superior imaginative faculty is needed to endow them with the warmth and color of humanity, still there are those who just do not so endow them. After all, Columbus and Vespucci and Hakluyt and De Bry have long been in their graves — Columbus, indeed, in two graves at once. But the men who pointed the way to the West are only of the day before yesterday. After life's fitful fever they, too, sleep full as well as Cortez and the Cabots, but grandchildren who clearly remember them are discussing golf handicaps at this very minute.

No one of these mid-century emigrants, presumably, paused to reflect that he was making history, or that, when he began to set down the record of his travels, he was bequeathing to posterity data of transcending importance. Often this voyager into the untracked West was either the town's addlepate or its ne'er-do-well, or at any rate was so regarded by his less mobile neighbors — who else would embark on such a giddy enterprise? When he returned, he was a better-than-nine-days' wonder, and was doubtless importuned by his friends (abetted by the local job-printer) to put his narrative into permanent form.

The permanence often proved transient enough. Produced usually in a small quantity (perhaps one hundred or two hundred copies), printed on any available paper, and protected only by the flimsiest wrappers, these records of early Western travel have become, as a class, among the scarcest of collector's items. Many of them have certainly vanished forever and will never be recorded even as hypothetical entries in any bibliography. And from time to time a new one is discovered, to take its place on the glamorous roster of argonautic archives.

As recently as 1932 there was announced from Boston the discovery of an early Western narrative which was unknown to any bibliographer. It is Riley Root's *Journal of Travels from St. Josephs to Oregon, with Observations of That Country, Together With a Description of California, Its Agricultural Interests, and a Full Description of Its Gold Mines*, printed at Galesburg, Illinois, by the Intelligencer Print in 1850. Below the imprint, mortised into a fearful ornamental border, appears inconspicuously the name 'Southwick Davis, Compositor.' Thus the wrapper — the title-page is almost identical with it, the phrase 'Some Description of California' being substituted for 'A Description of California' and 'Gazetteer and Intelligencer Print' for 'Intelligencer Print.' Root left home in April, 1848, and reached Oregon City in September, continuing to California the following spring. In October, 1849, he sailed for home, crossed the Isthmus of Panama dryshod, and took ship to New Orleans, reaching his starting-point on January 8, 1850, after an absence of one year, nine months, and five days. His record is a compound of narrative, first-hand (and good second-hand) observations, historical data, and advice to emigrants.

213

Root's story enjoyed the tremendous advantage (to collector and bibliographer) of being unrecorded; as a narrative it is doubtless no better and no worse than any of scores of others. Such of these as are known (or were known in 1921, when it was published in San Francisco) are described in Wagner's *The Plains and the Rockies: A Bibliography of Original Narratives of Travel and Adventure, 1800–1865.* Wagner's summary, as these dates show, is by no means confined to the gold-rush period. His first entry is Alexander Mackenzie's *Voyages from Montreal, on the River St. Laurence, Through the Continent of North America, to the Frozen and Pacific Oceans* (London, 1801) and his first with an American imprint, *Message from the President of the United States, Communicating Discoveries Made in Exploring the Missouri, Red River and Washita, by Captains Lewis and Clark, and Mr. Dunbar* (Washington, 1806). There is space here to list only a few of the guides and narratives that helped put gold in the pockets of local printers without putting them to the trouble of going to California for it: *California. A Trip Across the Plains, in the Spring of 1850, Being a Daily Record of Incidents of the Trip over the Plains, the Desert, and the Mountains, Sketches of the Country, Distances from Camp to Camp, Etc., and Containing Valuable Information to Emigrants, as to Where They Will Find Wood, Water, and Grass at Almost Every Step of the Journey. By James Abbey* (New Albany, Indiana, 1850); *A Journal of the Overland Route to California! And the Gold Mines, by Lorenzo D. Aldrich, late of Lansingburgh, Rensselaer Co. N. Y.* (Lansingburgh, 1851); *A Trip Across the Plains, and Life in California; Embracing a Description of the Overland Route; Its Natural Curiosities, Rivers, Lakes,*

Springs, Mountains, Indian Tribes, Etc., Etc.; the Gold Mines of California: Its Climate, Soil, Productions, Animals, Etc.... By Geo. Keller, Physician to the Wayne County Company (Masillon, Ohio, 1851); *Journal of the Sufferings and Hardships of Capt. Parker H. French's Overland Expedition to California, Which Left New York City, May 13th, 1850, by Way of New Orleans, Lavacca and San Antonio, Texas, El Paso, on the Rio Grande, the River Gila to San Diego on the Pacific, and Landed at San Francisco, December 14. By Wm. Miles, of Carlisle, Pa.* (Chambersburg, Pennsylvania, 1851); *California in 1850, Compared with What It Was in 1849, With a Glimpse at Its Future Destiny. Also a Concise Description of the Overland Route, from the Missouri River, by the South Pass, to Sacramento City, Including a Table of Distances, from Point to Point. With Notes on the Facilities Along the Route for Constructing a Railroad.... By Franklin Street* (Cincinnati and Louisville, 1851); *Overland Route to California, Description of the Route, Via Council Bluffs, Iowa; Keeping the North Side of the Platte River... By Andrew Child, of Wisconsin* (Milwaukee, 1852); and, later, but still in the covered-wagon era, *Notes by the Way. Memoranda of a Journey Across the Plains, from Dundee, Ill., to Olympia, W. T. May 7, to November 3, 1862. By R. H. Hewitt* (Olympia, 1863).

Productions of this type defy the hunter; they are as shy as gazelles; dozens of them are probably as extinct as the great auk. Of those which are listed and identified, many are known by but a few copies (three or four); others survive as unique examples. A few years ago, a New York bookseller who specializes in Americana adopted an ingenious device in an effort to bring to light additional copies (at least one, he hoped) of an early narrative of trans-Mississippi travel which had been printed as a pamphlet by the job plant in a small Middle Western town. It was reasonable to suppose that if any copies survived, they were as likely to survive in their birthplace as anywhere else. The bookseller asked the manager of the local motion-picture house to exhibit a slide at every show for a week (at the regular rate for such service) announcing that the bookseller was prepared to pay a specified figure for a copy of such-and-such a pamphlet, described in detail, which had been printed in that community in 1851. It is fair to assume that before the week was out, the entire adult population of the village was acquainted with a description of the pamphlet that would have enabled any of them to recognize it on sight, that they were all amazed at the amount offered, and that every conceivable hiding-place was ransacked. But not a single copy was found.

CHAPTER XII

Means — and an End

WHEN Stephen Daye or one of his sketchy crew pulled the first rough proof of *The Freeman's Oath* from the Widow Glover's primitive Cambridge press in 1638, nobody present appreciated the historic fact that there was then being initiated in the United-States-that-was-to-be an art and an industry which within two centuries would be reproducing in an endless whirr of machinery an incalculable quantity of vehicles of the printed word.

Printing was not Stephen Daye's trade; destiny had projected him into it; he was happy soon to be relegated to his proper calling of locksmith. How good or how bad a locksmith he was the world has no means of knowing. The locksmith's trade, too, has advanced immeasurably since 1638. Stephen Daye might be infinitely more amazed at sight of the tenderly balanced steel doors of a bank-vault than at the spectacle of a super-elephantine rotary press in the roaring crypt of a modern newspaper plant.

But if Stephen Daye could thus be translated into a newer time, and if he were endowed in his twentieth-century semblance with a sly appreciation of the fitness of things (which there is some reason to suppose he would not be), he would readily note the potentialities of a happy alliance between the two callings about which he knew most, without, in all likelihood, having been a master of either. For he would find every piece of printing with which he himself had had any concern whatever carefully

217

preserved in strong-rooms and guarded by elaborate mechanical devices against the incursions of moth, rust, thief, dust, fire, and excesses of aridity and humidity.

It would not do for him to think, as in his simplicity he might, that every scrap of paper covered with printer's ink that had been produced in the generations immediately following his own was similarly babied. The question of rare-book values has been deliberately avoided in these notes, for a multitude of what have seemed to the compiler excellent reasons. Book values are far from constant; all that can be said is that at a given moment a specific copy of a certain book is worth what an intending buyer is prepared to give for it. Nor can it be said that an example of a specific first or rare edition is 'worth' a definite figure even to an intending buyer; the element of condition is a determining factor in the computation of values, and while an eager collector might be willing to pay x dollars for a superb copy of Bryant's *Poems* of 1821 in the original wrappers, he might be willing to pay only $x/20$ for a tattered copy in sheep with the front flyleaf missing and a corner torn from the title-page. In fact, if he were a discriminating collector, he might not want it at any price.

It is wholly reasonable, however, that a person who owns a copy of what he thinks or knows is a rare book should want to know how to secure some information that might indicate its approximate value. One cannot learn, outside the actual test of marketing it, what a book will fetch, but one can learn whether a copy of a Boston imprint of the early 1700's should be worth closer to ten cents than to a thousand dollars — or *vice versa*.

FIRST SEPARATE AMERICAN EDITION (1846) OF KEATS'S
POEMS

Which is the earlier state of binding?

If a book is sufficiently rare and sought for to
command any kind of a market (and if, at the same
time, it is common enough, even to the extent of a
single copy's turning up in a generation, to have
commanded a definite market), there will exist a
record, not of what it is worth, but of what somebody
once paid for it, which might be a tenth of what it
was worth or ten times what it was worth. That
record exists in black and white in *American Book-
Prices Current*, an annual publication established in
1895. Each of these manuals contains the auction
prices of the previous season (extending in general
from October of one year to May of the next), together with brief descriptions, summarized from the
auction catalogues themselves, of the condition and
binding of each lot sold. Here are statistics every
unit of which is a condensed drama — the climax of
a struggle, mild or frenetic, between two or more who
want where only one may have. Its romance is set
down in fascinating case-histories in Dr. A. S. W.
Rosenbach's *Books and Bidders* (Boston, 1927).

The book-auction houses in New York, Chicago,
Philadelphia, and elsewhere issue catalogues which
are sent to inquirers either gratis or on payment of a
reasonable fee. The descriptions of the lots offered as
given in these catalogues are naturally more detailed
than the summaries presented in *American Book-
Prices Current*. The auction houses will supply
priced copies of catalogues after sales have been
conducted, the charge for this service being cus-
tomarily one dollar for each session of the sale (an
average of three hundred lots is sold at a session).
Only the professional bookmen usually avails himself of this service — and hundreds of professional
bookmen do not — but it is essential to a running

familiarity with the trend of rare-book prices. The amateur, however, can maintain an excellent contact with trends in the book market by securing the catalogues issued with more or less regularity by rare-booksellers, whose shops extend (not quite in unbroken line) from New York and Boston to San Francisco and Los Angeles, and from Glasgow and Edinburgh to Florence and Rome. They are happy to have him on their mailing-lists; they expect an occasional order by way of reciprocity, and generally they are not disappointed.

Not every rare book, obviously, gets into an auction catalogue or a bookseller's, and this comment has not yet quite solved the problem of the perplexed owner of a supposedly valuable item who cannot find it catalogued anywhere or listed in *American Book-Prices Current* and who is even more anxious on that account to learn its value.

Local librarians will often be able to give some indication of whether a book is an exemplar of a rare edition or not; they may have the means of determining whether the book is likely to be of value; they can at any rate suggest the names of reputable booksellers with whom they are doing business, who can be consulted.

Unless the inquirer has at least some rudimentary information, some slight trace of technical bibliophilic knowledge, to give him a hint that his prize may be valuable, the chances are a thousand to one (or worse) that the prize is worthless. This unfortunate but impressive truth has caused more heartaches than the bookseller likes to think about. In inquiring about the value of a supposedly valuable book, it is well to begin with the assumption that it is worth nothing at all — and if this proves to be the case, the owner is not disappointed. The average family Bible, for instance, regarded as an article of commerce, is not worth its weight in flour. Owners of supposedly priceless old editions of the Scriptures which were printed in English in America need feel their pulses beat the quicker only if their copies bear the imprint of Robert Aitken, of Philadelphia, and the date 1782. If their copies bear British imprints, their hopes can be nurtured by a little more variety; there exists the highly remote chance that the volume may be a copy of 'the greatest book in the world,' in A. Edward Newton's just phrase — the original edition (1611) of the King James version.

If one is eager to learn the value of a book, it does not follow that he is anxious to dispose of it — he may want simply to acquire it. Here, fortunately, it is possible to give him a genuine counsel of perfection: let him consult a rare-bookseller and ask him how much the book will cost. Because a book is rare, it does not follow that a fortune is required to possess it. Seymour de Ricci, a world authority on medieval manuscripts as well as on early printed books, contributed to Part II (May, 1930) of the *Colophon* an illuminating paper on 'Book-Collecting for All Purses' in which he said: 'I can quite conceive of a large, valuable and interesting library in which no volume would have cost more than one dollar.' While it would be nonsense for a collector to limit himself arbitrarily to this maximum unless his pocket strictly compelled him to or unless (as Mr. de Ricci suggests) he were doing it on a bet, still the basis of the idea is eminently sound, and if one admit an occasional exception beyond the dollar limit, its execution is eminently practicable. It would not, of course, be practicable in many or most of the special fields which are already pre-empted by well or moderately pursed collectors. But for every pre-empted field there are a score of others in which the collector can operate without competition that is likely to be serious enough to elevate prices beyond his reach. There is one rule, of course, that every book-collector, for his soul's comfort, should apply to himself, regardless of the quantity of time, thought, and money he is able to devote to his pursuit: he should acquire only those books in the subject matter of which he has a definite personal interest.

Local history, local biography, local imprints, offer a whole combination of fields to which the beginner can devote his attention and which will repay him rich rewards of interest the further he progresses — and local can here be interpreted as including one's immediate community, a county, a state, or a geographical division. The bookseller himself occasionally forms collections of this sort which, from trifling beginnings, grow by their very bulk into impressive and valuable assemblages of printed material. He carefully sets aside, say, everything that comes to his hands relating to Arkansas — books, pamphlets, leaflets, broadsides, an occasional old newspaper — regardless of its intrinsic importance or lack of it; bank statements, dance cards, school graduation programs, reports of any and all sorts of organizations, the lesser with the greater; anything, however apparently trifling, of Arkansas origin or interest; and by the time he has garnered a thousand pieces, he has a collection which cost him (and was worth, unit by unit) virtually nothing, but which he has little difficulty in marketing.

Collecting books relating to one's trade or profession is a wholly fascinating pursuit. Some of the best and most extensive libraries on hairdressing have been assembled by barbers. A bank president's collection includes a presentation copy of Alexander Hamilton's first report as Secretary of the Treasury (1790), an excessively rare pamphlet. Physicians and surgeons are among the most indefatigable of acquirers. An inclusive collection of non-medical books by American doctors would embrace many hundreds of volumes. Even the most technical of medical books frequently have a high romantic interest. Let the medical collector attempt, for example (the search may require many years), to secure a copy of William Beaumont's *Experiments and Observations on the Gastric Juice and the Physiology of Digestion*, which the author published at his own expense in an edition of a thousand copies at Plattsburg, New York, in 1833. Victor E. Vaughan says of it in the *Dictionary of American Biography*: 'The paper was poor; the illustrations were crude; typographical errors were many; but the contents constituted the greatest contribution ever made to the knowledge of gastric digestion.' All honor to William Beaumont; some honor, at least, to his most famous if occasionally intractable patient, Alexis St. Martin, into whose stomach an aperture was made by the accidental discharge of a gun, permitting Beaumont to study the digestive processes as physician had never had opportunity of doing before.

Members of social, civic, and fraternal organizations (there is a collector in Pittsburgh who gathers books written by members of Phi Delta Theta) who attempt to assemble libraries relating to their specific interests will be astonished at the ease with which the start is made. Not long thereafter they will be equally amazed at the difficulty of securing certain mildly elusive items; next they will become coldly infuriated at the apparent impossibility of laying hands on a tiny cluster of desiderata (all of which, with perhaps two or three exceptions, they will ultimately own); come weal, come woe, they will be enslaved forever, to their durable delight and dissatisfaction. They can split their hobbies into innumerable re-sections, lengthwise and crosswise; they can define the field as narrowly as they choose; yet they will never be able to encompass it, nor will they ever cease from trying. Nor ought they.

To attempt to list the departments open to the collector would be to attempt the impossible; to attempt a large fraction of them would be to bore the reader to utter tediousness (for it is part and parcel of the collecting tradition that one's own hobby is the only hobby, and that all others' hobbies are bilge and tosh). Anyone who is catholic enough in his views to be capable of enjoying a reasonably broad conspectus of the collecting panorama will find it in *Private Book Collectors in the United States and Canada With Mention of Their Hobbies*, an occasional manual issued at New York which is much consulted by the bookseller. From this convenient compilation, and from consultations with the book trade generally, one learns that plots already staked out by the collector include American transportation in all its phases (stage-coach, canal-boat, railroad, automo-bile, airplane; try, for instance, to obtain a copy of *Lindbergh's Own Story of His New York–Paris Flight*, a pamphlet issued by the *New York Times* in 1927 that antedated *We* by a month — a veritable Columbus letter of aerial navigation); books by or biographies of the alumni of a certain school or college; sports and games, preferably one at a time, which permits plenty of excitement (let the devotee of baseball try to assemble a set of the *Guides* of the seventies); American archæology, anthropology, and ethnology (here again the collector will do well to circumscribe his field, at least at the outset); poetry by periods or localities; anthologies of American poetry, general or local (the localized anthology flourished mightily during the middle third of the nineteenth century); American art (a vast area with much neglected acreage, as, for example, the rise and fall of magazine illustrating); first American editions of English classics (whether, for instance, the earliest separate American edition of Keats — New York, 1846 — should be designated 'Keat's Poems' or 'Keats's Poems' on the shelfback is not so easily determined as might appear); American caricature, by persons or by periods; early American cookery (where, for example, will one find the earliest reference in print to chicken à la King?); the literature of American songs, from the aboriginal to Irving Berlin, and the first appearances of the songs themselves (witness the matchless Stephen Collins Foster collection of J. K. Lilly at Foster Hall, Indianapolis); the history of special immigrant groups (and remember that even the Lowells and the Cabots were once immigrants) and of their contribution to American culture; the history of great social, political, and economic movements (slavery, free silver, prohibition); the Atlantic telegraph; the telephone; radio; lighthouses; the United States Navy and the American merchant marine (President Roosevelt is the ranking exponent of this department of collecting activity); crime (all-embracing or limited to a single group of manifestants, such as the James brothers);

tobacco; boundary disputes between the States; playing cards (consider the potentialities of a collection devoted to poker alone); the Negro, his songs and his folklore; the thousand and one collecting trails marked by the story of the American Indian; books by Presidents of the United States; witchcraft and related delusions; Confederate imprints; the history of romantic community ventures (Oneida, New Harmony, the Shaker settlements); the development of a specific religious denomination; Mormonism; Christian Science; early American schoolbooks, as a group, or, better, as a start, by a special subject; military art and science (again, as a start, the literature of a particular campaign, or books by or about a great military leader, from Myles Standish to John J. Pershing); American Christmas booklets, from John Greenleaf Whittier to A. Edward Newton.

The collector of things is by that token all but compelled (a not disagreeable compulsion) to collect books about them. The literature of coins and stamps is formidable; there is an abundance of printed material concerning antiques, both in general and by particular groups (furniture, firearms, glass, china, prints, all the handicrafts). Bookplate collectors, also, will find the pursuit of their hobby a haphazard and uninformed endeavor unless they are guided by the *Bibliography of Bookplate Literature* edited by George W. Fuller and compiled by Verna B. Grimm (Spokane, 1926). A collection of old but not particularly costly books containing the charming old booklabels (as distinguished from the more formal bookplate) of the late eighteenth and early nineteenth centuries would be a source of inexhaustible interest.

What sort of books a book-collector collects is de-

termined by sundry considerations, but chief of these,
as has been said before (it is worth stating again),
must be the intimate desirability to the collector of
the collected books. Lacking this impulse, his whole
impulse becomes pointless and void, a mere bootless
attempt to keep up with the Joneses — the Herschel
V. Joneses and the Huntingtons and the Brinleys and
the Wakemans and the Quinns and the Newtons.

But the desirability of the collected book is only
the *primum mobile* of the enterprise. There is the
problem of the availability of the desired books —
are there copies to be had for love or money, and if
for money, how much?

The collector must want the books, he must be
able to afford them, and — Point Three — he must
be able to house them. For of equal importance with
desirability and possessibility is mass — the sheer
physical bulk of the material which is the concretion
of the will to own. The collector who inhabits a shal-
low hall bedroom need not on that account alone be
deterred from sheltering all the essential items in a
set of the first editions of Charles Brockden Brown,
but the denizen of a Newport villa would think at
least twice, however strong the urge, before he began
assembling an impressive collection of Lincolniana.
There would doubtless be more collectors of books and
pamphlets relating to the Civil War if that struggle
had not produced (and been produced by) so vast a
cataract of printed material. And what is true of the
Civil War is true in far more striking degree of the
World War, even if one reduce the gross tonnage of
its typography to a mere fraction of what it might be
by limiting one's activities to the American participa-
tion.

World War material will one day be eagerly sought

227

by the collector — indeed, when one considers such a remarkable collection as the Hoover War Library at Stanford University, one has definite assurance that from an institutional point of view at least that day is already here. The individual World War collector, assuming that he does not have a storage warehouse at his disposal, will for his own convenience limit himself to some special phase of the business — American fiction with a war background, soldier-produced verse, soldier-edited periodicals, sheet music, Y.M.C.A.-ana, the various issues of the Treaty of Versailles, the personal narratives of privates and/or generals, the pro and con of specific controversies (as the taking of Montfaucon and Grand-Pré), espionage and counter-espionage, the activities of the various technical arms, the art of camouflage by land and sea, histories of combat organizations.

Each of these pursuits, or of a hundred others that might be named, has its romance and its fascinations. The assembler of organization histories, for instance, may seek during diligent years before he acquires copies of such casual overseas productions as *102nd [Ammunition Train] Yesterday, To-day and To-morrow* (Laval, L. Barnéoud et Cie.); *History of the 311th Infantry*, published at Flavigny-sur-Ozerain (Côte-d'Or) with the imprint of J. Delorme, of Dijon; *History of the Fifth Division*, printed at Luxembourg by Joseph Origer; *The Story of the Sixteenth Infantry in France* and the chronicle of its brigade-mate, *The Twenty-sixth Infantry in France*, both with the imprint of Martin Flock, Montabaur-Frankfurt o. M.; *Commendations of Second Division American Expeditionary Forces, France 1917–1919 Germany*, published at Cologne, by whom is not specified in the pamphlet; *The Second Division [:] Syllabi of the Histories of Reg-*

iments and Separate Organizations, with the imprint of the *Coblenzer Volkszeitung; Company 'M' 356th Infantry 89th Division Camp Funston, Kansas to Schweich,Germany,* printed by Gebrüder Koch at Trier. All of these are dated 1919, or, if undated, are 1919 nevertheless, for at the beginning of that anticlimactic year the A.E.F., having made history, was settling down to the writing of it. Many units, of course, waited until they were home again; some are still waiting. But many, wisely, would not wait; they set these matters down while the memory of them was hot — and the worth of definitive histories is not impaired by the quantity of comparative trivia that has gone before.

Yet even if these ephemera were of no historical value (and it is easy to underestimate their historical value), sentimentally they are of superlative importance, and sentiment is the basis of book-collecting. They were produced, many of them, in the enemy's country during the Allied occupation — produced by technically hostile printers who were themselves freshly demobilized (lending them an advantage over the occupiers which may have partially compensated for the occupation), by printers who may well have borne scars recently given them by their new customers, who set strange copy in a strange tongue, and printed on *ersatz* paper that began to crumble a few weeks later, and the durability of which has not been augmented in the intervening years. They were produced, too, these tabloid narratives, so very close to the birthplace of printing from movable types that there is about them a kind of postponed incunabularian interest. If only the Mainz instead of the Coblenz bridgehead had been assigned to the Third American Army, then certainly a memorable cluster of A.E.F.

unit histories would have been handed down to posterity with the imprint of the home town of Master Gutenberg himself.

If he collects by author rather than by subject, the beginner is likely to find a greater abundance of bibliographical assistance at his service. There are three kinds of bibliographies: good, bad, and indifferent. The indifferent far outnumber the good and the bad — (this is a hazy generalization but a safe one, based on the expectation of error in any sublunar enterprise). But indifferent bibliographies enjoy one advantage which many indifferent undertakings do not — they are better than none. Even the bad bibliographies are better than none, unless they are utterly, irretrievably, and irremediably bad. It is the other side absurdity for a bad bibliography to be wholly wrong. And it is a little further the other side absurdity for a good bibliography to be wholly right.

The bibliographer's trinity of requisites for his task are a modicum (at least) of knowledge of the mechanics of book production, familiarity with his special subject, and some measure of enthusiasm for that subject. This enthusiasm need not amount to blind or even one-eyed adoration. A bookseller, for instance, can hardly afford, for his own good and for his worth as a public benefactor, to bow down to a single god, yet booksellers have produced some of the most serviceable bibliographies that are available to the rapt devotee. The reason behind the badness of much bad bibliography is that many bibliographers bring to their task only the last of the three requisites, and if one requisite must be dispensed with, the last is the one. There was recently issued a 'bibliography' of a living English author, the compiler of which marveled at the signature marks which he found at regular intervals throughout the text (he even failed to notice that they occurred at regular intervals). Doctors, lawyers, motorists, and peddlers must have licenses; firemen, policemen, letter-carriers, soldiers, sailors, and marines must pass certain examinations. But bibliographers do not have to be licensed or to undergo examinations. Paper, pen, ink, access to a few books, and the itch to be at it — these sometimes are the sole weapons in their armories, and therewith, paradoxically, they can often inflict greater havoc than if they were properly accoutered.

A bibliography, moreover, is likely to be accurate and serviceable according to the intelligent measure by which the compiler plans it with a certain clearly defined audience in view. That audience, in perfect instances, should be broad enough to include the student (casual or concentrated), the librarian, the collector, and the bookseller. The two last may be on different sides of the fence, but it is the same fence. The collector as collector (to distinguish him from the collector as reader) is interested in externals, in the romantic husks of books. He already knows, or should know, their withins, and he consults his bibliography in order to know their withouts.

It is safe to venture another generalization: that the utility of a bibliography is likely to increase according to the breadth of its plan. The bibliography designed purely for the collector is apt to be the poorer bibliography. It is not quite so safe to carry this premise to its logical conclusion; namely, that the closer a bibliography approaches serviceability to a general audience, the better bibliography it should be. Yet it would be possible to cite excellent bibliographies that are books to be read as much as they are books to be consulted.

231

Any properly compiled bibliography offers a superb conspectus of the development of the fledgling scribbler into an authentic spokesman of his day or of all days — offers a more significant, comprehensive, and comprehensible panorama of his growth than does the most ample and painstaking biography. A glance through Evans presents a lightning-flash survey of the cultural growth of America to the end of Washington's Presidency. The curious posthumous odysseys of Thoreau's manuscripts transcend in romantic interest any chronicle of the external incidents of his life, and any Thoreau biographer who goes into the story must thereby innocently encroach on a field already properly pre-empted by Francis H. Allen's bibliography. A good bibliography is itself a biography — not merely a birth-record of books, but a life-history of books that have put on immortality.

Collecting tastes are continually shifting and evolving, a fact due partly to an unfortunate and uninspired (as well as uninspiring) tendency on the part of some collectors to follow the pack regardless of where it is heading, and partly to a wholly rational reappraisal of literary values from one generation to another. In his invaluable *History of American Magazines*, already heavily consulted, Frank Luther Mott reproduces an engraved frontispiece showing nine 'Eminent Living American Poets' which accompanied the issue of the *New-York Mirror* for January 26, 1828. Eight small portraits enclose a larger portrait; the eight small portraits depict William Cullen Bryant, Fitz-Greene Halleck, Edward C. Pinckney, Charles Sprague, James G. Brooks, John Pierpont, Washington Irving, and Samuel Woodworth. The central representation — the pre-

sumed cynosure of every eye — is of James Gates
Percival. Bryant's eminence is not to be disputed;
Halleck, Pierpont, and Woodworth wrote each at least
one set of verses which posterity has not forgotten
(though posterity may not generally link the verses
with the authors' names); Pinckney, Sprague,
Brooks, Irving (as poet), and Percival had their day
and ceased to be. A similar grouping of the contemporary great at any period of a nation's literary
development (including the present) must in later
years display a similar apparent critical unsoundness.
Hindsight is never compelled to yield a single round
to foresight.

Ten years earlier, in the *North American Review* for
July, 1818, Bryant himself had discussed the past and
present states of American poetry. In this survey, as
John Bigelow summarizes it, 'he passes in review all
the writers of verse on this side of the Atlantic who
had yet ventured into print, save some "whose passage to that oblivion, towards which, to the honor of
our country they were hastening," he did not wish to
interrupt.' The poets 'whose passage to oblivion he
thought worthy of being interrupted, though [adds
Bigelow] at this day it is not so easy to see why,' included John Adams (not the President), Joseph
Green, Francis Hopkinson, Benjamin Church, Philip
Freneau, John Trumbull, Timothy Dwight, Joel
Barlow, David Humphreys, Lemuel Hopkins, William
Clifton, St. John Honeywood, and Robert Treat
Paine. 'At this day,' when Bigelow wrote, meant
1889; Freneau's fame has since taken on a touch of
fresh luster; so may one day the fame of the others —
certainly no man living or yet to live will dare say it
never shall.

Glance now for a moment at the other end of the

nineteenth century. The equivalent of several generations in the metamorphosis of collecting tastes and
in the multiplication of collectors has elapsed since
P. K. Foley's *American Authors, 1795–1895; A Bibliography of First and Notable Editions Chronologically
Arranged With Notes* was issued (Boston, 1897). The
passage of another like interval, with heaven knows
what evolution and involvement in the collecting
panorama, will still find this modest manual within
ready reach of the bookseller's hand, and on the
shelves of those shrewd amateurs for whom any copies may be left over.

The book-collector of 1897 had not yet discovered
Ambrose Bierce, on the one hand, or, on the distant
other, Emily Dickinson. There was, to be sure,
reason enough for this lack of discernment in instances
where there was as yet little to discern. *The Education of Henry Adams* was not to be issued until 1907,
and even then its circulation was to be restricted, for
eleven years more, to a small and fortunate group of
the author's friends; Stephen Crane was riding the
tide as a best-seller, as little aware of his impending
eminence as James Abbott McNeill Whistler was con-
vinced of his; readers of the *Century* and *Harper's* bestowed passing glances of appreciation on the drawings of Howard Pyle without realizing that the level
of the art of illustrating in America was rising to a
new plane of accomplishment before their eyes.

But the bibliophile of the McKinley epoch did,
apparently, devote some attention to the work of, and
presumably exert a modicum of his purchasing power
toward the acquisition of books by Henry Abbey,
Oscar Fay Adams, John Albee, William Livingston
Alden, Anne Reeve Aldrich, Thomas Gold Appleton, George Arnold, Jane Goodwin Austin, Maturin

Murray Ballou, George Bancroft, John Bartlett, John Russell Bartlett, Arlo Bates, Park Benjamin, S. G. W. Benjamin, William Henry Bishop, Gertrude Bloede, Frank Bolles, H. H. Boyesen, Charles Frederick Briggs, Charles Astor Bristed, Charles Timothy Brooks, Maria Brooks, John Brougham, Henry Howard Brownell, Daniel Bryan, William Henry Burleigh, and Edwin Lassiter Bynner. The list could be extended to appalling length, but this hand-picked selection from the A's and B's gives abundant indication of what one may expect to find, and does find, in the C's, the L's, the R's, and the W's. Mr. Foley's goal properly was inclusiveness; there were doubtless contemporary American purchasers of *American Authors* who wondered who Herman Melville might be — he came between Grenville Mellen and George Henry Miles.

It will not do to dismiss casually the Abbeys and the Albees and the Appletons, the Bishops and the Bloedes and the Bristeds. Some of them may never have merited collecting, some may never be collected again, some as certainly one day will be. Some of them were universally read in their own time and have left a permanent but anonymous imprint on American thought, some of them wrote books that were standard for half a century, not a few wrote books that are still in print, and at least one or two produced that which is likely to be in print forever.

Three hundred and fourteen authors are listed in Foley. The A's and B's total forty-eight, of whom twenty-eight are cited above as authors for whose first editions there is now a minimum demand (to put the case at its most sanguine). Assuming that this proportion holds throughout the bibliography, one hundred and eighty-odd of Mr. Foley's grand total are in like situation.

The purpose of this bandying of statistics has been rather to point a moral than to adorn a tale. The simple fact that many of these writers are now neglected by reader and collector alike gives the new collector (and the old as well) a golden opportunity to investigate for himself and to determine whether the neglect is merited. An abundance of biographical and critical references are available; a little exploration will uncover a few titles for the student's examination (although in general the first editions of an uncollected author are apt to be harder to find than those of a collected author), and there is always the possibility that some rich vein of delight will be uncovered that will well repay the explorer's search and justify (to himself at least, which means complete justification) his status as a collector. And let him remember that the collector has many times been the pioneer in the rehabilitation of a literary reputation.

Such an exploration holds two practical allurements. It is not likely to be formidably expensive, and yet it has all the compensating difficulty that makes both rocky and roseate the path of him who seeks, say, for first editions of Edgar Allan Poe. Take, for example, from the above list, George Bancroft. Born within a year after the death of Washington, Bancroft survived into the Presidency of Benjamin Harrison. His productive period covered sixty-two years, from his *Poems* of 1823 to a sketch of Martin Van Buren issued in 1889, two years before Bancroft's death. Half a dozen school texts which Bancroft edited or translated in his early years are probably next to impossible to find in first edition. His *History of the United States* in ten volumes covers a creative span

236

which far exceeds that of any comparable performance. Gibbon projected his *Decline and Fall of the Roman Empire* in 1764; the first volume was published in 1776 and the fourth and last in 1788. Macaulay began his studies for his *History of England* in 1839; the first two volumes appeared in 1848, and the fifth was issued posthumously in 1881. But the first volume of Bancroft's history was published in 1834 and the tenth and last in 1875 — and when the collector has assembled a set, he can leave room beside it (the vacancy is likely to persist for some time) for one of the fifty copies of the large-paper edition which appeared between 1861 and 1875. Acquisition of a copy of the large-paper issue (also in fifty copies) of the *Memorial Address on the Life and Character of Abraham Lincoln* (Washington, 1866) is also likely to cause some embarrassment, for here the Bancroft enthusiast — and by this time our hypothetical collector will certainly have become one — must cross the trail of the Lincoln specialist; and where collecting trails cross, there irresistible forces meet immovable bodies, and gnashing of teeth ensues.

Foley's *American Authors* is itself today none too easy of acquisition. This condition, fortunately, is not yet true of Merle Johnson's *American First Editions*, published at New York in 1932 in an edition of a thousand copies, although these were quickly exhausted. *American First Editions* gives bibliographic check-lists of one hundred and forty-six authors, and while some of these inevitably duplicate Foley (plus, where it has become available, later information), attention is paid both to later writers, of whom some were not born when the Foley manual appeared, and to some of the earliest.

Among the youngest authors listed in *American*

First Editions are Stephen Vincent Benét and Ernest Hemingway. Both were born in 1898. That was the year, as more ancient readers of these notes will recall, of the *Maine* disaster and the War with Spain (an episode, by the way, to which the book-collector has not paid the attention it deserves). For purposes of the present discussion, however, the War with Spain can hardly be regarded as early, though it may so appear to Mr. Benét and Mr. Hemingway. A thousand years hence, the ordered distortion of perspective may lump the whole panorama, and Ernest Hemingway, Stephen Vincent Benét, Anne Bradstreet, and Michael Wigglesworth, plus Stephen Daye and Bruce Rogers, will perchance be mentioned together in the introductory chapter of the definitive chronicle of early American printing and early American books.

THE END

INDEX

INDEX

Abbey, Henry, 234
Abbey, James, 214
An Act for Making... Bills of Publick Credit, 39
An Act for raising Six Thousand Pounds, 57
An Act to Incorporate the City of Chicago, 170
Adams, Henry, 234
Adams, James, 63
Adams, John, 233
Adams, Oscar Fay, 234
Addison, Joseph, 115
The Advantages and Disadvantages of the Marriage State, 48
Aitken, Jane, 121
Aitken, Robert, 118 ff.
Alabama, earliest printing in, 162
Albee, John, 234
Alcuin (Brown), 154
Alden, William Livingston, 234
Aldrich, Anne Reeve, 234
Aldrich, Lorenzo D., 214
Alideo, Cardinal Pedro, 20
Allen, Francis H., 232
Allen, Paul, 154
Allibone, S. Austin, 196
Almanacs, 27, 41, 42, 51, 52, 64, 66, 67, 83 ff.
Alta California, 208
American Antiquarian Society, 107, 109
American Authors, 1795–1895 (Foley), 234
American Bibliography (Evans), 43, 63, 65
American Book-Prices Current, 219, 220
American Broadside Verse (Winslow), 145
The American Collector, 104

American First Editions (Johnson), 237
The American Instructor, 100
The American Jest Book, 166
American Legion, 111
The American Magazine, 113, 114
The American Magazine and Historical Chronicle, 115, 122
The American Magazine and Monthly Chronicle, 115
The American Magazine, or General Repository, 123
American Museum, 165
American Poems (ed. Smith), 148
American Publishers' Circular, 173
American Publishing Company, 40
The American Querist (Cooper?), 103
The American Singing Book (Reed), 48
American Verse, 1625–1807 (Otis), 149
The American Village (Freneau), 146
American Weekly Mercury, 94
The Americans Roused, 103
Ames, Nathaniel, 64, 67
Analectic Magazine, 182, 183
Androborus (Hunter), 157
Annuals, 202
Appleton, Thomas Gold, 234
Apthorp, Frances, 151
Armbruster, Gotthard, 86
Arnold, George, 234
Arthur Mervyn (Brown), 154
The Association of the Delegates... Versified, 103
Astronomical Diary (Ames), 64
Atkins, Samuel, 52 ff., 175
Atlantic Souvenir, 202
Austen, Jane, 196

241

Austin, Jane Goodwin, 234
Autobiography (Franklin), 89, 133

A Bag of Nuts, Ready cracked, 109
Bailey, Francis, 147
Ballou, Maturin Murray, 234, 235
Bancroft, George, 235 ff.
Barlow, Joel, 143, 233
Barlow, S. L. M., 21
Barlow, William, 15
Bartlett, John, 235
Bartlett, John Russell, 235
Baseball Guides, 225
Bates, Albert Carlos, 46 ff.
Bates, Arlo, 235
Bay, Jacob, 130
Bay Psalm Book, 28 ff., 45, 118, 201
Beaumont, William, 223
The Beauties of Poetry (ed. Carey), 166
Becker, Carl L., 85
The Beginnings of Printing in Utah (McMurtrie), 60
Behaim, Martin, 13
Beissel, Conrad, 83
Belknap, Jeremy, 123, 124
Bell, Robert, 120
Bellamy, Joseph, 65
Be Merry and Wise, 109
Ben-Hur (Wallace), 17
Benét, Stephen Vincent, 238
Benjamin, Park, 235
Benjamin, S. G. W., 235
Berlin, Irving, 225
Beste, George, 14
Bible in English (Aitken), 36, 59, 120, 121, 221
Bible in English (Bradford proposal), 58
Bible in English (Douai version), 166
Bible in English (King James version), 221
Bible in German (Sauer), 36, 131
Bible in Indian (tr. Eliot), 34 ff.
Bible in Latin (Gutenberg), 3, 5, 6

Bibliographical Society of America, 46
Bibliography of American Newspapers (Brigham), 108
Bibliography of Bookplate Literature (Fuller and Grimm), 226
Bibliography of the History of California (Cowan), 206
Bibliography of the Spanish Press of California (Cowan), 206
Biblioteca Ambrosiana (Milan), 9
Bibliotheca Americana Vetustissima (Harrisse), 21
Bibliothecae Americanae Primordia (Kennett), 19
Bibliothèque Royale (Brussels), 10
Bierce, Ambrose, 234
Bigelow, John, 190, 191, 233
Biglow, William, 116, 117
Biographical Sketches of Loyalists (Sabine), 102
Biography of James Lawrence (Irving), 183 ff.
Bishop, William Henry, 235
Blackburn, Philip C., 175, 184, 199
Blackstone, Sir William, 108
Blair, Hugh, 166
Bland, Harry MacNeill, 184
Bleyer, Willard Grosvenor, 93, 96
Bloede, Gertrude, 235
Blow at the Root of Antinomianism (Bellamy), 66
Böhm, Johannes, 86
Bolles, Frank, 235
Book of Lawes and Liberties, 33
Books and Bidders (Rosenbach), 219
Boston, early printing in, 33
Boston Gazette, 94
Boston Magazine, 123
Boston News-Letter, 93, 94
Bowles, Samuel, 135
Bowtell, Samuel, 137
Boydell, James, 65
Boyesen, H. H., 235
Boynton, Henry Walcott, 194, 198
Brackenridge, Hugh Henry, 146, 152, 153, 157

Bradbury, John, 167, 168
Bradford, Andrew, 76, 77, 94 ff., 113, 114
Bradford, Fielding, 162
Bradford, John, 162
Bradford, Thomas G., 162
Bradford, William, 50 ff., 62, 76, 77, 94, 95, 115, 127, 157
Bradsher, E. L., 166
Bradstreet, Anne, 137, 138, 140, 238
Brandt, Sebastian, 13
Brannan, Samuel, 208
Braud, Denis, 164
Briefe and True Report of Virginia (Hariot), 14
Briggs, Charles Frederick, 235
Briggs, Samuel, 67
Brigham, Clarence S., 108
Brinley, George, 21, 29
Bristed, Charles Astor, 235
The British Prison-Ship (Freneau), 147
Bronson, Walter C., 177
Brooker, William, 94
Brooks, Charles Timothy, 235
Brooks, James G., 232, 233
Brooks, Maria, 235
The Brother's Gift, 109
Brougham, John, 235
Brown, Charles Brockden, 154, 178, 227
Brown, John Carter, 21
Brown, Nicholas, 177
Brown, William Hill, 151
Brown University, 22, 177
Brownell, Henry Howard, 235
Bryan, Daniel, 235
Bryant, Dr. Peter, 189 ff.
Bryant, William Cullen, 146, 189 ff., 204, 232, 233
Buckingham, Joseph T., 106, 117
Buell, Abel, 129, 130, 132
Bulletin of the New York Public Library, 175, 184
Burleigh, William Henry, 235
Byles, Mather, 143

Bynner, Edwin Lassiter, 235

Caines, George, 179
Caleb Williams (Godwin), 154
Calhoun, John, 169
California, earliest printing in, 206
California. A Trip Across the Plains (Abbey), 214
California Imprints (Wagner), 208
California in 1850 (Street), 215
California Star, 208
California State Library, 208
Californian, 207, 208
Cambridge, early printing in, 25 ff.
Cambridge History of American Literature, 137, 149, 153
Cambridge University, 41
Campbell, John, 93, 94
Campbell, Thomas, 181
Campbell, William J., 73, 81, 87, 89
A Candid Examination (Galloway), 102
Capital Lawes (of Massachusetts), 33
Carey, Mathew, 123, 165 ff.
Carriers' addresses, 68
Castell, William, 15
A Catalogue of Books Relating ... to America (Rich), 19
Cato Major (tr. Logan), 86
Cato's Moral Distichs (tr. Logan), 86
Caxton, William, 4
Centinel of the North-Western Territory, 163
Century Magazine, 234
A Century of Printing ... in Pennsylvania (Hildeburn), 52
Champlain, Samuel de, 14
Chandler, Thomas B., 102
Charge to the Grand Jury (Gooch), 62
Charles II, 36, 50, 51
Charless, Joseph, 165, 167
Charleston, first printing in, 62
Charlotte (Rowson), 151, 152

243

Charlotte's Daughter (Rowson), 152
Chattin, James, 38
Chicago, earliest printing in, 168 ff.
Chicago American, 169
Chicago Democrat, 169, 172
Chicago Historical Society, 170
Child, Andrew, 215
Church, Benjamin, 233
Church, E. Dwight, 22
Cicero, Marcus Tullius, 86
Cincinnati, earliest printing in, 163
Clara Howard (Brown), 154
Clark, Captain William, 214
Claypoole, David C., 110
Clemens, Samuel Langhorne, 40, 208
Clifton, William, 233
The Cloister and the Hearth (Reade), 4
Club of Odd Volumes, 140
Cole, George Watson, 22
The Collection of Franklin Imprints... of the Curtis Publishing Company (Campbell), 72, 77, 87
Collins, John, 76
The Colonial Mind (Parrington), 66
The Colonial Printer (Wroth), 66, 128
Colophon, 176, 208, 221
Colton, Walter, 207
The Columbiad (Barlow), 144
Columbian Magazine, 123, 154, 165
Columbus, Christopher, 3, 6 ff., 15, 17, 20, 212
Commendations of Second Division, 228
Commentaries (Blackstone), 108
Common Sense (Paine), 120
Company 'M' 356th Infantry, 229
The Compleat Angler (Walton), 136
Compleat Body of Divinity (Willard), 44
A Complete Guide for the Management of Bees, 108
The Complete Housewife, 100
Complete Letter Writer (Dilworth), 65

Confession of Faith. *See* Saybrook Platform
Conflagration (Byles), 143
Conley, Phil, 164
Connecticut, first printing in, 39
The Contrast (Tyler), 157
Cooper, James Fenimore, 194 ff.
Cooper, Myles, 103
Cooper, William, 195
The Coquette (Foster), 151
Cosby, William, 96
Cosmographiae Introductio (Waldseemüller), 2, 3, 212
Cowan, Robert Ernest, 206
Cowan, Robert Grannis, 206
Crane, Stephen, 198, 234
Cuneo Press, 170
Curiosities of Common Water, 77
Cyclopædia of American Literature (Duyckinck), 150

Dana, Richard Henry, 175, 180, 192, 204
Dana, Richard Henry, Jr., 204, 205, 208
Davis, James, 63
Davis, T. O., 169, 170
Davos-Platz press (Stevenson-Osbourne), 87
The Day of Doom (Wigglesworth), 141
Daye, Stephen, 26 ff., 131, 173, 217, 238
Deane, Samuel, 108
Deare, Lewis, 185
De Bry, Theodor, 14, 212
Decades (Martyr), 14
Declaration of Reasons... in the Province of Maryland, 62
Defoe, Daniel, 69
De Lancey, Susan, 196
Delaware, first printing in, 63
De Pons, F. R. J., 179
A Description of New England (Smith), 12
Detroit, first printing in, 168
Dickens, Charles, 187

Dickinson, Emily, 234
Dictionary of American Biography, 57, 85, 97, 154, 223
Dictionary of Authors (Allibone), 196
A Dictionary of Books Relating to America (Sabin), 23, 24, 46
Dilworth, W. H., 65
A Dissertation on Liberty and Necessity (Franklin), 79
Dockrill, Joseph, 208
The Doctrine of Absolute Reprobation Refuted, 77
Doolittle, Isaac, 132
The Dreadful Visitation of the Plague (Defoe), 68, 69
Duncan, Matthew, 168
Dunlap, John, 110, 150
Dunlap Society, 157
Dunlap, William, 154 ff.
Dunn, William, 209
Duyckinck, Evert A., 150
Duyckinck, George L., 150
Dwight, Timothy, 233
Dying Speech of Bristol, a Negro Boy, 67

Eames, Wilberforce, 29, 57
Early American Fiction (Wegelin), 153
Early American Plays (Wegelin), 156, 157
Early American Poetry (Wegelin), 141, 149
East-Florida Gazette, 164
Edgar Huntly (Brown), 154
Edgeworth, Maria, 196
The Education of Henry Adams, 234
Eliot, John, 28, 34 ff.
Elizabeth, Queen, 12
Ellis, Albert G., 172
Ellis, John Harvard, 138
Ellis, Milton, 151
The Embargo (Bryant), 190, 191
Emerson, Ralph Waldo, 203
An Englishman's Answer (Lind), 102

Engraving, earliest in British America, 118
Entertainment for a Winter's Evening (Green), 143
Evans, Charles, 43 ff., 63, 65, 232
Evans, David, 88
Everett, Alexander H., 20
Every Man His Own Lawyer, 100
Experiments on the Gastric Juice (Beaumont), 223

A Faithful Narrative of Elizabeth Wilson, 48
The Family Female Physician, 108
Fanshawe (Hawthorne), 201
Farmer's Library, 163
The Father (Dunlap), 158
Faulkner, William, 208 ff.
The Federalist, 146
Fenner, Mary, 41
Fenning, David, 42
Field, Robert, 159
Figueroa, José, 206, 207
The First Printers of Chicago (McMurtrie), 170
The First Year of Printing in New York (Eames), 57
Florida, first printing in, 164
The Flourishing State of Pennsylvania (Holme), 58, 127
Foley, P. K., 234 ff.
Folger, Henry Clay, 142
Folger, Peter, 142
Ford, Paul Leicester, 73, 84, 100, 167
Forget-me-not, 202
Foster, Hannah Webster, 151
Foster, John, 118, 138
Foster, Stephen Collins, 225
Fowle, Daniel, 41, 42, 62, 105
Fowle, Zechariah, 105
Fox, Justus, 130
Franklin, Anne, 41
Franklin, Benjamin, 40, 61, 62, 70 ff., 113, 114, 119, 165
Franklin, James, 40, 62, 72 ff., 94, 132

Franklin, Josiah, 70 ff.
Franklin, William Temple, 89
Franklin and His Press at Passy (Livingston), 87
The Freeman's Oath, 25, 217
Freer, Samuel, 111
Freer, Samuel S., 111
Freneau, Philip, 146 ff., 233
A Friendly Check from a Kind Relation, 74
Frobisher, Martin, 14
Fuller, George W., 226

Gaine, Hugh, 65, 99 ff., 134, 147
Gaine, John, 36
Galloway, Joseph, 102, 132
Gavin, Mrs. Michael, 184
Gavit, Joseph, 112
Gay, Ebenezer, 48
General Magazine and Historical Chronicle, 114
The Gentleman from Indiana (Tarkington), 32
Georgia, first printing in, 63
Gesamtcatalog der Wiegendrucke, 5
Gibbon, Edward, 136, 237
Glover, Jose, 25, 26, 34, 41
Goad-Ballinger Post, American Legion, 111
Goddard, Mary Katherine, 133
Goddard, William, 41, 65, 132 ff.
Godey's Lady's Book, 117
Godfrey, Thomas, 84
Godwin, William, 154
Gooch, William, 62
Good Newes from New England (Winslow), 143
Goodall, Baptist, 15
Goodrich, S. G., 148, 200 ff.
Graham's Magazine, 117
Grands Voyages (De Bry), 14
Green, Bartholomew, 39, 94
Green, Joseph, 143, 233
Green, Samuel, 35, 40, 130
Green, Thomas, 39, 40, 130
Green, Timothy, 37, 39, 47, 130
Green Bay Intelligencer, 172

Gridley, Jeremiah, 115
Grimm, Verna B., 226
Grolier Club, 87, 128
Gutenberg, Johann, 3, 4, 230

Hakluyt, Richard, 11, 12, 212
Hall, David, 86
Halleck, Fitz-Greene, 232, 233
Hamilton, Alexander, 97, 103, 148, 223
Harding, George L., 208
Hariot, Thomas, 14
Harper's Monthly Magazine, 234
Harris, Benjamin, 37, 91 ff.
Harrison, Benjamin, 236
Harrisse, Henry, 21
Hartford, first printing in, 39
Hartford Wits, 143, 200
Harvard, John, 25
Harvard College, 25, 33, 65, 192, 194
Hawthorne, Nathaniel, 145, 154, 201 ff.
Heartman, Charles F., 38, 153
Hebrew Grammar (Sewall), 65
Hemingway, Ernest, 238
Hewitt, R. H., 215
Hildeburn, Charles P., 52, 89
Hillhouse, James A., 195
Histoire de la Nouvelle France (Lescarbot), 14
History of American Journalism (Lee), 92
History of American Literature (Tyler), 67
History of American Magazines (Mott), 121 ff., 232
History of the American Theatre (Dunlap), 158
History of the Arts of Design (Dunlap), 158
History of Brown University (Bronson), 177
History of Columbus (Irving), 20
History of the Fifth Division, 228
History of New-England (Johnson), 15

History of New Netherlands (Dunlap), 158
A History of New York... by Diedrich Knickerbocker (Irving), 181, 189
History of Printing in America (Thomas), 41, 104, 161
History of the... Quakers (Sewell), 82, 88
History of the 311th Infantry, 228
History of the United States (Bancroft), 236, 237
Der Hoch-Deutsch Pensylvanische Geschicts-Schreiben, 131
Holme, John, 58, 127
Holmes, Oliver Wendell, 203
Holmes, Thomas J., 176
Holt, Howard Judson, 140
Honeywood, St. John, 233
Hood, John B., 162
Hooped Petticoats Arraigned, 74
Hoover War Library, 228
Hopkins, Lemuel, 233
Hopkinson, 150, 233
House, E. G., 191
How, Samuel, 65
Howell, John, 206
Hudson, Frederic, 96, 99, 106, 107, 172
Humphreys, David, 233
Hunnewell, J. F., 140
Hunter, Robert, 157
Huntington, Henry E., 22
Huntington Library, 22, 37, 157
Hylacomylus, see Waldseemüller, Martin

Illinois, first printing in, 168
Incunabula, definition of, 6
Incunabula and Americana (Stillwell), 43
Indiana, first printing in, 163
Irving, Catharine, 178, 179
Irving, Peter, 179
Irving, Pierre M., 175, 178 ff.
Irving, Washington, 19, 20, 175, 177 ff., 232, 233

Irving, William, 180
The Isle of Man, 74
Ives, Brayton, 14

James the Printer, see Printer, James
Jane Talbot (Brown), 154
Jefferson, Thomas, 118, 120, 148, 189, 190
Jennings, Samuel, 56
John Calhoun Club, 56, 60
John Carter Brown Library, 31, 59
John Hammett's Vindication, 41
Johnson, Edward, 15
Johnson, Marmaduke, 35
Johnson, Merle, 237
Johnston, James, 63
Journal of... Capt. Parker H. French's Overland Expedition (Miles), 215
Journal of the Overland Route (Aldrich), 214
Journal of Travels from St. Josephs to Oregon (Root), 213, 214
Journalism in the United States (Hudson), 96, 106, 107, 172
The Journals of Hugh Gaine (Ford), 100

Kalendarium Pennsilvaniense, 51 ff., 175
Keats, John, 225
Keimer, Samuel, 60, 61, 76 ff.
Keith, Sir William, 77, 78
Keller, George, 215
Kennett, White, 18, 19
Kentucky, first printing in, 162
Kettell, Samuel, 148, 149, 191
Kimball, Harlow, 169
Kite, Nathan, 58
Klacht van Nieuw-Amsterdam (Steendam), 143
Kneeland, Samuel, 37, 66
Knickerbocker Magazine, 117
Knoxville, first printing in, 163
Kustler, Bartholomew, 10

INDEX

Langfeld, William R., 175, 183, 186
Las Casas, Bartolomé de, 7, 20
The Last of the Mohicans (Cooper), 198
Lawrence, Captain James, 183 ff.
The Laws & Acts of ... New York, 57
Lechford, Thomas, 15
Lee, James Melvin, 92
Lenox, James, 21
Lescarbot, Marc, 14
A Letter from One in the Country, 74, 77
A Letter to a Friend in Ireland, 77
Letters of Jonathan Oldstyle (Irving), 178
Lewis, Joseph, 68
Lewis, Captain Meriwether, 214
Lighthouse Tragedy (Franklin), 72
Lilly, J. K., 225
Lincoln, Abraham, 152, 184, 237
Lind, John, 102
Lindbergh's Own Story of His New York–Paris Flight, 224
A List of American Newspaper Reprints (Gavit), 112
The Literature of the Middle Western Frontier (Rusk), 168
Livingston, Luther S., 87
Logan, James, 86
Longfellow, Henry Wadsworth, 202, 203
Longworth, David, 180
A Looking Glass for the Times (Folger), 142
Lothian, Marquis of, 15
Louisiana, first printing in, 164
Louisville, first printing in, 162, 163
Lowell, James Russell, 194, 203
Lyne, James, 57
Lyon, Matthew, 162

Macaulay, Thomas Babington, 237
Mackenzie, Alexander, 214
Madison, James, 146
The Magazine in America (Tassin), 123

Main Currents in American Journalism (Bleyer), 93
Maine, first printing in, 42
The Many-Sided Franklin (Ford), 73, 74
Marshall, James Wilson, 210
Martyr, Peter, 14
Maryland, first printing in, 62
Massachusetts, early printing in, 25 ff.
The Massachusetts Magazine, 116
Mather, Cotton, 40, 64, 138, 140, 176
Mather, Increase, 40, 176
Mather, Moses, 176
Mather, Richard, 28, 31, 32, 118, 176
Mather, William G., 176
Maxwell, William, 163
McFingal (Trumbull), 143
McMurtrie, Douglas C., 56, 60, 164, 170, 174
Meat Out of the Eater (Wigglesworth), 141
Mellen, Grenville, 235
Melville, Herman, 203, 235
Memoirs of Carwin the Biloquist (Brown), 154
Memorial Address on ... Lincoln (Bancroft), 237
Mencken, H. L., 32
Merchant Freighter's Assistant (Boydell), 65
Meredith, Hugh, 81 ff.
Mexico, early printing in, 28
Michigan, first printing in, 168
Miles, George Henry, 235
Miles, William, 215
Miller, James M., 168
Miller, Samuel, 162
Mississippi, first printing in, 164
Missouri, first printing in, 161, 167
Mobile Centinel, 162
Modern Chivalry (Brackenridge), 153
Moniteur de la Louisiane, 164
The Monster of Monsters, 41

Montalboddo, Fracanzano de, 14
Monterey, first printing in, 206
The Monthly Anthology, 117
Moody, Eleazar, 42
Morrell, William, 138, 139
Morton, Sarah Wentworth, 150, 151
Mother Goose's Melody, 109
Mother Midnight's Comical Pocket-Book (Lewis), 68
Mott, Frank Luther, 121, 232
Mundus Novus, 2
    Mystische und Sehr Geheyme Sprueche (Beissel), 82

A Narrative of an Attempt ... upon the Mohaques Country, 57
Nash, John Henry, 207
Navigators Supply (Barlow), 15
New-England (Morrell), 138, 139
New-England Courant, 40, 74, 75, 94
New England Primer, 36 ff., 65
New Englands Crisis (Tompson), 140
New-England's Spirit of Persecution Transmitted to Pennsylvania, 55
New Englands Tears (Tompson), 140
New Hampshire, first printing in, 41, 42
New Haven, first printing in, 39
New Jersey, first printing in, 59 ff.
New London, first printing in, 39
New Orleans, first printing in, 164
New Set of Copies for the Use of Schools (Thorne), 65
New-Year Verses ... Pennsylvania Gazette, 68
New-Year Verses ... Pennsylvania Journal, 68
New York, first printing in, 55 ff.
New-York Gazetteer, 101
New York Historical Society, 158
New-York Loyal Gazette, 101
New-York Mercury, 99
New-York Mirror, 232
New York Printing MDCXCIII (McMurtrie), 56

New York Public Library, 9, 37, 175, 184
New York State Library, 112
New-York Weekly Journal, 96 ff.
Newbery, John, 109
Newman, Henry, 37
Newport, first printing in, 40, 41
News from the Moon, 74
News from the Stars (Newman), 37
Newspapers, early American, 91 ff.
Newton, A. Edward, 221, 226, 227
Nichols, Charles L., 110
North American Review, 117, 175, 180, 191, 192, 204, 233
North Carolina, first printing in, 63
Notes ... of a Journey Across the Plains (Hewitt), 215
Nuremberg Chronicle, 13
Nuthead, Dinah, 62
Nuthead, William, 61, 62

Ohio, first printing in, 163
The Ohio Valley Press (Thwaites), 162
102d Ammunition Train, 228
Opie, Amelia, 196, 197
Ormond (Brown), 154
Osbourne, Lloyd, 87
Oswald, Eleazer, 165, 166
Oswald, John Clyde, 78
Otis, William Bradley, 149
Overland Route to California (Child), 215
Ovid's Metamorphosis Englished (Sandys), 136

Pacific News, 208 ff.
Paesi Nouamente Retrovati (Montalboddo), 14
Paine, Robert Treat, 233
Paine, Thomas, 119, 120
Palmer, Samuel, 78
Paltsits, Victor Hugo, 57, 101, 146
Pannartz, Arnold, 4
Paper, early manufacture of in America, 58, 127 ff.
Paper money, 57, 59, 60, 87

INDEX

A Paraphrastical Exposition (Philly), 56
Parker, James, 38, 39, 41, 61, 99, 132
Parks, William, 62
Parley, Peter. *See* Goodrich, S. G.
Parrington, Vernon L., 66
Parson Weems (Wroth), 167
Passy press (Franklin), 87
Pattee, Fred Lewis, 145
Paulding, James Kirke, 180
Paullin, George W., 170
Pearson, Edmund, 68
Peary, Robert E., 171
Peddie, R. A., 59, 164
Peirce, William, 27
Pendleton, Emily, 151
Penn, William, 50
Pennsylvania, first printing in, 51 ff.
Perfect Description of Virginia, 15
Pershing, John J., 226
Peter Parley's Universal History (Hawthorne), 201
Petits Voyages (De Bry), 14
Phelps, William Lyon, 194, 197
Philadelphia, first printing in, 51 ff.
Philenia (Pendleton and Ellis), 151
Philips, Willard, 191, 192
Phillips, Eleazer, Jr., 62, 63
Philly, John, 56
Pierpont, John, 232, 233
The Pilgrim's Progress (Bunyan), 109
Pinckney, Edward C., 232, 233
Pittsburgh, first printing in, 162
Plain Dealing: or, Newes from New England (Lechford), 15
The Plains and the Rockies (Wagner), 214
Poe, Edgar Allan, 154, 187, 194, 201, 203, 236
A Poem on the Rising Glory of America (Freneau), 146
Poems (Bancroft), 236
Poems (Bryant), 193, 218
The Poems of Philip Freneau, 147

Poems Written between...1768 & 1794 (Freneau), 147
Poetical Meditations (Wolcott), 143
The Poetical Works of Thomas Campbell (ed. Irving), 181
Poole, W. F., 16
Poor Richard almanacs, 83 ff.
Poor Robin almanacs, 84
Posa, Pedro, 9
The Posthumous Papers of the Pickwick Club (Dickens), 187
Potowmac Guardian, 163
The Power of Sympathy (Brown), 150, 151
Precaution (Cooper), 197, 199
Press, earliest made in British America, 131 ff.
A Pretty Story (Hopkinson), 150
Primer of the Massachusetts Indian Language (Eliot), 34
Prince, Thomas, 30
Principall Navigations (Hakluyt), 12
Printer, James, 35
Printers (journeymen), 133 ff.
Printing: A Short History (ed. Peddie), 59, 164
Private Book Collectors in the United States, 224
Private Presses and Their Books (Ransom), 87
Providence, first printing in, 41
Publick Occurrences, 91, 92
Purchas, Samuel, 12
Pyle, Howard, 234
Pynson, Richard, 14

Ramusio, Giovanni Battista, 14
Ransom, Will, 87
Read, Deborah, 83
Reade, Charles, 4
Recollections of a Lifetime (Goodrich), 148, 200, 201
Reed, Daniel, 48
Reed, Ebenezer, 168
Relation of a Journey (Sandys), 136

INDEX

The Religion of Nature Delineated (Wollaston), 79
Revere, Paul, 117
Rhode Island, first printing in, 41
Rhode Island College. *See* Brown University
Ricci, Seymour de, 221
Rich, Obadiah, 19, 20
Rider, Sidney S., 31
Riley, Isaac, 179
Rivington, James, 101 ff., 147
Robinson, Edwin Arlington, 32
Robinson Crusoe (Defoe), 69, 100, 109
Rodd, Horatio, 21
Rodd, Thomas, 21
Rogers, Bruce, 238
Roosevelt, Franklin D., 225
Roosevelt, Theodore, 6
Root, Riley, 213, 214
Rose, Aquila, 77
Rosenbach, A. S. W., 56, 219
Rowson, Susannah, 151, 152
Royal American Magazine, 116, 117
Royal Gazette, 101
Royle, Joseph, 134
Rusk, Ralph Leslie, 168
Rutherfurd, Livingston, 98

Sabin, Joseph, 23, 24, 46
Sabine, Lorenzo, 102
St. Louis, first printing in, 161, 167
St. Martin, Alexis, 223
Salmagundi (Irving and others), 180
Sanchez, Gabriel, 8
Sandys, George, 86, 136, 137
San Francisco, first printing in, 207 ff.
Santangel, Luis de, 8, 9
Santayana, George, 66
Sargent, George H., 104
Sauer, Christoph, 36, 68, 120, 130, 131
Savannah, first printing in, 63
Saybrook Platform, 39
The School of Good Manners (Moody), 42

Scott, Walter, 196
Scull, John, 153, 162
The Second Division, 228
Select Poems, Chiefly American (ed. Carey), 166
Select Reviews, 182
Semple, Robert, 207
Sermons (Blair), 166
Several Poems (Bradstreet), 138
Sewall, Jonathan, 103
Sewall, Joseph, 30
Sewall, Samuel, 65
Sewell, William, 82, 88
Shakespeare, William, 11, 159, 160
Sheldon, John P., 168
Short, Thomas, 39, 46, 47
Short Catechism (Stone), 74
Short Discoverie of the Coasts of America (Castell), 15
A Short, Plain Help for Parents (Evans), 88
Shurtleff, Nathaniel, 31
The Shyp of Folys, 14
The Simple Cobler of Aggawam (Ward), 139
The Sister Years (Hawthorne), 145
The Sister's Gift, 109
Skeel, Emily Ellsworth Ford, 167
The Sketch Book of Geoffrey Crayon, Gent. (Irving), 175, 182, 186 ff., 203
Smith, Elihu Hubbard, 148
Smith, Captain John, 12
South Carolina, first printing in, 62
Southern Literary Messenger, 117
Sowle, Andrew, 51
Specimens of American Poetry (ed. Kettell), 148, 149, 191
Specimens of Newspaper Literature (Buckingham), 106
Spiller, Robert E., 199
Spooner, Alden, 42
Spooner, Judah Padock, 42, 162
Sprague, Charles, 232, 233
Springfield Republican, 135
The Spy (Cooper), 198, 199
Standish, Myles, 226

251

INDEX

Stanford University, 228
Steele, Richard, 115
Steendam, Jacob, 143
Stevens, Benjamin Franklin, 21
Stevens, Henry, 20
Stevenson, Robert Louis, 87
Stillwell, Margaret Bingham, 43
Stockton, Robert Field, 207
The Story of the Sixteenth Infantry in France, 228
Stout, Elihu, 163
Street, Franklin, 215
Stuart, Gilbert, 195
Stutler, Boyd B., 164
Sufficiency of the Spirit's Teaching (How), 65
Summario (Ramusio), 14
The Summe of Certaine Sermons (Mather), 32
Sutter, John Augustus, 210
Sweynheim, Conrad, 4
Sydenham, John V., 172

Table of the Value of the Lawful Money Bills, 65
Tamerlane (Poe), 201
Tarkington, Booth, 32
Tassin, Algernon, 123
Ten Nights in a Bar Room (Arthur), 17
Tennessee, first printing in, 163
The Tenth Muse (Bradstreet), 137
Thacher, John Boyd, 8, 10
Thackeray, William Makepeace, 187
Thanatopsis (Bryant), 191, 192
Thatcher, B. B., 193
Thomas, Isaiah, 41, 61, 104 ff., 116, 117, 119, 121, 131, 161
Thomas, Moses, 182, 183, 185
Thoreau, Henry D., 203, 232
Thorne, William, 65
Thwaites, Reuben Gold, 162
Time's Portraiture (Hawthorne), 145
Timothy, Elizabeth, 63
Timothy, Lewis, 62

Titcomb, Benjamin, 42
To a Waterfowl (Bryant), 191
Token, 202
Tompson, Benjamin, 140
The Torrent and the Night Before (Robinson), 32
Treatise on Conversion (Stoddard), 74
A Trip Across the Plains (Keller), 214, 215
The True Travels ... of Captaine Iohn Smith, 13
Trumbull, James Hammond, 29
Trumbull, John, 143, 200, 233
The Tryall of Travell (Goodall), 15
Tucker, Samuel Marion, 137
The Twenty-Sixth Infantry in France, 228
Twice-Told Tales (Hawthorne), 202
Two Years Before the Mast (Dana), 204
Tyler, Moses Coit, 67
Tyler, Royall, 157
Type-founding, earliest in British America, 129 ff.

Ulster County Gazette, 111
The Ulster County Gazette and Its Illegitimate Offspring (Vail), 111
United States Military Academy, 194
Universal Instructor ... and Pennsylvania Gazette, 83
Universal Spelling-Book (Fenning), 42
Utah, first printing in, 60

Vail, R. W. G., 111
Vail, Samuel, 162
Van Buren, Martin, 236
Van Doren, Carl, 154
Vanity Fair (Thackeray), 187
Vaughan, Victor E., 223
Ventures into Verse (Mencken), 32
Vermont, first printing in, 42
Vespucci, Amerigo, 2, 212
Virginia, first printing in, 61, 62

INDEX

The Vision of Columbus (Barlow), 143, 144

Voyage from Montreal... to the Frozen and Pacific Oceans (Mackenzie), 214

Voyage to the Eastern Part of Terra Firma (De Pons — tr. Irving), 179

Voyages of the Companions of Columbus (Irving), 20

Wagner, Henry R., 208, 214
Wait, Thomas B., 42
Wakeman, Stephen H., 193
Waldseemüller, Martin, 1, 2, 3, 212
Wallace, John William, 58
Walton, Izaak, 136
Ward, Nathaniel, 139
Washington, George, 102, 122, 236
Watts, John, 79
We (Lindbergh), 224
Webbe, John, 113, 114
Webster, Noah, 124
Weems, Mason Locke, 166, 167
Wegelin, Oscar, 141, 149, 153, 156
Welde, Thomas, 28
Wells, Charles William, 164
Wells, John, 164
Wells, Robert, 105
West Virginia, first printing in, 163
The West Virginia Encyclopedia (ed. Conley), 164
Wharton, Thomas, 132
What think ye of the Congress Now? (Chandler), 102
Wheatley, Phillis, 143

Whistler, James Abbott McNeill, 194, 234
Whitman, Elizabeth, 151
Whitman, Walt, 203
Whitmarsh, Thomas, 62
Whittier, John Greenleaf, 203, 226
Whole Booke of Psalmes. See Bay Psalm Book
Wieland (Brown), 154
Wigglesworth, Michael, 140, 141, 238
Wiley, Charles, 198
Willard, Samuel, 44
Williams College, 193
Willis, Nathaniel, 163
Willis, Nathaniel Parker, 163
Winslow, Edward, 143
Winslow, Ola Elizabeth, 145
Winthrop, John, 27
Wisconsin, first printing in, 172
Wolcott, Roger, 143
Wollaston, William, 79
Woodworth, Samuel, 232, 233
A Word of Comfort to a Melancholy Country, 74
The Writing Scholar's Assistant, 108
Wroth, Lawrence C., 59, 60, 61, 66, 128, 131, 134, 164, 167
Wüster, Johannes, 86

Yale University, 39, 207
Young, Brigham, 60
The Young Clerk's Vade Mecum, 100

Zamorano, Agustin Vicente, 207
Zenger, John Peter, 96 ff.

A CATALOGUE OF
SELECTED DOVER BOOKS
IN ALL FIELDS OF INTEREST

A CATALOGUE OF SELECTED DOVER
BOOKS IN ALL FIELDS OF INTEREST

RACKHAM'S COLOR ILLUSTRATIONS FOR WAGNER'S RING. Rackham's finest mature work—all 64 full-color watercolors in a faithful and lush interpretation of the *Ring*. Full-sized plates on coated stock of the paintings used by opera companies for authentic staging of Wagner. Captions aid in following complete Ring cycle. Introduction. 64 illustrations plus vignettes. 72pp. 8⅝ x 11¼.   23779-6 Pa. $6.00

CONTEMPORARY POLISH POSTERS IN FULL COLOR, edited by Joseph Czestochowski. 46 full-color examples of brilliant school of Polish graphic design, selected from world's first museum (near Warsaw) dedicated to poster art. Posters on circuses, films, plays, concerts all show cosmopolitan influences, free imagination. Introduction. 48pp. 9⅜ x 12¼.
23780-X Pa. $6.00

GRAPHIC WORKS OF EDVARD MUNCH, Edvard Munch. 90 haunting, evocative prints by first major Expressionist artist and one of the greatest graphic artists of his time: *The Scream, Anxiety, Death Chamber, The Kiss, Madonna,* etc. Introduction by Alfred Werner. 90pp. 9 x 12.
23765-6 Pa. $5.00

THE GOLDEN AGE OF THE POSTER, Hayward and Blanche Cirker. 70 extraordinary posters in full colors, from Maitres de l'Affiche, Mucha, Lautrec, Bradley, Cheret, Beardsley, many others. Total of 78pp. 9⅜ x 12¼.   22753-7 Pa. $5.95

THE NOTEBOOKS OF LEONARDO DA VINCI, edited by J. P. Richter. Extracts from manuscripts reveal great genius; on painting, sculpture, anatomy, sciences, geography, etc. Both Italian and English. 186 ms. pages reproduced, plus 500 additional drawings, including studies for *Last Supper,* Sforza monument, etc. 860pp. 7⅞ x 10¾. (Available in U.S. only)
22572-0, 22573-9 Pa., Two-vol. set $15.90

THE CODEX NUTTALL, as first edited by Zelia Nuttall. Only inexpensive edition, in full color, of a pre-Columbian Mexican (Mixtec) book. 88 color plates show kings, gods, heroes, temples, sacrifices. New explanatory, historical introduction by Arthur G. Miller. 96pp. 11⅜ x 8½. (Available in U.S. only)   23168-2 Pa. $7.95

UNE SEMAINE DE BONTÉ, A SURREALISTIC NOVEL IN COLLAGE, Max Ernst. Masterpiece created out of 19th-century periodical illustrations, explores worlds of terror and surprise. Some consider this Ernst's greatest work. 208pp. 8⅛ x 11.   23252-2 Pa. $5.00

DRAWINGS OF WILLIAM BLAKE, William Blake. 92 plates from Book of Job, *Divine Comedy, Paradise Lost,* visionary heads, mythological figures, Laocoon, etc. Selection, introduction, commentary by Sir Geoffrey Keynes. 178pp. 8⅛ x 11. 22303-5 Pa. $4.00

ENGRAVINGS OF HOGARTH, William Hogarth. 101 of Hogarth's greatest works: *Rake's Progress, Harlot's Progress, Illustrations for Hudibras, Before and After, Beer Street and Gin Lane,* many more. Full commentary. 256pp. 11 x 13¾. 22479-1 Pa. $7.95

DAUMIER: 120 GREAT LITHOGRAPHS, Honore Daumier. Wide-ranging collection of lithographs by the greatest caricaturist of the 19th century. Concentrates on eternally popular series on lawyers, on married life, on liberated women, etc. Selection, introduction, and notes on plates by Charles F. Ramus. Total of 158pp. 9⅜ x 12¼. 23512-2 Pa. $5.50

DRAWINGS OF MUCHA, Alphonse Maria Mucha. Work reveals draftsman of highest caliber: studies for famous posters and paintings, renderings for book illustrations and ads, etc. 70 works, 9 in color; including 6 items not drawings. Introduction. List of illustrations. 72pp. 9⅜ x 12¼. (Available in U.S. only) 23672-2 Pa. $4.00

GIOVANNI BATTISTA PIRANESI: DRAWINGS IN THE PIERPONT MORGAN LIBRARY, Giovanni Battista Piranesi. For first time ever all of Morgan Library's collection, world's largest. 167 illustrations of rare Piranesi drawings—archeological, architectural, decorative and visionary. Essay, detailed list of drawings, chronology, captions. Edited by Felice Stampfle. 144pp. 9⅜ x 12¼. 23714-1 Pa. $7.50

NEW YORK ETCHINGS (1905-1949), John Sloan. All of important American artist's N.Y. life etchings. 67 works include some of his best art; also lively historical record—Greenwich Village, tenement scenes. Edited by Sloan's widow. Introduction and captions. 79pp. 8⅜ x 11¼. 23651-X Pa. $4.00

CHINESE PAINTING AND CALLIGRAPHY: A PICTORIAL SURVEY, Wan-go Weng. 69 fine examples from John M. Crawford's matchless private collection: landscapes, birds, flowers, human figures, etc., plus calligraphy. Every basic form included: hanging scrolls, handscrolls, album leaves, fans, etc. 109 illustrations. Introduction. Captions. 192pp. 8⅞ x 11¾. 23707-9 Pa. $7.95

DRAWINGS OF REMBRANDT, edited by Seymour Slive. Updated Lippmann, Hofstede de Groot edition, with definitive scholarly apparatus. All portraits, biblical sketches, landscapes, nudes, Oriental figures, classical studies, together with selection of work by followers. 550 illustrations. Total of 630pp. 9⅛ x 12¼. 21485-0, 21486-9 Pa., Two-vol. set $15.00

THE DISASTERS OF WAR, Francisco Goya. 83 etchings record horrors of Napoleonic wars in Spain and war in general. Reprint of 1st edition, plus 3 additional plates. Introduction by Philip Hofer. 97pp. 9⅜ x 8¼. 21872-4 Pa. $3.75

THE CURVES OF LIFE, Theodore A. Cook. Examination of shells, leaves, horns, human body, art, etc., in *"the* classic reference on how the golden ratio applies to spirals and helices in nature . . . ."—Martin Gardner. 426 illustrations. Total of 512pp. 5⅜ x 8½.   23701-X Pa. $5.95

AN ILLUSTRATED FLORA OF THE NORTHERN UNITED STATES AND CANADA, Nathaniel L. Britton, Addison Brown. Encyclopedic work covers 4666 species, ferns on up. Everything. Full botanical information, illustration for each. This earlier edition is preferred·by many to more recent revisions. 1913 edition. Over 4000 illustrations, total of 2087pp. 6⅛ x 9¼.   22642-5, 22643-3, 22644-1 Pa., Three-vol. set $24.00

MANUAL OF THE GRASSES OF THE UNITED STATES, A. S. Hitchcock, U.S. Dept. of Agriculture. The basic study of American grasses, both indigenous and escapes, cultivated and wild. Over 1400 species. Full descriptions, information. Over 1100 maps, illustrations. Total of 1051pp. 5⅜ x 8½.   22717-0, 22718-9 Pa., Two-vol. set $15.00

THE CACTACEAE,, Nathaniel L. Britton, John N. Rose. Exhaustive, definitive. Every cactus in the world. Full botanical descriptions. Thorough statement of nomenclatures, habitat, detailed finding keys. The one book needed by every cactus enthusiast. Over 1275 illustrations. Total of 1080pp. 8 x 10¼.   21191-6, 21192-4 Clothbd., Two-vol. set $35.00

AMERICAN MEDICINAL PLANTS, Charles F. Millspaugh. Full descriptions, 180 plants covered: history; physical description; methods of preparation with all chemical constituents extracted; all claimed curative or adverse effects. 180 full-page plates. Classification table. 804pp. 6½ x 9¼.
23034-1 Pa. $10.00

A MODERN HERBAL, Margaret Grieve. Much the fullest, most exact, most useful compilation of herbal material. Gigantic alphabetical encyclopedia, from aconite to zedoary, gives botanical information, medical properties, folklore, economic uses, and much else. Indispensable to serious reader. 161 illustrations. 888pp. 6½ x 9¼. (Available in U.S. only)
22798-7, 22799-5 Pa., Two-vol. set $12.00

THE HERBAL or GENERAL HISTORY OF PLANTS, John Gerard. The 1633 edition revised and enlarged by Thomas Johnson. Containing almost 2850 plant descriptions and 2705 superb illustrations, Gerard's *Herbal* is a monumental work, the book all modern English herbals are derived from, the one herbal every serious enthusiast should have in its entirety. Original editions are worth perhaps $750. 1678pp. 8½ x 12¼.
23147-X Clothbd. $50.00

MANUAL OF THE TREES OF NORTH AMERICA, Charles S. Sargent. The basic survey of every native tree and tree-like shrub, 717 species in all. Extremely full descriptions, information on habitat, growth, locales, economics, etc. Necessary to every serious tree lover. Over 100 finding keys. 783 illustrations. Total of 986pp. 5⅜ x 8½.
20277-1, 20278-X Pa., Two-vol. set $10.00

CATALOGUE OF DOVER BOOKS

THE STANDARD BOOK OF QUILT MAKING AND COLLECTING, Marguerite Ickis. Full information, full-sized patterns for making 46 traditional quilts, also 150 other patterns. Quilted cloths, lame, satin quilts, etc. 483 illustrations. 273pp. 6⅞ x 9⅝. 20582-7 Pa. $4.95

ENCYCLOPEDIA OF VICTORIAN NEEDLEWORK, S. Caulfield, Blanche Saward. Simply inexhaustible gigantic alphabetical coverage of every traditional needlecraft—stitches, materials, methods, tools, types of work; definitions, many projects to be made. 1200 illustrations; double-columned text. 697pp. 8⅛ x 11. 22800-2, 22801-0 Pa., Two-vol. set $12.00

MECHANICK EXERCISES ON THE WHOLE ART OF PRINTING, Joseph Moxon. First complete book (1683-4) ever written about typography, a compendium of everything known about printing at the latter part of 17th century. Reprint of 2nd (1962) Oxford Univ. Press edition. 74 illustrations. Total of 550pp. 6⅛ x 9¼. 23617-X Pa. $7.95

PAPERMAKING, Dard Hunter. Definitive book on the subject by the foremost authority in the field. Chapters dealing with every aspect of history of craft in every part of the world. Over 320 illustrations. 2nd, revised and enlarged (1947) edition. 672pp. 5⅜ x 8½. 23619-6 Pa. $7.95

THE ART DECO STYLE, edited by Theodore Menten. Furniture, jewelry, metalwork, ceramics, fabrics, lighting fixtures, interior decors, exteriors, graphics from pure French sources. Best sampling around. Over 400 photographs. 183pp. 8⅜ x 11¼. 22824-X Pa. $6.00

Prices subject to change without notice.

Available at your book dealer or write for free catalogue to Dept. GI, Dover Publications, Inc., 180 Varick St., N.Y., N.Y. 10014. Dover publishes more than 175 books each year on science, elementary and advanced mathematics, biology, music, art, literary history, social sciences and other areas.